[1] �... ᚠᚨᚺᚱᚱᚤᚾᚾᛒᚨ:

[2] ᛁ:ᛇᛒᚦᛜᚨᛏᛋᛏᛩᚷᚱᚹ:ᚹᚱᚨ:

[3] ᛩᛁᛏᚠᛜᛏᚦᛆᛩ:ᛩᛏᛋᛏ:ᛩᛁ:

[4] ᚼᛜᚦᚨ:ᛚᛪᛘᚨᚱ:ᛩᛏᚦ:ᚠ:ᛋᛏᚠᛜᚱ:ᚾᚾ:

[5] ᚦᛜᛦᛋ:ᚱᛁᛋᛏ:ᚻᚱᚱ:ᚹᚱᚨ:ᚦᛏᚾ:ᛋᛏᚾ:

[6] ᛩᛁᛩᛜᚱᚨᚾ:ᚹᛋᛏᛏᚾ:ᚦᛜᛦᚼᛪᛒᛁᚱ:

[7] ᛩᛁ:ᛇᚨᛩ:ᚾᛏᛩ:ᚹᛜᛏᛩ:ᛩᛜᛏ:ᚱᚨᚦᚨ:

[8] ᛜᚹ:ᛒᛚᚨᚦ:ᛋᚾ:ᚦᛏᚦ:ᛆᚢᛘ:

[9] ᚹᚱᚼᛏᛚᛋ:ᛜᚹ:ᛁᛚᛚᛦ:

[10] ᚼᛜᚱ:ᛩ:ᛩᛜᛏᛋ:ᛩᛏ:ᚼᛜᛩᛏᛏ:ᛜᛏ:ᛋᛏ:

[11] ᛪᛒᛁᚱ:ᛩᛇᚱᛏ:ᛋᛁᛒ:ᛚᛆ:ᚦᛜᛦᚼ:ᚱᛁᛋᛏ:

[12] ᚹᚱᛇᛩ:ᚦᛏᚾ:ᛜᛆ:ᛜᚨᚱ:ᛚᚠᚠ:

THE KENSINGTON STONE

A MYSTERY SOLVED

The Kensington Stone

a mystery

solved

ERIK WAHLGREN

THE UNIVERSITY OF WISCONSIN PRESS

Madison, 1958

TO MY WIFE BEVERLY

Preface

This book is the expansion of a research paper, "Runic Letters, Archive Study, and the Kensington Inscription," presented at a meeting of the Modern Language Association of America at Chicago, on December 28, 1953. The necessary field work and archive research in Minnesota were conducted in the summer of 1953 with the aid of a research grant from the Committee on Research of the Academic Senate, Southern Section, of the University of California. Important references were subsequently checked in the Royal Libraries of Stockholm and Copenhagen during the writer's sabbatical sojourn in Scandinavia in 1954–55 for the purpose of general runological study and the preparation of a work on runes, with the support of a grant from the American Philosophical Society. To the officials of the Society as well as to the Committee on Research, mentioned above, the author expresses his gratitude for generous support of this project at several stages of its development.

It is a pleasure to acknowledge the friendly coöperation of the Minnesota Historical Society and in particular of Mr. W. M. Babcock, Curator of the Newspaper Room, who microfilmed numerous documents upon request. Thanks are likewise owing to Miss Lucile Kane, Curator of Manuscripts, Miss Lois M. Fawcett, Head of the Reference Department, and Miss Kathryn Johnson, Assistant Curator of Manuscripts. Mention must likewise be made of the special courtesy of the Douglas County Historian, Mr. Ralph S. Thornton, Attorney at Law, of Alexandria, Minnesota and of the Alexandria Chamber of Commerce and its secretary, Mr. L. W. Denstedt, for allowing the writer to inspect the Kensington stone in 1953, then stored in the vault of the Chamber of Commerce building. The author is grateful likewise to Mr. O. M. Hovde, Librarian of Luther College, Decorah, Iowa, who has kindly acceded to numerous requests for items from the Norwegian-American files at his disposition. Dean J. Jørgen Thompson of St. Olaf College, Northfield, Minnesota, has furnished valuable information in his capacity as Secretary of the Norwegian-American Historical Association. Mr. J. W. Reginald Scurr of the Chicago Public Library Newspaper service has been similarly helpful.

Very special mention must be made of the invaluable assistance rendered by Mr. J. A. Holvik, Professor Emeritus of Norse and Music at Concordia College, Moorhead, Minnesota. Professor Holvik has followed the rune stone controversy since 1908. Numerous items from his vast file on the subject have generously been shared with scholars and journalists in several countries. The fact that certain of his newspaper articles, letters, and bulletins have conflicted with numerous convenient assumptions put forth by defenders of the Kensington stone has created resentment in quarters that believe that the stone and its antecedents should be immune from investigation. This, coupled with occasional minor inaccuracies in Holvik's presentation—inadvertencies which he, with true scholarly humility, has been the first to rectify—has deprived some of his opinions of the audience which they deserve. The writer entered into correspondence with Professor Holvik in 1952, and this volume has profited greatly by his observations, his knowledge of early events, and his familiarity with the inhabitants and the terrain of Minnesota. Most of the photographs here reproduced have been secured through Holvik, who likewise was the writer's guide in Douglas County in August, 1953. His important positive contributions towards the elucidation of the complex Kensington problem have been gratefully recorded in numerous places throughout the volume. I wish also to express my thanks to Professor Holvik's former pupil, Mr. Ronald Johnson of Elbow Lake, Minnesota, who contributed his time so willingly to drive us about in Douglas County.

To the eminent runologists, Professor Sven B. F. Jansson of

Statens Historiska Museum, Stockholm, Erik Moltke of Natio-nalmuseum, Copenhagen, and Dr. Harry Andersen of Copen-hagen University, the writer wishes to express his gratitude not merely for the inspiration of their published writings, but for numerous personal courtesies extended in their home countries several years ago. A word of acknowledgement is due to Mr. Iørn Piø, Copenhagen, for supplying copies of his two articles on the Kensington stone in the Copenhagen newspaper, *Berlingske Aftenavis*. Professor Ivar Högbom, President of the Stockholm School of Economics, and Professor Axel Boëthius, President Emeritus of Gothenburg University, have both volunteered valuable references, while Professor Elias Wessén of Stockholm University was kind enough to comment on portions of this re-search, presented orally before Samfundet för Nordisk Språk-forskning, Stockholm, in 1954. Thanks are owing to the staff members of several Scandinavian libraries and museums, par-ticularly to Dr. Olov von Feilitzen, Associate Librarian of the Royal Library, Stockholm, for assistance in procuring and con-sulting materials.

Dr. Henry Goddard Leach, President Emeritus of the Ameri-can-Scandinavian Foundation, New York, has given steady en-couragement towards the prosecution of runological research. Professor Johannes Brøndsted, Director of the Nationalmuseum, Copenhagen, graciously supplied the excellent photographs of the Kensington stone which, with the permission of the Smith-sonian Institution, have been reproduced in this volume as Figs. 1 and 2, and as endpapers for the book.

Many helpful suggestions, of a broad and pertinent nature, have been made by the writer's long-time friend, Waldemar Westergaard, Professor of History, Emeritus, at the University of California, Los Angeles. Special assistance has been rendered in various ways by the author's colleagues at large, Professors Arthur G. Brodeur of the University of California, Berkeley; Lee M. Hollander, of the University of Texas; the late Albert Morey Sturtevant, of the University of Kansas. The writer wishes also to thank the following staff members of the Uni-versity of California, Los Angeles: Professor Victor A. Oswald, Jr., Professor of German and Chairman of the Department of Germanic Languages; Mrs. Dorothea Lantos, Secretary-Stenographer, Department of Germanic Languages; Miss Louise Mallinson (now deceased), Committee Secretary of the Academic Senate; Miss Verna B. Anderson, Principal Account Clerk, Controller's Office; Mrs. Esther Euler of the Library. Valuable courtesies have been extended to the writer by Dr. Harold von Hofe, Professor of German, University of Southern California, and by Mr. John L. Harris, Examiner of Questioned Documents, Los Angeles. Mr. Donald Oehlerts, of the library staff of the Wisconsin Historical Society, was of great assistance in tracking down a variety of newspaper references. Especially appreciated are the services of Mrs. Elizabeth Robinson, who at a critical juncture laid aside her other duties to type the larger portion of the final manuscript.

The author wishes to express his deep gratitude for the decision to publish this work through the University of Wisconsin Press. To Mr. Ronald O. Burnett fell the task of preparing the text, line by line, word by word, and illustration by illustration, for the printer. It is a pleasure to acknowledge the helpful solicitude with which he has shepherded the work through the laborious stages of editing and production.

In equal measure, this book has profited by the scholarly attentions of Professor Einar Haugen of the University of Wisconsin. Professor Haugen has read the manuscript at three separate stages of its development and offered a wealth of criticisms on philological and other points. Not the least valuable of his contributions is the suggestion that influence from Ignatius Donnelly is to be discerned in the Kensington inscription.

Archive materials referred to throughout the volume are found in Boxes 10 and 12, known respectively as the N. W. Winchell and W. Upham Collections, in the Archive of the Minnesota Historical Society at St. Paul.

Unless otherwise credited, all translations from foreign languages have been made by the author.

For all statements of fact or interpretation in the following pages, the writer alone bears full responsibility.

ERIK WAHLGREN

Santa Monica, California
April, 1957

Contents

Illustrations

THE KENSINGTON STONE

A MYSTERY SOLVED

CHAPTER I

An American Rune Stone

From February 17, 1948, until February 25, 1949, there was on exhibit at the Smithsonian Institution, Washington, D. C., the inscribed slab of stone which has subsequently won international fame as the Kensington Rune Stone (Figs. 1 and 2). In size, shape, and color the Kensington stone—named for the town of Kensington, Minnesota, near which it was found in 1898—is not unlike an old style tombstone. Apparently intended to stand upright, the gray stone is approximately two and a half feet high, sixteen inches wide, and five or six inches thick. It lacks, however, the neat contours and polished smoothness appropriate to a burial marker, for its rectangular form is somewhat skew, its face rough-hewn and pockmarked. On the face and one edge the tablet bears a lengthy inscription in a form of the Swedish language, carved in letters that are clearly related to Scandinavian runic alphabets of an early era, together with one word (or set of initials) in Latin lettering, and the date 1362. The runic message can be rendered into modern English somewhat as follows:

8 Swedes and 22 Norwegians on an exploration journey from Vinland westward. We had our camp by 2 rocky islets one day's journey north of this stone. We were out fishing one day. When we came home we found 10 men red with blood and dead. AVM save us from evil. We have 10 men by the sea to look after our ships, 14 days' journey from this island. Year 1362.[1]

3

Although some four thousand runic inscriptions are known in Scandinavia, very few Americans have ever seen a runic symbol, let alone an entire stone carved with runes. That the Smithsonian, under any circumstances whatever, should have an example of runic epigraphy on exhibit, was thus mildly sensational in itself. Far more sensational was the drastic revision of American history for which the Kensington stone seemed to vouch. According to the inscription, white men had not only explored North America, but had penetrated far into the interior of the continent 130 years before Columbus and 300 years ahead of the French explorers. If the Kensington account is what it purports to be, the known history of Minnesota must of necessity span a period of six centuries instead of three, and certain generally held concepts in the history of exploration must be radically modified. The prospect, or even the mere possibility of this, furnishes legitimate cause for the excitement that has prevailed, not merely in Scandinavian-American circles, but among historically minded Americans generally. In the Scandinavian countries, as well, there has been occasion for more than a casual interest in the putative exploits of this medieval expedition from Norway and Sweden some three and a half centuries after the time of Leif Erikson and his adventures in Vinland.[2] The crux of the matter, then, is whether the Kensington inscription is a genuine medieval document, or a modern deception.

During the half century separating the Kensington stone's initial discovery and its public celebration a few years ago by our national museum, the antecedents of the petroglyph had repeatedly come under fire, but despite a certain discord among the scholarly inclined and the contentious, so nebulous a controversy had never seriously engaged the public mind, outside of Midwestern counties largely populated by Scandinavian immigrants. The evidence of the daily press and the news weeklies is that a new era in the life of the Kensington stone—and with it a radically new stage in the controversy over its authenticity— was brought about by the Smithsonian sponsorship. According to the best information available, the Smithsonian has never guaranteed the authenticity of the runic inscription; but evidence on the point is sufficiently ambiguous to have influenced both scholars and the public at large.

The *National Geographic*, for example, carries in its September, 1948 issue, a photograph of Neil M. Judd, Curator of Archaeology at the Smithsonian, as he studies the stone, and a statement regarding the inscription from which is quoted the following: "Later studies indicate that it was carved by white men who had traveled far into North America long before Columbus's first voyage."[3] On March 12, 1949, Dr. M. W. Stirling, Director of the Bureau of American Ethnology, Smithsonian Institution, was quoted in the *Washington Times-Herald* as stating that the Kensington stone is "probably the most important archaeological object yet found in North America."[4] And in 1951 the Smithsonian brought out a little monograph which attracted the attention of the entire world to the disputed rune stone. This was an English translation of the Danish scholar William Thalbitzer's study, *Two Runic Stones from Greenland and Minnesota*.[5] Comparing the Kensington inscription with the runic carving on the stone from Kingiktorsoak, Greenland from the year 1328, Thalbitzer concludes that they belong roughly to the same tradition and hence that the Kensington runes are genuine.

Since that time, the Kensington stone has clearly been in the ascendancy. The very large measure of approval accorded it by the Smithsonian Institution, and its gradual acceptance by historians, geographers, and archaeologists in various parts of the world,[6] despite expressed repudiation of the inscription by specialists in runology,[7] is generally credited to the several books and ceaseless researches, the ingenuity and indomitable perseverance of the Wisconsin writer, Hjalmar Rued Holand.[8] His lifetime of labor was crowned with publicly acknowledged success when the Kensington stone, after fifty years of orphanage, was housed under the hospitable roof of the Smithsonian Institution. This success was confirmed by two subsequent events of note. The first took place on March 15, 1949, when the Kensington stone was unveiled at St. Paul in honor of Minnesota Day on the occasion of the Minnesota Centennial. The second event rep-

resented the achievement of a more permanent goal: the establishment of an enduring monument to the Kensington stone
near its place of discovery in Douglas County, Minnesota. On
August 12, 1951, in "Runestone Memorial Park" at the
eastern entrance to the Douglas County seat of Alexandria,
quite the most impressive rune stone in all of history was unveiled. This was a gigantic reproduction of the Kensington stone
in rune-inscribed granite: an eighteen-ton stone on a four-ton
base. Sponsored by the Alexandria Kiwanis Club, the monument is flanked by a tablet on either hand, one containing an
English translation of the runes, the other a succinct account of
the stone's discovery by Olof Ohman in 1898, its rediscovery by
Holand in 1907, and its current status.

Other replicas of the Kensington stone are in existence. The
model of the stone now on exhibit at the Smithsonian, mistaken
by many visitors for the original, is a tolerably exact replica of
the original stone. A twin to this was long on exhibit in the front
window of the Chamber of Commerce at Alexandria, Minnesota,
where it was likewise often taken for the original. In addition to
this, small-sized replicas of the stone have been made for the
tourist trade and may be purchased at Alexandria, along with
descriptive brochures and automobile stickers that depict the
carving of the rune stone and its importance. As this book was
about to be set in type it was learned from Professor Einar
Haugen (July, 1957) that the original stone has once again been
put on display at Alexandria. And there, for the time being,
we must leave it in order to go back to the year 1898.

CHAPTER II

The History of the Rune Stone

At some time during the latter half of the year 1898, a Swedish immigrant farmer named Olof Ohman, engaged in clearing a piece of farmland about three miles from the village of Kensington in Douglas County, Minnesota, assertedly uncovered a flat slab of gray stone which had been lodged beneath the roots of a poplar tree (Figs. 7 and 8).[1] At first he noticed no special peculiarities in the stone; but some time later his ten-year-old son, we are told, chancing to dust off the stone with his cap, noticed that it was carved with a series of unfamiliar symbols. Neither Ohman nor his neighbor on the adjoining farm, Norwegian-born Nils Flaten, had any opinion as to the origin or meaning of these markings, and a rumor spread in the vicinity that they had been carved by white or Indian robbers in connection with a buried treasure. However, a series of excavations with pickaxe and shovel failed to turn up any treasure, and soon the stone was hauled in to Kensington and there exhibited, we are told, in the window of a bank, where it was the object of widespread interest. Eventually it began to be rumored that the symbols on the stone represented an inscription in Scandinavian runes, this rumor being corroborated by persons who had seen similar inscriptions reproduced in Scandinavian books.

The result of this discovery was that a copy of the inscription was forwarded to Professor O. J. Breda, who taught the Scandinavian languages at the University of Minnesota. Though not a runic specialist, Breda was able, on the basis of the material sent him, to interpret the larger part of the inscription, with the conspicuous omission of the numerals (Fig. 13). At the same time, Professor Breda expressed as his opinion that the inscription was not genuine, but rather a modern joke, launched by someone who knew runes and wanted to have a little fun with the learned professors. It does not appear certain that Breda had seen the stone at the time he worked out his translation, although the evidence on this point is conflicting.[2]

Breda's rejection of the stone was reported in the press towards the end of February, 1899. At about this same time, the stone was being shipped to the Germanic philologist, Professor George O. Curme, of Northwestern University. Before the arrival of the stone, however, Professor Curme had received a copy of the inscription, and his translation of the copy, together with his recorded expectation that the inscription would prove genuine, received wide newspaper publicity along with Breda's views to the contrary. By March 1, 1899, Curme had received the stone and decided that the inscription on it varied from the copy that had been sent him, for which reason a slightly differing translation was indicated.[3] After considering the evidence, Curme came to regard the rune stone as spurious. He did not rely on his own knowledge of runes, however, and according to newspaper accounts, he made a copy of the inscription and sent it to the famed linguistic authority, Professor Adolf Noreen of Uppsala University, Sweden.[4] Meanwhile, Professor Breda had suggested that photographs of the rune stone be sent to Professor Sophus Bugge of Christiania, Norway, and Professor L. V. A. Wimmer of Copenhagen, Denmark.[5] There is no proof that photographs were sent at this time, but it seems likely enough that either hand-drawn copies of the inscription or newspaper reproductions of such copies were sent both to these and to other European and American scholars, for there is mention of this in various contemporary newspaper accounts.

What most of these Scandinavian specialists thought of the Kensington inscription has not been made a matter of record, but in at least one quarter the reaction was as condemnatory as it was prompt. Reproduced in the *Minneapolis Tribune* for April 16, 1899 is the telegram sent by Professors Gustav Storm, Sophus Bugge, and Oluf Rygh of Christiania University: "The so-called rune stone is a crude fraud, perpetrated by a Swede with the aid of a chisel and a meager knowledge of runic letters and English."[6]

In the face of so harsh a denunciation, popular support of the Kensington stone as a genuine medieval record collapsed. The stone ultimately made its way back to its owner, Olof Ohman, who let it lie ("face down"?) on his property for a number of years.[7] For a long time, little or nothing was heard of the rune stone.

Then, in the summer of 1907, a Norwegian-American writer, Hjalmar Rued Holand, was touring Minnesota while engaged in collecting material for his forthcoming book on the history of the Norwegian settlements.[8] In the month of August he visited the Ohman farm, and presently he acquired the stone from Ohman.[9] A transcription and translation of the Kensington inscription was published in his book the following year, and this was followed by other articles and lectures by Holand during the years immediately succeeding.[10] As a result of this, the Minnesota Historical Society appointed a committee to investigate the stone in 1909–10.[11] During and immediately following the investigation, the inscription was condemned by specialists in Scandinavian philology, while the circumstances of the find were debated at length by geologists and by various persons concerned with the roots of the poplar tree under which the stone had purportedly been found. In 1911, Holand travelled abroad with the stone and exhibited it in France and in Scandinavia, where he debated or discussed the problem with various persons. This second phase of the Kensington stone's history was concluded in 1912 with the appearance of the Minnesota Historical Society's report (dated 1910) which was favorable to the stone. Holand, and those who believed with him that the Kensington inscription bore a true account of fourteenth century penetration into Minnesota by a party of Swedes and Norwegians, had won a major victory before the bar of public opinion.

CHAPTER III

Authorities For
and Against
the Stone

During nearly four decades it has scarcely been possible to discuss the Kensington question from any point of view whatever without referring to Holand, primarily because Holand's defense of the stone is so valiant, his publications so numerous, and his arguments so universally quoted by both believers and disbelievers in the runic inscription, that every discussant expressly or by implication must take a stand on Holand's arguments. Accordingly, although his reasoning will not be evaluated at this point, Holand's chief publications on the Kensington problem will be listed briefly.

In Holand's immigration study already referred to, *De Norske Settlementers Historie*, published in 1908, eight pages are devoted to the Kensington stone. A photograph of the stone and a reproduction of the inscription, together with a transcription of it, are included. In the next several years, Holand developed the subject in a series of magazine and journal articles that were prophetic of an activity that he has maintained down to the present.[1] His first major work on the subject was his book, *The Kensington Stone*, issued in 1932, which has an extensive bibliography of writings on the topic, including Holand's own articles from 1908 to 1928, and thirty-five illustrations. After a cursory account of the find, Holand discusses certain investigations that were made into the question a decade or so after the fact, together with the results arrived at in each case; the linguistic, runological, and human aspects of the case; the geographical, geological, botanical, and historical possibilities; the likelihood that certain arms and implements unearthed in Minnesota date from Scandinavian explorations in the pre-Columbian era. Various affidavits respecting either the Kensington stone or other finds are referred to and their wording reproduced.

Eight years later, Holand again considered the problem in his *Westward from Vinland*. Against a background of early sailings by Erik the Red, his son Leif Erikson, and their contemporaries, Holand returns to a contention made in the earlier volume that explorers referred to in the Kensington inscription were members of an official expedition authorized by King Magnus Smek of Sweden and Norway, which ostensibly took place under the direction of Paul Knutson during the years 1355–64. The rest of the volume is similar to the former book, save for a series of bibliographical notes which have been added. This book was reissued in 1942.

The Kensington stone plays a subordinate part in a book published by Holand in 1946, *America, 1355–1364: A New Chapter in Pre-Columbian History*.[2] The chief contribution of the new work was an extensive discussion of the famous stone tower at Newport, Rhode Island. Usually regarded as a seventeenth century colonial product originally serving the purpose of a windmill, the structure is by Holand claimed to be a watch tower or fortress from a much earlier period and of Scandinavian origin.

In 1956, Holand's *Explorations in America Before Columbus*[3] appeared, making several mentions of the Kensington stone, introducing new material and making a strong effort to discredit the results of recent investigations hostile to the stone. Adding to these books Holand's numerous articles and lectures on this subject, it is not surprising that his name is indissolubly connected with every phase of the intricate problems posed by the rune stone, and that writers favorable to the Kensington inscription explicitly base their arguments in most instances on his

demonstrations. It is from Holand, for example, that Professor
Hennig secured the recent (and inexplicable) information that
"the Scandinavianists of North America . . . in view of the convincing arguments for the contrary point of view, have already to
95% abandoned their objection to the genuineness of the rune
stone. . . ."[4] And the jacket of *America, 1355–1364* contains
extracts of laudatory reviews of *Westward from Vinland* from
which we quote the following:

"Mr. Holand [offers] probably the most important . . . contribution yet made to the pre-Columbian history of America.
His investigation has searched widely and probed deeply, and
his account of the assembling of his great mass of material is
capable and scholarly" (*New York Times Book Review*).

"The author gives evidence of great thoroughness and erudition. . . . The book is heartily recommended" (*Christian Science
Monitor*).

More impressive even than such praise is the amount of labor,
physical and mental, that Holand has devoted to the stone
throughout half a century, and the tremendous amount of
linguistic and other data accumulated and organized by him.

A number of other persons have either actively entered the
lists on Holand's side of the rune stone controversy, or are cited
by him as authorities in pertinent disciplines. In order not to
burden succeeding chapters with biographical digressions, the
more important of these persons will be identified here.

Among the prominent figures who, at an early stage of the
controversy, rallied to Holand's support, were Newton Horace
Winchell (1839–1914) and Warren Upham (1850–1934), geologists and archaeologists. Winchell was State Geologist of Minnesota, 1872–1900 and Professor of Geology and Mineralogy at
the University of Minnesota, 1873–1900. After 1906 he was the
archaeologist of the Minnesota State Historical Society. Along
with his friend and associate Upham, Winchell became deeply
interested in the Kensington stone, and he was principal author
of the sixty-six page report on the stone issued by the MHS in
1912.[5] Dr. Upham, who also published on the Kensington stone,
was secretary and librarian to the MHS, 1895–1914, and there-

after its archaeologist. Upham and Winchell studied the Kensington stone for more than a year before publishing their reports.

An investigation into the Kensington problem was conducted
independently in 1909 by Dr. Knut Hoegh, a physician in
Minneapolis, who published a report that same year which was
favorable to the authenticity of the stone.[6] Born in Norway and
a graduate of Christiania University, Dr. Hoegh had come to the
United States in 1869 and settled in Minneapolis in 1889. Although no special reason for his interest in the Kensington controversy is manifest, it is known that he was acting as chairman
of a committee of three appointed by Det Norske Selskab (The
Norwegian Society) of Minneapolis. The other two members
were the theologian, Professor E. Kr. Johnson, and Professor
Gisle Bothne, then chairman of the Department of Scandinavian
at the University of Minnesota. It must be observed, however,
that Bothne abstained from active participation in the work of
the committee, inasmuch as he was skeptical of the stone.

Among those who early manifested partiality to the Kensington stone must be mentioned at least two men of Norwegian
birth who wrote on the subject in the papers. The older of the
two was Peter P. Iverslie, born in 1844 and a student at Luther
College, Decorah, Iowa, 1862–64. According to one who knew
him, Iverslie at various times lived at Waupaca, Wisconsin, and
Milan, Montevideo, and Minneapolis, Minnesota, working as
farmer and teacher. The other was John J. Skørdalsvold, a
journalist born in 1853. He graduated from Augsburg Seminary
in 1881 and from the University of Minnesota in 1888. He taught
and did newspaper work in Minneapolis. Both are quoted in the
present book.

O. E. Hagen (1853–1926), professor and farmer, is several
times referred to by Holand and wrote at least one article on the
Kensington stone. Hagen studied at the University of Wisconsin
1882–86 and at Leipzig 1886–90. From approximately 1891 to
1900 he was professor of Hebrew, Greek, and Scandinavian at the
University of South Dakota. There is evidence that he was plan-
ning a second lengthy article on the Kensington problem at the

time of his death.[7] He is also associated with the recording of a certain Norwegian ballad which is of interest in the Kensington matter.

Professor Andrew Fossum of Northfield, Minnesota, is likewise referred to by Holand, who cites Fossum's book *The Norse Discovery of America* (1918) as well as several articles on the Kensington stone. Fossum (1860–1943) was a specialist in Greek and French languages, which he taught at St. Olaf College 1892–1910 and thereafter at Park Region Luther College and Concordia College, respectively.

In recent years, Holand has quoted a number of scholars to buttress his own views on the Kensington stone. The more important of these are: Professor Johannes Brøndsted, eminent Danish archaeologist, professor and Director of Nationalmuseum, Copenhagen; F. S. Cawley, 1890–1942, Scandinavian specialist and Assistant Professor at Harvard University; Stefán Einarsson, Icelandic born and Professor of Scandinavian Philology at Johns Hopkins University; S. N. Hagen (born 1872), Professor Emeritus of English at Franklin and Marshall College, who has published an eloquent defense of the stone;[8] Richard Hennig, 1874–1951, Professor of Geography at the Technical University of Düsseldorf, Germany, an enthusiastic Kensingtonian; G. L. Indrebø (1889–1942), Professor of Norwegian Dialectology at Bergen Museum, Norway; Hjalmar Lindroth (1878–1947), Professor of Scandinavian languages at the University of Gothenburg, Sweden; K. F. Söderwall (1842–1924), Professor of Scandinavian Languages at Lund University, Sweden, authority on medieval Swedish, and for eighteen years editor-in-chief of the Swedish Academy's great dictionary of the Swedish language; William Thalbitzer (born 1873), authority on Eskimo dialects and Professor Emeritus of Arctic Ethnology at the University of Copenhagen, Denmark, whose dissertation on the stone is well known; Andrew Adin Stomberg (1871–1943), Professor of Scandinavian languages at the University of Minnesota and author of *A History of Sweden*. The value and bearing of their respective utterances ill be examined at a later stage; suffice it to say here that the degree of approval of the Kensington stone, or of Holand's views respecting it, which is expressed or which may be extrapolated from their remarks, varies considerably from case to case.

From time to time, Holand has dipped into the philological treatises of two great Swedish linguists in order to establish or verify this or that detail of medieval Swedish grammar or orthography. These are Axel Kock (1851–1935), Professor of Scandinavian Languages, first at Gothenburg and then at Lund, and a pioneer in the study of Swedish phonology, and Kock's great rival, Adolf Noreen (1854–1925), a member of the Swedish Academy, Professor of Scandinavian Languages at Uppsala, and one of the basic founders of the modern study of Scandinavian philology. Holand does not cite any pronouncements on the Kensington stone by either of these Swedish linguists, but S. N. Hagen has found that Noreen expressed opposition to it.[9]

Let us now identify a number of other authorities who will figure in these pages chiefly as witnesses against the Kensington stone. It is pertinent to begin with those men who were the world's chief authorities on runic inscriptions at the time that the stone was being reinvestigated and debated in 1909, 1910, and 1911.

Sophus Bugge (1833–1907), Professor of Comparative Linguistics and Old Norse at the University of Christiania, Norway, was, along with his Danish colleague, Ludvig Wimmer, the cofounder of modern runology. Ludvig Wimmer (1839–1920) was Professor of Scandinavian Languages at the University of Copenhagen. Dr. Erik Brate (1857–1924), college teacher of Swedish, was one of Sweden's most productive writers on runology. Otto von Friesen (1870–1942), who trained an entire generation of Swedish linguists while Professor of Swedish at Uppsala, was a member of the Swedish Academy. Magnus Olsen (born 1878) was Professor of Old Norse and Icelandic Language and Literature at the University of Oslo for forty years, beginning in 1908. This brilliant quintet, together with their distinguished pupils and successors, made of runology a branch of epigraphical research which bears comparison with any other field of study.

Oluf Rygh (1833–1899) was an archaeologist, historian, and philologist who since 1875 had held the Chair of Scandinavian Archaeology at the University of Christiania, as Norway's capital was called for three centuries before resuming its original name of Oslo in 1924. A pioneer in the field of prehistoric archaeology, Rygh was also a prominent specialist in the branch of linguistics known as place name research.

Gustav Storm (1845–1903) had, at the time of his death, been Professor of History at Christiania since 1877, and had several years previous to the Kensington discovery published a work on the Vinland voyages.[10]

The Norwegian lexicographer and dialectologist, Marius Hægstad (1850–1927), became Professor of Norwegian Landsmål (Popular Speech) and its Dialects in 1899. Author of various texts and of a dictionary of Old Norse, Hægstad was particularly an authority on the period 1200–1350.

Helge Gjessing (1886–1924) was an archaeologist. From 1917 until his untimely death he was Assistant Director of Antiquities at the University of Oslo.

Best known of the recent writers who have attacked the disputed rune stone is Dr. Sven B. F. Jansson of Stockholm University, who simultaneously is Professor of Runology at The State Historical Museum and director of the great project to edit and interpret all of Sweden's rune stones.

Jansson's elder colleague, Professor Elias Wessén, is a member of the Swedish Academy and currently the dean of authorities on the Swedish language and runes.

Ivar Lindquist is Professor of Scandinavian Languages at Lund University, Sweden, and a writer on runological and other linguistic problems. Professor Karl Gustaf Ljunggren is Professor of Swedish at Lund and a prolific author of philological treatises, including a number on runology.

Dr. Assar Janzén, formerly assistant professor at the Universities of Gothenburg and Lund, Sweden, is Professor of Scandinavian Languages in the University of California, Berkeley.

In Denmark the most distinguished present-day commentator on the Kensington stone is Erik Moltke, archaeologist attached to the National Museum at Copenhagen. Co-editor of a great work on Danish runes, Moltke has devoted considerable time to the Kensington problem.

Associated with Moltke in this study is Dr. Harry Andersen, Assistant Professor at Copenhagen University, a linguistic specialist, and author of a grammar of Old Icelandic. The distinguished Danish runologist, K. M. Nielsen, author of many runic treatises, has also commented on the Kensington stone.

Professor Jón Helgason, Icelandic born, has been Professor of Icelandic Language and Literature at Copenhagen University since 1936, and has performed a vast labor as editor of numerous basic works from the Middle Ages.

The first American scholars to comment on the Kensington stone were O. J. Breda and George O. Curme. Breda (1853–1916) was born in Norway; in 1883 he became a professor of Scandinavian Languages at the University of Minnesota, resigning in 1898 to return to Norway. Curme (1860–1948), an internationally recognized authority on the German language, was Professor of Germanic Philology at Northwestern University. Neither Breda nor Curme was a runologist.

The most frequently quoted American philologist on this question has been George T. Flom (born 1871). A specialist in Scandinavian philology and a member of the University of Iowa faculty 1900–1909, Flom spent the next thirty years as Professor of Scandinavian Languages (and English Philology) at the University of Illinois, serving simultaneously as associate editor, then chief editor of the internationally recognized *Journal of English and Germanic Philology*. Now Professor Emeritus, Flom is a Fellow of the Norwegian Academy of Sciences.

Chester N. Gould (1872–1957), was for many years Associate Professor of German and Scandinavian Languages at the University of Chicago. He is the author of several treatises on ancient Scandinavian literature, folklore, and linguistics.

Gisle Bothne (1860–1934) was born in Norway, became Professor of Greek and Scandinavian at Luther College in 1881, and was from 1907 onward chairman of the Department of Scandinavian Languages at the University of Minnesota.

Axel Louis Elmquist (1884–1949) served as Instructor in Greek, Latin, and Scandinavian, and later as Assistant Professor of Germanic Languages, first at Northwestern University and subsequently at the University of Nebraska. For many years he was associate editor of the scholarly quarterly, *Scandinavian Studies and Notes*.

Julius E. Olson (1858–1944) was Professor of Scandinavian Languages at the University of Wisconsin.

J. A. Holvik (born 1878), Professor Emeritus of Norse at Concordia College, Moorhead, Minnesota, has a vast file on the Kensington question, which he has studied continuously since 1908, and during the course of which he has made several discoveries of great importance.

The author of the present study is Professor of Scandinavian Languages at the University of California, Los Angeles.

Lawrence M. Larson (1868–1938) was born in Norway. He served for many years as Professor of History at the University of Illinois, and edited several manuscripts from Norway's medieval period.

Milo M. Quaife (born 1880) was formerly Superintendent of the Wisconsin State Historical Society. An editor, librarian, and university teacher of note, Dr. Quaife is one-time president of the Mississippi Valley Historical Association.

The Canadian historian, Dr. W. S. Wallace, has published extensively on historical questions. Formerly a professor, Wallace is now Librarian Emeritus of the Toronto Public Library.

Dr. Roberto Almagià has edited and published widely in the field of geography and is an authority on the history of exploration. President of the Academy of Rome, Almagià has served for decades as Professor of Geography at the University of Rome.

Wilhelm Krause, formerly of the University of Koenigsberg, is Professor of Comparative Linguistics at the University of Goettingen, Germany. He has published, together with Helmut Arntz, a large work on the Germanic runic inscriptions of the European continent, and is one of the chief names in modern runology.

Dr. Helmut Arntz, formerly attached to the University of Giessen, is Guest Professor at Bonn, Germany, and a specialist in the history of writing and in epigraphical technique. He has published numerous works of importance in the runological field.

The Nature of the Problem

The present book will not attempt to solve the Kensington problem merely by the method of counting authorities for and against the rune stone, or by estimating the pagination on this or that aspect of the question. Nevertheless, inasmuch as a great deal of confusion exists as to who stands where in this controversy, some precise information will help give shape to the issues involved and dispel the fog of vagueness, half-truth, and misinformation which for too many years has obscured the issues upon which the genuineness of the Kensington inscription must be judged.

Since the Kensington stone purports to be a genuine rune stone and its chief proponent, Mr. Holand, a runologist,[1] it is appropriate to turn first of all to the world's great runologists—already identified in the previous chapter—in order to ascertain their attitude towards the question of whether the Kensington inscription can be a genuine runic carving from 1362.

Sophus Bugge telegraphed to Minneapolis from Norway in 1899 that the stone was "a clumsy fraud."[2] Erik Brate, in describing the stone for Sweden's great encyclopedia, *Nordisk Familjebok*, wrote that "the inscription must be forged."[3] Magnus Olsen, in an important treatise on runes written for the great Scandinavian cultural series, *Nordisk Kultur*, has stated simply: "Norse runic inscriptions have never been demon-

strated in North America."[4] In 1948 he affirmed that "scholarship completely rejects the Kensington inscription, which must
have been made in modern times."[5] Documents pertaining to the
stone have been found among the papers of both Otto von Friesen[6] of Sweden and Ludvig Wimmer[7] of Denmark, both of whom
had been approached on the matter, and both of whom considered the inscription a forgery. As a matter of fact, von Friesen
sent an expression of his views to the Minnesota Historical
Society.[8] Ivar Lindqvist and K. G. Ljunggren stated in the 1950
edition of the Swedish encyclopedia, *Svensk uppslagsbok*, that
"there can be no doubt that the Kensington stone is a forgery."[9]
Wilhelm Krause, the German runologist, gives the stone short
shrift;[10] his younger colleague, Helmut Arntz, does not even mention the stone in his manual of runology.[11] K. M. Nielsen of
Denmark suggests that dialect research will help ascertain what
province of nineteenth century Sweden is responsible for the
language of the inscription.[12] Elias Wessén has declared both
orally and in writing that the inscription is a fake.[13] The most
extensive and convincing of the arguments that have been
brought up against the inscription in recent years are those of
the Danes, Erik Moltke,[14] and Harry Andersen,[15] and the Swede,
Sven B. F. Jansson.[16] Each, in his own way, has declared that
the rune stone from Kensington is bogus.

By the testimony, then, of the men who have devoted their
lives to studying runic inscriptions, who, among them, have
scrutinized, photographed, drawn, made plaster or paper pulp
casts of, and extensively analyzed and commented, edited and
published most or all of the rune stones known to exist in the
world, the Kensington stone is not genuine. Even though most
of these scholars have had to study the inscription through
photographs merely, their opinions merit respect. When Jansson,
commissioned in 1948 by the Swedish Academy of Sciences, came
to this country and examined the Kensington stone at firsthand,
the last remaining doubt was dispelled: As far as modern runology was concerned, the inscription was of no interest.[17] Which
is not to say, of course, that it does not have interest from other
points of view.

It happens that the study of runology calls for a type of train-

ing possessed by very few people anywhere in the world. Not only the ordinary layman, but even scholars, in such fields as history, geography, ethnology, geology, archaeology, and even general linguistics are little equipped to deal with runological problems, particularly when they cannot read modern Scandinavian languages out of a printed book, let alone read Old Norse, Old Swedish, etc., from manuscripts and carved stones. A superficial familiarity with runes can, to be sure, be acquired through perusal of runic alphabets reproduced in encyclopedias and historical works on early Scandinavia. And as with most other branches of science and learning, this has been the undoing of incautious amateurs.

Haziness of definition with respect to what runology is has been an additional factor in the Kensington controversy. This is best exemplified by the widespread references in the American press a few years ago to a treatise on the question by Professor William Thalbitzer of Copenhagen, which the Smithsonian Institution caused to be published in English translation.[18] In the attendant publicity, Thalbitzer was referred to as a "runologist." The fact is that Thalbitzer is not, and never has been, a runologist. It was noted above that his specialties are the Eskimo languages and arctic ethnology (Chapter III). Very few Americans had the opportunity of knowing that the original Danish version of Thalbitzer's article had been discredited in Scandinavia long before the translation could be brought out in the United States.

Now, apart from the runic symbols themselves and the problems they raise, there is another set of primary linguistic criteria upon which the Kensington inscription can and must be judged, and these have to do with the identity of the language which the symbols express. Most commentators, including Holand, agree that the language of the inscription is a form of Swedish, or at least chiefly Swedish, with Holand claiming it as medieval Swedish and his critics asserting it to be modern. An occasional commentator, for reasons which will be illuminated in a separate chapter on the linguistic features of the case, considers the language to be rather a form of modern (Dano-) Norwegian. This introduces the necessity of judging the inscription in accordance with all that is known and recorded concerning the Swedish and Norwegian languages from older times to the present. If any-thing more than casual familiarity with Scandinavian linguistics prevails anywhere, it will inevitably be found among those men whose professional training and life work has revolved around solving practical problems in this field. As this is true of medicine, law, engineering, so it is true of language study that the practical and the theoretical go hand in hand. The chief authorities on Scandinavian linguistics are those who have com-piled the etymological and historical dictionaries of the languages involved, written reference grammars, and edited the basic texts, to mention some principal criteria. What have such men had to say regarding the Kensington inscription?

Of such scholars, whether in the United States or abroad, who have made pronouncement on the authenticity of the inscrip-tion, not one researcher of the first rank has ever stated that he favored it. Several, like Hjalmar Lindroth, have been puzzled by the Kensington stone. But what has puzzled them has chiefly been the discrepancies between linguistic evidence on the one hand and the alleged circumstances of the finding of the stone on the other. To quote Professor Lindroth:

There exists a sharp conflict between the data which have reference to the find as such and those which concern the language. In the in-scription are several linguistic forms that speak strongly against the possibility that the inscription was made in the fourteenth century. The runic characters also appear to be divergent from the types which we have assumed represented the fourteenth century. To be sure, the material available for comparison is somewhat scarce. On the other hand, the reliableness of the testimony as regards the circumstances of the find seems to me to be very strong.[19]

This is to say that, speaking of such matters as he can in-dependently judge as an authority on Scandinavian philology, Lindroth is skeptical of the Kensington stone. What he finds in its favor is something that at a remove of 5000 miles, he was never in a position to investigate for himself: the testimony per-taining to the discovery. This testimony concerned the finding of the Kensington stone under the roots of a tree, and thus had nothing to do with linguistic considerations.

Professor F. S. Cawley of Harvard is another linguist whom Holand quotes with approval:

Skeptical as the reader may be (and properly so) when he begins the book, he will find it difficult as he proceeds to resist the force of Mr. Holand's affirmative arguments, and still more difficult to answer the pertinent questions which he puts to the advocates of the hoax theory. The very irregularities are an argument against the assumption of a learned forger, and it is hard to conceive an ignoramus who would have had the necessary knowledge of history to fabricate such a record. No impartial person will deny, at least, that this book [*The Kensington Stone*] reopens to debate a question which had been generally regarded as a *res adjudicata*.[20]

In other words, Cawley, following his philological instincts, had always suspected a hoax, until Holand's eloquence persuaded him that a suitable hoaxer could not have had access to the Kensington stone before it was produced in public. The arguments which he tentatively accepts are, once again, circumstantial ones. If a reasonable hoaxster could be shown, one whose qualifications were neither those of a "learned forger" nor those of an "ingnoramus," it is strongly implied that Cawley would revert to his original opinion. This was written by Cawley in 1933, half a generation before the controversy was indeed "reopened to debate."

Also delivered in 1933 was a cautious opinion by another philologist of note. Professor Stefán Einarsson stated that some of Holand's linguistic evidence cannot be easily refuted, and that for this reason as well as for

. . . the well documented story of its origin, its weathered appearance, the plausible connection with fourteenth-century Scandinavian history, etc.—it is my conviction that linguists and runologists would do well to take the matter under renewed consideration before rendering their final verdict. Let us hope that the Swedish and Norwegian scholars working on this period will give us their opinion before long.[21]

It should be noted that Einarsson was impressed by "the well documented story" of the finding of the stone. He speaks also of mineralogical and historical factors. His final appeal is to those authorities whose final opinion he will accept: "the linguists and runologists" of Norway and Sweden. And for the present, he finds a score of errors and irrelevancies in the book by Holand that he is reviewing.

Also cited by Holand is Professor A. A. Stomberg of the University of Minnesota. Writing in 1932, Stomberg considered that the circumstances of the runic find and the historical background of the fourteenth century pointed towards the genuineness of the runic inscription. However, when it came to the runes and the language of the inscription, Stomberg, whose specialty was literature rather than linguistics, would not trust himself to venture an opinion.[22]

Professor Gustav Indrebø of Bergen, is another linguistic authority relied upon by Holand.[23] But what has Indrebø had to say about the Kensington inscription? Holand translates Indrebø's letter of 1928: "If it can be proven that the inscription on the Kensington stone is as much as a hundred years old, then one must, in my opinion, because of historical reasons, assume, that it is in fact much older, and genuine—in spite of the fact that it contains various uncommon and unexpected linguistic things."[24] The phrase "If it can be proven" is of course the joker in Indrebø's communication. On linguistic grounds, the Norwegian scholar will not accept the stone.

To sum up: No scholar of eminence in the field of Scandinavian philology has called the Kensington inscription genuine. In the few cases in which such linguists have granted any measure of approval to the disputed stone, they have done so chiefly for other than linguistic reasons, and indeed, in spite of linguistic reasons and on the basis of arguments organized for them and "guaranteed" by Mr. Holand. Conversely speaking, the historians and geographers who have come out in favor of the Kensington stone have usually been most impressed by those portions of Holand's reasoning which they themselves are least equipped to deal with: the linguistic arguments. It is not mere accident that among historians, those in the Scandinavian countries have been the least inclined to place credit in Mr. Holand's theories regarding fourteenth century Scandinavian penetration into Minnesota.

In the present book, each aspect of the Kensington problem, whether linguistic, historical, geological, or otherwise will be dealt with in its separate place. But inasmuch as the Kensington inscription is primarily a written document—a message in a Scandinavian dialect and carved in Scandinavian runes—the linguistic and runological aspects assume a definite primacy. In the final analysis the Kensington inscription stands or falls by its own testimony. Mr. Holand goes into linguistic matters at some length, stating, "The language of the inscription, being the principal means by which the writer reveals himself, presents one of the best fields for testing its authenticity."[25]

Professor Brøndsted, who thinks that from the viewpoint of archaeology the rune stone might well be genuine, asserts however, that the decisive opinion on the matter must come from the runologists.[26] S. N. Hagen, a prominent American defender of the stone, agrees that linguistics must carry the day with respect to the question of the medieval origin, and the arguments he uses in its favor are limited to the linguistic.[27] The present author attacked Hagen's views in general, but agreed to the primacy of linguistic arguments.[28] C. N. Gould has stated: "Not until after this question [*i.e.*, the linguistic aspect] is settled can these other questions be deemed pertinent."[29] G. O. Curme wrote: "The question is solely a linguistic one."[30] G. T. Flom and H. Gjessing each have published basic attacks on the stone, chiefly from the linguistic point of view.[31]

In short, both sides agree as to the importance of linguistics in this dispute. Unfortunately for the average person interested in an artifact of this kind, the problem has been complicated by at least three factors of importance. The first of these is that when such a person reads the Kensington inscription, he is not reading the original but something twice removed from it. He is reading a translation based on a transliteration. That is, the runes—and they are strange and disputed ones—have been converted into their assumed alphabetical equivalents in order to form a communication in a—similarly disputed—Scandinavian dialect, which then has been translated into English.[32] Once translated, the message might, for all the reader can tell, have originally been expressed in Arabic or Eskimo. A translation becomes the (not always accurate) possible common denominator of an endless array of dialects whose divergencies from the translation language and from one another may vary incalculably. Thus, the Kensington history has rid itself of certain discrepancies in grammar, orthography and idiom which induce philologists to regard the inscription as nothing more than an unsuccessful imitation—or a humorous take-off—on an earlier mode of writing, in short, as a *pastiche.*

A second factor is that, just as a prolonged and intense training in mathematics is required for the solution of problems of astronomy or physics, so a problem involving medieval languages calls for special skills. For runological study, certain extra skills are involved. As previously stated, it does not suffice to have learned to read Swedish, even older forms of Swedish, nor even to be able to spell through the runes, since what is needed above all is the judgment and ability to *evaluate* linguistic evidence. Not only does this type of ability mature very slowly in a given individual, but except in the graduate schools of our universities it seldom has any occasion for developing at all.

In the third place, those who have written in favor of the stone have chiefly done so in English. This has vastly facilitated quotation from pro-Kensington sources. Of those who have attacked the Kensington stone with linguistic arguments, and in English, none has directly reached the public with his arguments: Gould's article remained in typescript and was never published; Flom's article was better known, but has been out of print for many decades; the author's article appeared in an academic *festschrift* or presentation volume of limited circulation; Moltke wrote, besides an article in Danish, a special article which, translated into English, appeared in an American quarterly with a circulation of 600 copies.[33]

That the public's familiarity with arguments in favor of the stone should preponderate over its acquaintance with those against is a simple product of statistics. Unfortunately this has led to the oft-repeated assumption that there are no valid arguments against the stone, else why has no one produced any? This proud boast by Mr. Holand has been repeated endlessly in the public press. Here is a characteristic quotation from Holand, the earliest of this nature that could be located: "The ablest runologists and linguists of two continents have critically scrutinized it but the runestone has triumphed spotless. . . . Serene in its defiance to all learned criticism, this old inscription is like some piece of forgotten art of pottery, a snowflake, or a piece of radium."[34] That was written in 1910. Forty-one years later Holand summarized what he claimed to be the chief reason for skepticism about reputed ancient Scandinavian relics in America: "It traces its origin from the totally preposterous introduction which the first of these finds—the Kensington stone— received when it was discovered 54 years ago."[35] This was in effect to repeat, if in slightly different form, the claim from 1910: that as of the year 1951, there were still no valid arguments against the stone, which had merely been the victim of a slight misunderstanding. Just because some professors assertedly were prejudiced against the Kensington stone in 1899, no one—except Mr. Holand—has been able to think straight about the matter ever since.[36]

This book will attempt to show that, not the rune stone, but Mr. Holand himself, has remained serenely defiant to "all learned criticism." It is the contention of this book, furthermore, that the entire problem of the rune stone has been misstated. The Holand school of thought has made excellent capital of the points at which the history of the disputed runic monument has been obscure. Holand and his followers have insisted that for want of conclusive proof of its modern fabrication, the inscription must be acknowledged as medieval. To claim that a rune stone, which all runologists and most philologists have condemned outright, must be a genuine medieval product, simply because we cannot lay our hand on some specific modern author or authors, is sadly to pervert the logic of the situation. To adapt slightly a simile from the Icelandic linguist, Professor Helgason of Copenhagen: If a telephone book for the year 1957 were to be found under the roots of a 500-year-old tree (the tree roots that figure in the Kensington case were of an age estimated at from ten to seventy years at the most), one would indeed admire the skill with which it had been placed there; but one should not find it necessary to accept the antiquity of the volume in question.[37] Holand himself attempts to make much of linguistic evidence, which he debates at length with the professors.

Each time that he finds himself in linguistic straits, however, he suddenly abandons this tack and seeks to overcome philological objections through the production of dendrological, historical, geological, or testimonial evidence, and it is this shifting, poly-morphous approach that has obstructed the true issues involved. No comprehensive solution to this vexed question—one that includes not merely negative arguments, however valid, but like-wise a positive demonstration of what the Kensington is—having previously been attempted, the present investigation has aimed at covering all essential aspects of the case.

The problem in our day is no longer one of showing that the Kensington carving cannot be of ancient origin, for the runolo-gists have already established this. The problem is merely whether one can successfully dispose of certain alleged stumbling blocks to the treatment of the carving as a modern lithography. If it can be shown that the carving of such a document as the Kensington stone in the late nineteenth century was not only possible, but in fact quite easy, and that the commission of such a hoax during that period in Scandinavian-populated Minnesota, far from being the inexplicable phenomenon that is so regularly postulated, was the eminently logical outcome of various cul-tural circumstances; if contributory human factors can be shown; if pertinent textual materials are demonstrated to have been available in the area of the "find," in short, to such persons as had opportunity to make practical use of them; if something resembling a "family tree" for numerous features of this par-ticular inscription can be brought to light; if it can be established that the principal objections relied upon to disprove the "mod-ern" theory rest on unproven allegation, errors, and even mis-representation of fact; then the original linguistic arguments will regain the hearing they deserve and it will not be necessary to go further. If, in addition, something can be indicated regarding the Kensington inscription's real purpose and merits—since it lacks neither—then this book will have made some contribution to the history, not of Pre-Columbian exploration, but of American immigration in the nineteenth century. Such a demonstration will be attempted here.

It is possible to construct a satisfactory genealogy for the inscription and even a reasonable motive, the two constituting a unified whole without inconsistent details.

Everything necessary to the fabrication of such a hoax existed in the immediate vicinity: an ample supply of stone, piled along the edges of the fields, as a geologist's report described them in 1910; an atmosphere conducive to the hoax; the requisite human material, that is, a local population of Scandinavian immigrants; and *textual materials* which can account for the more puzzling features of the Kensington inscription. Though clever in many respects, the Kensington inscription is *not* the sophisticated product that myth would have it. Its principal author, whoever he was, was clearly not the fabled "man of much learning in philology and history."[38] It is obvious that his book learning was limited and that he possessed no library on Old Swedish philology. Just as obviously, he did have access to a circumscribed amount of reference material, between which and the inscription there is a positive correlation. Mr. Holand furnishes a valuable lead: "The discussion concerning [the stone in the fall of 1898] finally resulted in the conclusion that the stone contained a runic inscription, *several persons recalling that they had seen illustrations of similar inscriptions in Scandinavian books.*"[39] (Italics supplied.)

In these discussions we shall not name a perpetrator or perpetrators as such but will discuss freely the names of several men unavoidably associated with any such investigation. The name most frequently mentioned in this connection is, of course, that of Olof Ohman. It is necesssary to assert here that a statement circulated in 1954 by *Time* magazine that the author had positive proof of the deceased Ohman's authorship of the Kensington inscription, is categorically false and was never made.[40] Indeed, the original interview carried a specific disclaimer on this point which was ignored by the editor of the periodical. For the purpose of this book, the author of the Kensington inscription remains as a "person X," for neither legally nor scientifically is proof of a given person's authorship now possible. What one may claim to have *proof* of is that the Kensington inscription is modern; the aims of a scientific investigation are fully satisfied by such a demonstration.

Pains have been taken to consult several local persons, including the two sons of Olof Ohman who continue to reside on the old farm, and who reacted with great courtesy. Oral information is specifically identified and credited in the following pages. In no case have the conclusions of this volume been based on rumor.

CHAPTER V

The Discovery of the Stone in 1898

Of all the arguments employed to establish the authenticity of the Kensington inscription, the argument upon which the greatest reliance is placed by the Holand school of thought concerns the initial discovery of the stone under the roots of a certain tree (Figs. 7 and 8).[1] The tree in question is referred to as an aspen or poplar (*Populus tremuloides*) growing on the premises of the Swedish immigrant farmer Olof Ohman. We are told by Holand that, one day in 1898, while Ohman was clearing a rough and timbered section of his land, he discovered a stone under the roots of this tree, or perhaps more accurately, under the roots of the stump of the tree; he was at this point "grubbing," or clearing trees and stumps. After extracting the stone from the roots of the tree, and noticing nothing odd about it, Ohman let the stone lie on the ground. Some time later—whether minutes or hours we are not told—Ohman's ten-year-old son Edward chanced to dust the stone off with his cap and thereupon discovered that it was inscribed with strange characters. Father and son jointly speculated that these might be signs from some Indian almanac. Ohman informed his neighbor, Norwegian-born Nils Flaten, owner of the adjoining farm, of the discovery, and

Flaten came over "that same afternoon" to inspect the curiosity, the existence of which he had not previously suspected.

Eleven years later—in July, 1909—the two farmers made affidavits respecting certain features of this discovery (see Chapt. VI).[2] The affidavits pertained to the uncovering of the stone under the roots of the tree, to the location of the tree, the size of the tree and its roots, and to the date of the find.

The age of the tree standing over the stone has been the subject of endless discussion during the last half century, with Holand and his followers seeking to establish that the tree was of such age that the carving and placing of the stone must antedate the earliest Scandinavian settlement of the Kensington area. The effect of this would be practically to guarantee its medieval character. Most critics of the stone assume that it was "planted" in the '80's or '90's of the nineteenth century, and either inserted between the roots of a young tree, or simply given a shallow burial, after which a tree was allowed to grow over it. According to this view, the tree was probably only ten or twelve years old at the time of the discovery in 1898.

In Holand's book (published 1908) on the Norwegian settlements he describes the tree as having been, by his estimate, twenty-five years old in 1898.[3] In 1910 he refers to it as being "at least 40 years old."[4] In his later works he describes the retroactive age as "at least 70 years."[5] This estimate purports to be based on U. S. Forestry reports on the growth rings of trees. It also appears, however, that the estimate of greater age, and the energy devoted to supporting the estimate's validity, reflect a growing need, on the part of proponents of the stone, to give the latter a more unassailable certificate of antiquity the more it was attacked on runological and linguistic grounds.

Great uncertainty attaches to the age of the tree. Professor Thalbitzer estimated its age, as of 1898, at over fifty years.[6] J. J. Skørdalsvold, who believed in the inscription, stated in 1913 that it would be impossible to determine the age of the tree, which had been estimated at from ten to forty years.[7] According to an article by Dr. Henrik Nissen of Minneapolis, one witness had said that the tree was five years old; Nissen himself calculated that it might be ten to twelve years old.[8] In every case, however,

the hypothetical age of the tree was a derivative of its alleged
diameter rather than anything independently ascertainable.
And estimates of the diameter have varied from as little as 4
inches to as much as 10. If we dwell briefly on this matter, it is
not because a determination of the precise diameter and age of
the poplar tree are necessary to proof of the falsification thesis. It
is only to Mr. Holand that these factors are urgently vital. The
function of our discussion is to illustrate the basic uncertainty
of one of his key arguments.

The jeweler, Mr. Samuel Olson of Kensington, told Professor
Flom in very definite terms in April, 1910, that the stump of
the poplar, sawed off to a length of approximately 12 inches, was
4 inches in diameter.[9] Three months later, Holand induced Olof
Ohman, finder of the rune stone, to point out on his own property some examples of trees similar to the one under which he
had discovered the stone. Ohman pointed out three trees, respec-
tively $8\frac{1}{2}$, $8\frac{3}{4}$, and $5\frac{1}{2}$ inches in diameter.[10] Polished cross sections
of these trees are preserved at the Minnesota Historical Society.
Ohman indicated that the "rune stone tree" had been 3 inches
greater in diameter than the smallest of the sections, which is to
say that it had had a diameter of from 8 to 9 inches. Shown the
three sections by Holand, Samuel Olson then thought the Kensington tree had been slightly larger than the $5\frac{1}{2}$ inch section,
i.e., probably 6 inches.[11] This was at a distance of 18 inches
above the ground. Seeking to refute Flom's version of Olson's
opinion, the MHS Report merely corroborates in effect what
Flom had reported.[12] Claiming that Flom labored under a "mis-
apprehension," the MHS Report states: "Mr. Olson says that
he said that the tree tapered so that at fifteen or eighteen
inches above the stone it was about four or five inches in diameter."[13] Affidavits secured meanwhile from Olof Ohman and his
neighbor Nils Flaten placed the estimate at, respectively, "10
inches in diameter at its base" and "8 inches to 10 inches in
diameter at its base."[14]

As Dr. Quaife has pointed out, it is unfortunate that Flom did
not examine Ohman on discrepancies regarding the diameter of
the tree.[15] However, Samuel Olson made for the MHS a drawing of his recollection of the poplar stump, and this drawing

makes it perfectly clear how the tree could have been described by him as 4, or 4 or 5, inches in diameter at from 12 to 18 inches above the ground, while others described it as 8 to 10 inches across at the base (Fig. 8).

The three-inch root which ran across the sixteen-inch top of the stone was practically on the surface of the ground, and Ohman's and Olson's estimates of the diameter of the aspen at its base comprehend the normal enlargement produced by this "almost horizontal" root. The measurement of the trunk proper, on which any estimate of the age of the tree must be based, must obviously be taken at a point where this surface root ceased to be a factor. A tree which immediately above its roots is four inches in diameter is properly described as being four inches thick.[16]

Samuel Olson's drawing of the roots of the tree should now be compared with Mr. Holand's (Fig. 7). The two are grossly at variance. Whereas Holand quotes and relies on a statement made in writing by Olson to Dr. Knut Hoegh that the poplar was nine inches in diameter at its base, thereafter tapering so as to be perhaps 6 inches across at 18 inches from the base, Holand's drawing amounts to a falsification of that testimony and of Olson's diagram alike.[17] The "Holand poplar" is clearly intended to be a uniform 8, if not 10, inches thick from top to bottom. Nowhere does Holand explain the justification for his substitute sketch. Readers should bear this discrepancy in mind when the map used by Holand to establish the location of the runesite is discussed.

The diameter, or supposed diameter, of the poplar has resulted in a wide variety of estimates as to its age. Dr. Nissen describes a fourteen-year-old poplar with a diameter of eleven inches.[18] One of a group of men who, along with Samuel Olson, dug into the runesite in April, 1899, stated in response to an inquiry from the MHS that "we judged the tree to be about twelve years old."[19] What is one to make of all this?

In the first place, not one of the estimates cited above is in any sense contemporary with the discovery of the stone in 1898 or even of the digging on the runesite the following spring. All of the approximations date from 1909 or 1910, if we make exception for Holand's own expanding estimates at later dates. Carefully examined, furthermore, not even these statements purport to be warranties based on actual measurements or on recollections of actual measurements made at any time, or by any person, of the poplar tree in question. They are only guesses made more than a decade after the fact.

Interestingly enough, although Olof Ohman at one time stated that the poplar was a dwarf tree,[20] nowhere can a statement be found estimating the height of the tree in question. The tireless Holand has never seen fit to inquire into this, or at any rate, to report it. Professor Flom ascertained nothing on this score.[21] The MHS Report has nothing to say about it. Nils Flaten, who allegedly was called to the runesite by Olof Ohman on the day the stone was found, was never questioned on this point, so far as can be learned at so late a date. Is this the result of mere chance? Was the height of the tree really a matter of indifference to those who have claimed a retroactive age of from thirty to seventy years for the tree which, above all other evidence, is relied upon to prove the antiquity of the disputed Kensington stone? Or were facts, inconvenient facts, at one time discovered about the tree which its protagonists have not deemed it necessary to produce for scholarly assessment?

It seems legitimate to put such a question in view of the fact that the height of a tree—while by no means conclusive—yet might be supposed to have such an important bearing on any conclusions as to its age, that its conspicuous omission from Mr. Holand's elaborate structure of speculation is a cause for wonder. At all events, the Kensington tree was never to our certain knowledge seen by anybody. Cut from its stump at a point from 12 to 18 inches above its roots, it was speedily removed from the runesite, one must suppose, and converted into firewood before questions could be asked.

Meanwhile, the only tangible evidence ever offered respecting the alleged tree was a certain stump with the roots. Such a stump, with roots which had evidently clasped an object somewhat similar in width (this would be 16 inches; the length and thickness of the stone were not subject to estimate by these criteria, according to Samuel Olson's diagram. See Fig. 8) to the Kensington stone, was assertedly shown to Flaten and, a good five months later (or eight, as future discussion will indicate as a possibility)[22] to a group of local residents who came to excavate the premises in search for buried treasure.[23] And the tangibility of this evidence is materially attenuated by the circumstances that another ten or twelve years had passed before the various parties concerned were called upon to fashion their respective estimates and thus willy nilly take sides in the rune stone controversy then raging. At the outset there are thus two tremendous gaps in the chain of evidence. And yet this is the type of evidence submitted by Holand as *incontrovertible proof* of the authenticity of the most disputed artifact in American history.

One of the more remarkable features of the rune stone discovery is the lack of agreement by its supporters over just when it was found. Respecting this, there are two main lines of tradition, mutually contradictory, yet both accepted, without critical comment, by the pro-Kensington school of thought. It is reported, on the one hand, that the Kensington rune stone was uncovered in the month of August, 1898, and on the other, that its date of discovery was November 8 of that same year. Mr. Holand himself subscribes to both opinions, or to neither of them, as suits his purpose. For example, writing in the *Journal of American History* in 1910, he states the month as August.[24] In his book of 1932 he refers to the time of the find as August,[25] and as the "summer of 1898,"[26] printing likewise affidavits to establish the date as August.[27] In his book of 1940, reprinted in 1942, Holand repeats these statements, together with the affidavits.[28] In an article in 1951, Holand avoids stating a specific date, but indicates by a reference to the search party of April, 1899 (" . . . only five months after the stone was found . . . "),[29] that the find must have taken place in November. By the time of his article of 1953, Holand had evidently decided to keep silent on the date entirely and allow readers to guess for themselves.[30]

Helge Gjessing in Norway was told "August."[31] Dr. Upham of the MHS wrote "August" in an article from 1910.[32] Simultaneously, his colleague Professor Winchell printed in the MHS Report that the true date was November, 8.[33] Both Upham and Winchell believed in the stone. Professor Flom was told "the fall" of 1898.[34] Professor Breda reports having heard around New

Year of 1899, from Kensington, that the stone had been found in November.[35] In 1934, Holand was challenged by Dr. Quaife to explain the discrepancy in these conflicting versions.[36] Purporting, in a countering article the following year to have "answered, fairly and squarely, every argument and objection which Mr. Quaife has made against the authenticity of the Kensington rune stone," Holand nevertheless said nothing whatever about the troubled matter of dates.[37] Five years later, as indicated above, he was still clinging stoutly to the month of August as the date of the rune find, directly in conflict with the date of "November 8" as ascertained by the MHS, whose Report Holand simultaneously upheld as a model investigation.[38]

But Holand's thinking on this subject was meanwhile undergoing a revolution, as his article of 1951 intimates. To be sure, he does not use the word "November," but allows readers to calculate this for themselves by counting backwards from the spring of the following year, a calculation somewhat less than precise for those readers who lack access to the fact, elsewhere recorded, that the digging party of 1899 took place in the month of April.[39] In his article of 1953, Holand avoids the matter of the date. In his book of 1956, he boldly declares the date to be "November."[40] The affidavits (which contain the date of "August") are once again referred to, but only in general terms, and this time they are not included for comparison.[41] Thus Holand manages to eat his cake and have it too by utilizing as corroborative evidence for his theories, documents which his own statement specifically discredits. He has also, over a period of thirty years, reversed his own statements on the date, and he has done this without the slightest explanation. If the matter were unimportant, Holand would not have changed his story. To be sure, an investigator is entitled to change his mind with the discovery of new evidence, or through a reinterpretation of evidence, but if his work is to inspire confidence as a true work of research rather than a partisan presentation of arguments, the nature of the new evidence, or the reasons for the reinterpretation, must be set forth. This Holand fails to do. It should be noted that Holand is discrediting not only his own arguments, but likewise the word of Olof Ohman, on whose evidence he must rely for the existence of a rune stone—inscribed, and found under the roots of a tree—in the first place. Significant also is the fact that, in dating the runic find in his book of 1956, Holand does not say "November 8," but merely "November." Perhaps this should be taken as representing Holand's tactful conclusion that Professor Winchell, in preparing the MHS Report in 1910, was right after all in ascertaining November, rather than August, as the correct date, but not right to the extent of fixing it so precisely as November 8. But there is also another possibility, namely, that the date "August" had become inconvenient and must be disposed of as quietly as possible, since it represented a potential danger to the rune stone story. This matter will be discussed more fully below, some attention being given first to the location of the runic find.

The Kensington stone was assertedly turned up on the farm belonging to Olof Ohman, specifically, "upon a timbered elevation, surrounded by marshes, in the southeast corner of my land, about 500 feet west of my neighbor's, Nils Flaten's, house, and in the full view thereof."[42] According to Professor Winchell and the MHS Report, the stone was found 44 feet above a former lake (See Figs. 3 and 6): "The exact location was on the southern slope of one of two knolls which together form the higher part of what has been called an 'island' because formerly surrounded by a lake and now surrounded by a grassy marsh. These knolls have an extreme height, above the surface of the marsh, of fifty-five feet, the smaller knoll rising about fifty feet. The stone lay forty-four feet above the marsh."[43]

Holand's description the same year is roughly similar: "The spot was a rough and inaccessible one, being a hilly knoll surrounded by a small and shallow lake, which of late years had dried up and become a swamp."[44]

Compare the MHS Report:

The stone is said [in the inscription] to have been located on an island, but when found it was not on an island. It was on a morainic hill which is now surrounded by a grassy marsh, and which may have been an island in a small lake prior to the desiccation of the country which has converted many lakes into marshes and many marshes into meadows. This gradual drying up of the country is a well-known feature throughout the western part of the state. It has been known and many times noted throughout the western part of the state.[45]

Holand's diagnosis of 1956, "No one would think of calling this elevation an island now, because it is merely a slight rise on a rolling prairie"[46] takes on an interesting significance when one thinks of the obvious implications of the statement. "No one," not Olof Ohman, nor Flaten, or any of the other residents would think of calling the rise an island, and since they would not think of this it would be ridiculous to assert that any one of them could have carved the stone. But is any such implication accurate? It should be noted here that Winchell's observation did not purport to be a recent discovery of his own of a fact ascertainable only by a person of geological, or at least scholarly, training. Quite the reverse, Winchell reports in a matter of fact tone that the place "has been called an 'island,'" presumably by the local residents that is (and this would certainly include Ohman and Flaten), and he proceeds to explain the logical basis for this.

The date of the reduction of the lake to a swamp "of late years" cannot be ascertained. In the warm month of August, 1953, the onetime lake, on which some cattle were grazing, was muddy and difficult to walk across.[47] There appears, then, to be a perfectly simple and natural connection between the reference to "this island" in the Kensington inscription and the appellation of "island" reportedly used for the immediate area of the runesite by at least some local persons who had occasion to reflect on the nature, past or present, of the terrain in question. In this particular field, at least, a runic hoaxer would not have had to be a scholar.

In the year 1938, Mr. Edward Ohman, Olof Ohman's son, planted a pipe on the slope of the knoll on which the rune stone allegedly was found.[48] Although the location could not be accurately checked in 1953, inasmuch as the pipe had been removed, its former location, as pointed out, seemed to agree with the location assigned to the discovery by Winchell (see Figs. 3 and 6). An interesting problem, however, is involved at this point. Holand has repeatedly insisted, and demonstrated with his affidavits, that the runesite was "500 feet" from Nils Flaten's house, and he has in two of his books printed a map which supposedly indicates this distance (Fig. 9).[49] Edward Ohman, as a boy of ten, was assertedly on the spot at the time the Kensington stone was uncovered. The spot at which he planted the pipe in 1938 was measured by Professor J. A. Holvik as being 156 feet west of the eastern boundary of the Ohman farm as it adjoins the Flaten farm. The boundary, according to survey, is 80 rods, or 1320 feet, or a quarter of a mile from the highway just east of Flaten's house. Standing in the marshy pasture at a spot 500 feet west of Flaten's house, one still has 580 feet to go toward the west before reaching the nearest boundary of Ohman's farm (Figs. 3–5). As measured by Professor Holvik and an assistant with a 100-foot steel tape, with two per cent margin for error, the distance from Flaten's house to the runesite is not 500 feet as Holand claims and his *ad hoc* map distinctly shows, but nearly two and a half times that—1241 feet.[50] Holand's map has greatly foreshortened the width of the marshy area.[51] It also shows Flaten's house much closer to the runesite, and farther from the road, than it now is or formerly was. A thick grove of trees stands immediately to the west of Flaten's house, and the evidence of the stumps is that it was there during the last century as well, in conformity with general reports by Holand and others as to the overgrown character of this terrain (Figs. 5 and 6). Flaten's house could not have stood farther to the west without being situated in the swamp; nor has Holand made any claims concerning removal of the Flaten house.

Holand's meretricious map and any allegations based on it ought consequently to be withdrawn. There is an additional point. The thick grove of trees just mentioned obscures the vision between Flaten's house and any spot 500 feet west of it. The unsupported but constantly reiterated assertion that the location of the find, 500 feet west of Flaten's house, was "in plain view" of the house, is obviously untenable and should likewise be striken from the evidence.

But to suppose for a moment that Holand and the affidavits he has gathered, are right about the 500 feet. (And indeed, one who has reconnoitered that area as often and as thoroughly as

Holand, ought to be well informed on the topic.) The net result of this is to place the runesite in the middle of the marshland. Now, any spot so located, that is, 500 feet west of Flaten's house, or even as much as 1000 feet west of it, is now and was in 1898 on Flaten's land rather than Ohman's.

To be sure, the reputed affidavits by Ohman and Flaten state that the Kensington stone was uncovered by Ohman, who then summoned Flaten to the scene.[52] But Professor Winchell reported at the meeting of the MHS on December 13, 1909, that it was Flaten who had uncovered the stone and found no writing on it, after which the stone lay neglected for a long time. This was after Winchell had been conferring in person or by mail with both Holand and his own associate, Dr. Upham, for over a year.[53] This extraordinary information, however acquired by Winchell, was soon suppressed and not again referred to, either in the printed Report of the MHS or in any of Holand's exhaustive commentaries.

In *Westward from Vinland*, Holand goes to the trouble to print a curious letter by Flaten to cinch the matter of the precise location of the runesite:

"Kensington, Minn., July 20, 1909.

"This is to certify that I live only 500 feet from the spot where the rune stone was found. This house faces directly toward this spot and there is only the open swamp between. I have lived in that house since 1884 and there has not been a day or night but that the house has been occupied by some members of my family.

"(Signed) Niles [*sic*] Flaten."[54]

This letter, whether purposely or not, fails to certify whether Flaten or any members of his family had intimate knowledge of the Kensington stone.

As a purported alibi for his neighbor Ohman, the letter is irrelevant, a veritable "joker." But the statement as to the swamp ties in very well with information sent to Professor Curme at Northwestern in February, 1899. According to Flom, the stone was forwarded to Curme by Sam Olson; in all probability, the information sent to Curme derives from the same source. As reported in the *Chicago Tribune* for February 20, 1899, the stone "is said to have been found in a swamp near Kensington,

Minn., by four Norwegian farmers and laborers." Curme was
also told that the proprietor was "draining."[55] Such a phrase is
applicable to swampland, less so to an elevation "forty-four feet
above the marsh."

In a letter of February 23, 1899, to the editors of *Skandinaven*,
and printed by them on March 1, E. E. Aaberg reproaches them
for reporting the previous day that the stone had been found "i
en myr." But there is no internal lack of probability in the
account by which a Norwegian farmer—Flaten—draining the
swamp in August at a point on his own property—as it would
have to be—*500 feet* west of his house, uncovered a large stone
which had *no inscription on it*. This version was, however,
superseded by a new one in which the stone was found by the
Swede, Ohman, *with* an inscription, at a time and place uncertain
(in "August" or in "November"). But the Norwegian tradition was strong down to the last, for Upham wrote to Winchell
on Nov. 27, 1909: "The Norwegian farmer who found the Rune
Stone on his land is Otto Öhman."[56] Writing to Winchell on
May 12, 1910, J. P. Hedberg states that "Flaaten" [*sic.*] helped
dig the stone.[57]

What is the explanation of so many conflicting assertions on
what should have been an easily ascertainable fact? Was the
Kensington stone found for the first time, in the marsh, in the
month of August, 1898, by Nils Flaten? Was it *reincarnated* in
the hill location on November 8 following by Ohman? Such a
hypothesis would explain many things, including various peculiarities in Holand's writings.

We know that a group of citizens dug in the excavation left by
a poplar tree some time in the spring of 1899, many months after
the supposed find of a rune stone.[58] They were assertedly told by
Ohman that the Kensington stone had been found by him under
the roots of this very tree (stump). These men jointly saw the
stump, the bent roots, and a hollow spot from which a bulky object had evidently at some time been removed; and although the
contemporary evidence on this point does not with certainty
establish the *location* of their digging (its identity with the spot
on the knoll has subsequently been presumed, but there is
neither proof nor an unequivocal statement on this score), the

matter is again not essential. We need not impugn the joint testimony of these men as to what they saw in 1899, for we have no proof that the Kensington stone had been inscribed when dug up the previous year. Secondly, there is no proof that the excavated stone was this particular stone in the first place. All claims that such was the case rest on the word of Ohman. It will not suffice to beg the question by citing his self-serving statements as proof, for it is exactly the validity of his claim that we are attempting at this point to determine through external criteria. It happens that an important letter is preserved that bears directly on the issue.

The letter was written on April 19, 1910, by Mr. C. W. Van Dyke, then director of the Miami Townsite Company at Miami, Arizona. Mr. Van Dyke, who had attended lectures on archaeology at the University of Minnesota, was Superintendent of Schools in the Kensington area at the time that the Kensington stone was being investigated early in 1899. He was a member of the digging party referred to above. His letter was written to Professor Winchell of the MHS, apparently in response to the latter's inquiry. Van Dyke states in part: "The tree, as indicated by its roots, had undoubtedly grown over some flat stone; *whether it was this stone I could not say as I had not seen it in place* [italics supplied]. As I remember it, we judged the tree to be about twelve years old. . . . Of course, I could not determine whether or not the stone was there before the growth of the tree."[59]

Van Dyke's letter is conspicuously omitted from the MHS Report and there is no quotation from it anywhere by Holand. In a single clause, Superintendent Van Dyke uncovered a fatal weakness in all stories pertaining to the roots, and the vague reference to Van Dyke in the Report[60] is satisfactory evidence that both Winchell and Holand realized this perfectly. For Van Dyke had not seen the stone in place. None of the other diggers ever claimed to have seen it in place. In fact, there is no record of anyone's claim to having seen it in place except that of Olof Ohman, the man most commonly suspected of forging the inscription. Without necessarily subscribing to that accusation, we may nevertheless insist that Ohman's remarkable statement regarding a circumstance so evidently in need of corroboration is no sort of proof. Summing up, one can conclude from an analysis of all available evidence bearing on the poplar tree and its roots, that a sizable stone actually was, at some time, found under the accommodated roots of a tree, the disputed age, girth, and disposition of which bear no necessary relation to the Kensington inscription.

How, then, was the exploit performed? The runes could easily have been carved a few months, or, for that matter, a very few days previous to the "find." It can be surmised that the stone was probably "found" twice, the first time uninscribed, in August (by Flaten, in the swamp, 500 feet from Flaten's house?), and the second time on the 8th of November, on Ohman's hillside, some 700 feet further west, but now inscribed with the runes. Perhaps there was even a substitution of stones, with the inscribed one taking the place of another stone—one of similar size—a "twin" which had been previously extracted from the roots of the tree. After all, there are many stones in this area, of which 5 per cent, according to Winchell's geological report, resemble the graywacke of the Kensington stone.[61] As for the testimony concerning the tree, the roots, and the hollow spot— this would be equally applicable to a quite different situation, a situation in which a stone with dimensions approximating those of the known Kensington stone had been removed from under a tree with witnesses then invited to inspect the truncated roots and reconstruct, mentally, a tree they had never seen as "proof" of a strictly non-relevant allegation, *i.e.*, an allegation as to the identity of the removed stone with that which bore the Kensington inscription.

There is no reason for assuming that the Kensington carving antedates the year 1898.[62] When one inquires whether the stone, in its *inscribed* state, was found in August or in November of that year, some curious contradictions come to light. These contradictions reveal themselves in the evidence of Ohman and Holand, on the one hand, and in that of a prominent Kensington resident, J. P. Hedberg, on the other. Olof Ohman, in an affidavit quoted by Holand (see the following chapter), states that the date was "August," and goes on to recite: "I kept the stone in my possession for a few days; and then left it in the Bank of Kensington, where it remained for inspection for several months. During this interval, it was sent to Chicago for inspection and soon returned in the same state in which it was sent."[63]

Holand himself writes: "In the summer of 1898 a farmer in western Minnesota named Olof Ohman made a strange discovery. . . . The news of this discovery was soon noised about and many persons came to inspect the stone. . . . This discovery was much more than a nine days' wonder, and as the stone was on exhibition in one of the bank windows of Kensington it was inspected by thousands."[64]

We turn now to J. P. Hedberg, who was a real estate and insurance man and travel agent at Kensington. On January 1, 1899, Hedberg wrote a letter regarding the stone to the prominent Swedish-American publisher, Swan J. Turnblad, of Minneapolis. Still extant, this letter is discussed more fully in Chapter XIV, below. The letter (see Fig. 11) begins as follows: "I Inclose you a Copy of an inscription on a stone found about 2 miles from Kensington by a O. Ohman he found it under a tree when Grubbing—he wanted I should go out and look at it and I told him to haul it in when he came (not thinking much of it) he did so and this is an excest Copy of it. . . ."[65]

We have independent evidence that the Kensington stone was sent to Chicago (Evanston) and received by Professor G. O. Curme of Northwestern University at the end of February, 1899. It is likewise established that the stone before long—in March or April of that same year—was returned to Kensington and its owner, Olof Ohman. What we know about these circumstances can therefore be summed up as follows: The stone was known to Hedberg on January 1, 1899, as evidenced by his letter of that date; secondly, the stone was in Evanston, Illinois at the end of February, 1899. The rest of the evidence, or purported evidence, regarding the stone, may be organized into two accounts, the Ohman-Holand version, and the Hedberg version.

According to Ohman and Holand, as quoted above, the Kensington stone, inscribed, was found in August, 1898. Within a few days it was placed on display in the bank window at Kensington, where it was "inspected by thousands." On or about

February 16, 1899, it was sent to Chicago and Evanston, from where it later was returned in good shape. The implication of this account is that the stone was on continuous exhibit at the Kensington bank for a probable period of five months: September, October, November, December, January.

Hedberg's evidence, above, is that he heard of the stone directly from Ohman, who reported to him the discovery of an inscribed stone and asked him to "go out and look at it." But Hedberg, "not thinking much of it," "told him to haul it in when he came." Since Hedberg's letter to the newspaper editor is dated January 1, 1899, it seems likely that the stone had been brought in to him shortly before this date.

The "thousands" who assertedly inspected the Kensington stone in the late summer and fall of 1898 must really have created a sensation, amounting as they would have to many times the population of little Kensington, which even today boasts a mere 354 inhabitants.[66] It is, then, rather strange that so sensational a pilgrimage was not reported in the newspapers as an extraordinary thing in itself, long before the following January; but no such accounts are known. And, under such circumstances, why would not the local realtor, J. P. Hedberg, have written his letter about the mysterious stone earlier than the first of January? Most probably because he had not seen the stone.

How could it happen that Hedberg had failed to see the "nine days' wonder" during the four months that it was in a bank window down the street of the village to which "thousands" of curious persons were streaming in order to view that very stone? The likeliest answer is that it was *not on display at all*.

If the stone was not on display from within "a few days" of its discovery in August until (and well past) the January date of Hedberg's letter, as claimed by Holand and Ohman, why was it not on display? And where was it? One can assume that it was not on display for two excellent reasons, the first of these being that the stone, inscribed with runes, was almost certainly not found in August, but in November, as reported to the Minnesota Historical Society by Professor Winchell in 1910,[67] and as admitted by Holand in 1956.[68] The second reason is that the Kensington stone, far from being in any bank window, as an attraction for the multitude, was several miles out in the country, on Ohman's farm. Why else would Hedberg have to ask Ohman to "haul it in" so that he, Hedberg, could see it?

The Kensington stone may well have been exhibited at some time, indeed more than once, in a bank or other public place; but this would have been subsequent to the rather late hauling into town reported by Hedberg: just prior to the stone's journey to Chicago, perhaps, or upon its return to Kensington after it had been discussed in the press of the world. The presumably inadvertent admission of the date "August" into public discussion of this affair reflects the probability—discussed earlier in this chapter—that the stone had acquired its inscription at some time between a first uncovering in August and a second, "official" discovery in November.

The absurdity of all this is manifest insofar as it pertains to the genuineness of the runes. If the rune stone was turned up on November 8, as determined by Professor Winchell, a period of six weeks passed before the stone was seen by a single person whose name is known and whose account is contemporary and dated. If the stone was found in August, the gap is widened to four months. In either interval, there was time, and more than enough, for the carving of a dozen Kensington stones.

CHAPTER VI

The Affidavits

One of the seemingly most impressive aspects of Mr. Holand's argumentation on behalf of the Kensington stone is the affidavits to which he constantly refers and the texts of which he has several times reproduced. The first, and obviously the most important, of these was secured from Olof Ohman. It is here quoted from *Westward from Vinland:*[1]

I, Olof Ohman, of the town of Solem, Douglas County, State of Minnesota, being duly sworn, make the following statement:

I am fifty-four years of age, and was born in Helsingeland, Sweden, from where I emigrated to America in the year 1881, and settled upon my farm in Section Fourteen, Township of Solem, in 1891. In the month of August, 1898, while accompanied by my son, Edward, I was engaged in grubbing upon a timbered elevation, surrounded by marshes, in the southeast corner of my land, about 500 feet west of my neighbor's, Nils Flaten's, house, and in the full view thereof. Upon removing an asp, measuring about 10 inches in diameter at its base, I discovered a flat stone inscribed with characters, to me unintelligible. The stone lay just beneath the surface of the ground in a slightly slanting position, with one corner almost protruding. The two largest roots of the tree clasped the stone in such a manner that the stone must have been there at least as long as the tree. One of the roots penetrated directly downward and was flat on the side next to the stone. The other root extended almost horizontally across the stone and made at its edge a right angled turn downward. At this turn the root was

48

flattened on the side toward the stone. This root was about three inches in diameter. Upon washing off the surface dirt, the inscription presented a weathered appearance, which to me appeared just as old as the untouched parts of the stone. I immediately called my neighbor's, Nils Flaten's, attention to the discovery, and he came over the same afternoon and inspected the stone and the stump under which it was found.

I kept the stone in my possession for a few days; and then left it in the Bank of Kensington, where it remained for inspection for several months. During this interval, it was sent to Chicago for inspection and soon returned in the same state in which it was sent. Since then I kept it at my farm until August, 1907, when I presented the stone to H. R. Holand. The stone, as I remember, was about 30 inches long, 16 inches wide, and 7 inches thick, and I recognize the illustration on page 16 of H. R. Holand's History of the Norwegian Settlements of America, as being a photographic reproduction of the stone's inscription.

(Signed) OLOF OHMAN

Witness:
  R. J. RASMUSSON
  GEORGE H. MERHES

State of Minnesota,
County of Douglas.

On this 20th day of July, 1909, personally came before me, a Notary Public for Douglas County and State of Minnesota, Mr. Olof Ohman, to me known to be the person described in the foregoing document, and acknowledged that he executed the same as his free act and deed.

(Signed) R. J. RASMUSSON,
Notary Public,
Douglas County, Minnesota.

(Seal)

Following this, Holand prints an affidavit by Ohman's neighbor, Nils Flaten:[2]

I, Nils Flaten, of the town of Solem, Douglas County, Minn., being duly sworn, make the following statement:

I am sixty-five years of age, and was born in Tinn, Telemarken, Norway, and settled at my present home in the town of Solem in 1884. One day in August, 1898, my neighbor, Olof Ohman, who was engaged in grubbing timber about 500 feet west of my house, and in full view of same, came to me and told me he had discovered a stone inscribed with ancient characters. I accompanied him to the alleged place of discovery and saw a stone about 30 inches long, 16 inches wide and 6 inches thick, which was covered with strange characters upon two sides and for more than half their length. The inscription presented a very ancient and weathered appearance. Mr. Ohman showed me an asp tree about 8 inches to 10 inches in diameter at its base, beneath which he alleged the stone was found. The two largest roots of the asp were flattened on their inner surface and bent by nature in such a way as to exactly conform to the outlines of the stone. I inspected this hole and can testify to the fact that the stone had been there prior to the growth of the tree, as the spot was in close proximity to my house. I had visited the same spot earlier in the day before Mr. Ohman had cut down the tree and also many times previously—but I had never seen anything suspicious there. Besides the asp, the roots of which embraced the stone, the spot was also covered by a very heavy growth of underbrush.

I recognize the illustration on page 16 of H. R. Holand's History of the Norwegian Settlements as being a photographic reproduction of the inscription on the face of the stone.

(Signed) NILS FLATEN.

Witness:
   R. J. RASMUSSON
   GEORGE H. MERHES

State of Minnesota,
County of Douglas.

On the 20th day of July, 1909, personally came before me, a Notary Public in and for Douglas County and State of Minnesota, Mr. Nils Flaten, to me known to be the person described in the foregoing document, and acknowledged that he executed the same as his free act and deed.

(Signed) H. [sic.] J. RASMUSSON,
Notary Public,
Douglas County, Minnesota.

In his earlier book, The Kensington Stone, Holand had printed two further affidavits, of which the first was a joint statement by Roald Bentson and Samuel Olson:[3]

We, the undersigned, residents of Kensington, Minn., and vicinity, hereby testify to the fact that we have seen a stone with an inscription in characters to us unintelligible, of which it was alleged and which we truthfully believe, was discovered and dug out of the ground in August,

Fig. 1
Front view

Fig. 2
Edge view

The Kensington Stone (courtesy the Smithsonian Institution)

Fig. 3. Facing west: Ohman's "Island"

Fig. 4. Facing east: Flaten's silo

Fig. 5. Facing east: Flaten's grove of trees

Fig. 6. Air photo of Flaten and Ohman farms. Flaten's house at extreme right of clearing in foreground. Indicated are spot (circled) in former marsh approximately 500 feet west of house, and pile of stones (arrow) at base of hill ("Island"). Rune stone was allegedly found on slope of this hill.

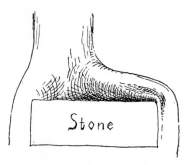

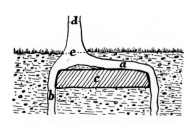

Fig. 7

Stone and roots according to
Holand (*Westward*, p. 114).

Fig. 8

Stone and roots according to Olson
(MHS Report, p. 245).

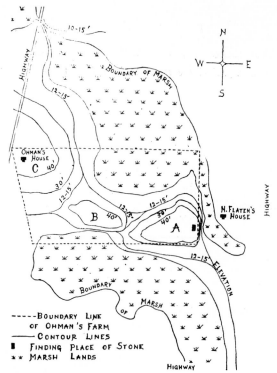

FIG. 5. SKETCH SHOWING TOPOGRAPHIC CONDITIONS OF THE FINDING PLACE
OF THE STONE AND VICINITY

Fig. 9. Holand's map (Westward, p. 123)

1898, about four miles N. E. of Kensington, Minn., on the S. E. corner of the S. W. ¼ of the N. E. ¼ of Section 14, Town 127, Range 40 W., by one Olof Ohman, and his son, Edward Ohman. We further testify that we saw the hole in the ground in which it was stated that the stone had been imbedded. The inscription as seen by us presented an ancient and weathered appearance, similar to the uninscribed parts of the stone. We saw the root of an asp that was from eight to ten inches in diameter at the bottom of the trunk, of which it was alleged that it had grown on one side of the stone, and in close contact with same. We saw the stump of this tree, and are convinced that it had been in close contact with the stone because of its peculiar shape. One of the roots that had pursued a perpendicular course downward was flattened on one side, as we think because of its contact with the stone.

We saw another root of the same stump about three inches in diameter which had taken an almost horizontal course from the body of the stump. About eighteen inches from its junction with the first-mentioned root, this second root made a right-angled bend and continued downward. It was flattened and expanded on its interior bend. We are convinced that the two roots above described exactly conformed to the configuration of the stone. The stone was about thirty inches long, sixteen inches wide and seven inches thick. We recognize the illustration on page 16 of H. R. Holand's History of the Norwegian Settlements as being a photographic reproduction of the inscription on the face of the stone.

[Signed] ROALD BENSON
S. OLSON

Witness:
R. J. RASMUSSON
GEORGE H. MERHES

State of Minnesota
County of Douglas

On this 20th day of July, 1909, personally came before me, a Notary Public in and for Douglas County and State of Minnesota, Mr. Roald Benson and Mr. S. Olson, to me known to be the persons described in the foregoing document, and acknowledged that they executed the same as their free act and deed.

[Signed] R. J. RASMUSSON
Notary Public,
[Seal] Douglas County, Minnesota

My Commission expires November 17, 1915.

The next affidavit was obtained of Edward Ohman:[4]

I, Edward Ohman, of the town of Solem, Douglas County, Minn., being duly sworn, make the following statement:

I am twenty years of age and was born in the town of Oscar Lake, Douglas County, Minn.; in August, 1898, when about 10 years of age, I was helping my father, Olof Ohman, in grubbing on the southeast corner of his land, about 500 feet west of Nils Flaten's house, and in full view of same; in removing an asp, a stone was found imbedded in the ground and embraced by two roots of said asp, one root going downward on one side of the stone and so close to it that its surface was flattened from contact; the other root pursuing a nearly horizontal course across the surface of the stone, where it bent down into the ground, forming a right-angle. The stump of the asp was about ten inches in diameter at the base, the horizontal root about three inches in diameter. I saw the stone in the ground, and the roots in their undisturbed position on the side and on the surface of the stone. After my father had got the stone out of the ground, and we had rolled it to one side, I noticed that some characters were inscribed on the stone and called my father's attention to it. The stone was taken to my father's house and from there sent to the Bank at Kensington, from which it was returned. It remained in my father's possession until he gave it to H. R. Holand, in the year 1907. The stone was about thirty inches long, sixteen inches wide and seven inches thick.

I recognize the illustration on page sixteen of H. R. Holand's History of the Norwegian Settlements as being a photographic reproduction of the inscription on the face of the stone.

[Signed] EDWARD OHMAN.

Witness:

R. J. RASMUSSON
GEORGE H. MERHES

State of Minnesota
County of Douglas

On this 20th day of July, 1909, personally came before me, a Notary Public in and for Douglas County and State of Minnesota, Mr. Edward Ohman, to me known to be the person described in the foregoing document, and acknowledged that he executed the same as his free act and deed.

[Signed] R. J. RASMUSSON
Notary Public,

[Seal]   Douglas County, Minnesota.

My Commission expires November 17, 1915.

The Benson-Olson affidavit is very precise about the arrangement of the poplar roots, differing somewhat from Olof Ohman's description. This can of course be attributed to mere forgetfulness, for we are reading estimates made eleven years after the events described. The Benson-Olson affidavit is equally precise about another circumstance: These two citizens saw the hole, the stump, the roots, and the inscribed stone, on a date not specified, and they were familiar with a variety of allegations made concerning these. Furthermore, the affiants were willing to state their belief—not their knowledge—that the allegations were true. The caution and preciseness of the affidavit conduces to a certain respect for the judgment of the men who allegedly made it. The diagram made that same year for the MHS by Samuel Olson (Fig. 8) is in perfect accord with the statement in the affidavit by Benson and Olson that the "root of the asp . . . was from eight to ten inches in diameter at the bottom of the trunk." This is exactly the explanation given in Chapter V, above: that the tree, as orally described to Flom, and as drawn on paper for Winchell of the MHS, was 4 inches in diameter (according to another interview, 5 or 6) at 15 or 18 inches above the roots, but materially thicker at its base. This was owing to the horizontal deviation of one of the roots in accommodation to the stone— or a stone—which lay just beneath the surface of the ground. The peculiar flattening of the roots observed by the two men does indeed strengthen the probability that some such object had been embraced by the roots.

Only one circumstance calls for comment. Unless this affidavit is entirely fraudulent, it establishes that the stone was inscribed by the time Benson and Olson saw it. Holand tells us that they saw the root, the hole and the stone "a few days after the stone was found."[5] There is no proof that they did not see the stone at this time, though even so, they were not in a position to guarantee the inscription. But why is a statement as to this so conspicuously omitted from an affidavit given for the purpose of strengthening credence in the stone? Why is this statement provided with no date whatever? Could it be that the rune stone and the other paraphernalia were seen by Benson and Olson at a considerably later date than August? Could it be, in short, that they were summoned to the runesite shortly after November 8, 1898? This would explain the story given to Winchell that November 8 was the true date of the find. In reducing the embarrassingly long gap between a discovery in August and the first reports to the public early in 1899, it might even explain Mr. Holand's latter-day reversal of himself and conversion to a November date. And it would render it unnecessary for us to believe that, in this particular, at least, the affidavits by Flaten and the Ohmans were false.

We should remember that the four affidavits reprinted above were all gathered, or at any rate signed, on the same day, July 20, 1909. The great similarity in language and phraseology shows that they were essentially the product of one and the same organizing intelligence. Such a fact does not of itself, of course, invalidate affidavits, for it is in the very nature of things that affidavits seldom arise spontaneously. They are typically the products of conflicts of interest, in which the several interested parties attempt to secure sworn support for their contentions. If an affiant is willing to sign and swear to a given statement before a competent notary—ostensibly of his own free will and with full knowledge of the contents of the statement—then the affidavit is valid as far as it goes. The value of an affidavit can easily be overrated by persons unaccustomed to legal proceedings. It does not have the value of a deposition, for example, in which question and answer and cross-examination by opposing counsel—members of the bar—serve to illuminate disputed points at issue. Still less does the affidavit approximate the net results of testimony given by contending parties during an open session of court. An affidavit presents only one set of opinions, affording no opportunity for cross-examination, prodding, or contradiction. Its application, then, is rather limited in courts of law. It must be equally limited in scientific investigations which have the duty of airing all the pros and cons of disputed theories.

The language of these four affidavits is formal, the phraseology of certain parts uniform or approximately uniform, to all of them. Particularly in the case of Olof Ohman is the formal English of the affidavit in distinct contrast to the language which he spoke.[6] According to both Winchell and Van Dyke, Ohman

understood, but scarcely spoke English.[7] A letter written by him
on December 9, 1909, is written in imperfect Swedish, with incorrect spellings and mixed Swedish-English expressions, as the
following extract will show:[8]

> Jag kottade af den ytre roten som ni ser på tekningen och afven
> jartroten pa samma plats som det visas på tekningen. Sedan fall
> trädet och stenen var blåtat. Jag såg att stenen var tun, jag helt enkelt
> sätte grubbhån under den och vände den undra sidan upp så att runorna
> kom upp i dagen. min pojk Edvard är född 1888. han var omkring 10
> år han såg forst at det var någonting ritat på stenen, pojkarna trodde
> att de har funnit en Indi almanacka Jag själf, såg ochså att det var
> någonting skrivit men att läsa hvar för mig et mysterie. . . .

On July 16, 1910, Ohman sent Professor Winchell another
letter, this one pertaining to the diameter of trees. It was translated for Winchell by Holand and printed in *The Kensington
Stone* and *Westward*, without indicating that the document was a
translation.[9] In English translation, the special features of the
original letter are inevitably lost. Perhaps one should not say
"original letter," for all that is preserved is a typed copy of the
original, and the typist, clearly ignorant of Swedish, has presumably added several errors of her own, although the quality
of the original is clearly observable in the result. In short, there is
a profound contrast between what Ohman wrote for himself—or
dictated to one of his sons, as may have been the case—and what
was composed for him by persons with a formal command of
English.

In *Westward*, Holand implies at one point, and states outright at another, that Dr. Knut Hoegh of Minneapolis secured
the affidavits from all five persons concerned.[10] On a third page,
he states that Olson and the two Ohmans "were separately in-
terviewed by Dr. Hoegh and the writer."[11] In his article of 1935
Holand asseverates that Dr. Hoegh wrote the affidavits.[12] On
the page following, he writes that three of them were by Hoegh,
but that the joint one by Benson and Olson was written by
them.[13] Which of these conflicting allegations has superior claim
to one's belief?

In the Norwegian-American publication *Symra*, for October 2,
1909, Dr. Hoegh printed the report on the Kensington stone which

he had been preparing,[14] and that same fall he reported orally to
the Norwegian society which had commissioned him. In the oral
report, according to the newspaper *Minneapolis Tidende*, no
mention was made of affidavits. In the printed report, one single
affidavit was mentioned, namely that by Roald Benson. The report also states that Hoegh and Holand had investigated the
rune stone area in the month of June, 1909. No subsequent visit
by the two men is mentioned. No fistful of affidavits is mentioned
beyond one by Benson. But all the affidavits, which according
to Holand were procured by Dr. Hoegh, are dated July 20,
1909. Decidedly, there is something mysterious about these affidavits. Dr. Hoegh surely would not have concealed these affidavits in his report, if they had existed, nor could he have forgotten
them.

Through Professor Holvik, inquiry has been made concerning
R. J. Rasmusson's certificate of notaryship. Holvik has ascertained through Douglas County records that Rasmusson was
appointed Notary Public for Douglas Couty on November 17,
1908. His certificate of notaryship was recorded by the Clerk of
District Court at Alexandria on November 22, 1910, a full sixteen months subsequent to the dates of the affidavits. Quite
apart from any internal value of the affidavits as evidence, it
would appear that they have little or no standing as legal documents. That in itself should suffice to divest them of any remaining shreds of the magic with which Holand has striven to invest
them. There is one final consideration.

Holand complains in 1940 that Dr. Quaife "rejects all these
five affidavits as being misleading and erroneous. Instead he
accepts without a doubt a statement made by Professor G. T.
Flom. . . ."[15] Holand's reference is disingenuous in the extreme.
For Dr. Quaife has done something much more important than
to point out the unsatisfactory nature of the affidavits. He has in
effect challenged Holand to *produce the affidavits*. That was in
1934. In Holand's answering article of the following year, that
challenge was ignored.[16] In 1940 it was ignored. In Holand's
articles of 1951 and 1953 it was ignored.[17] And in his most recent
pronouncement, *Norse Explorations in America Before Columbus*,

published in 1956, Holand still blandly pretends that all is well with his affidavits.[18] But are there, or have there ever been, any affidavits?

In a letter to Dr. Upham, dated at Sparta, Wisconsin, on December 27, 1909, Holand says: "Enclosed I send you copies of the other three affidavits. . . ."[19] The typewritten copies purport to be based on affidavits by Edward Ohman, Nils Flaten, and, jointly, Roald Benson and S. Olson. A previous affidavit by Olof Ohman himself is also represented in the MHS archive merely by a typed copy. These are the documents printed by Holand and considered above. Writing to Professor Winchell on May 19, 1910, Holand speaks of "eight affidavits declaring [the tree] to be about 10 inches in diameter."[20] But an affidavit is not a state of mind, nor a copy of anything, nor a printed assurance that something exists. An affidavit is a definite, formal document with signature, witness, and seal. Why are these documents not in the MHS Archive with the rest of the Kensington material? Why is it impossible to trace them? Why was Mr. Holand from the very start so reticent about their whereabouts? Did Dr. Hoegh or Mr. Holand really secure the originals of these affidavits (sworn before a notary whose commission remained unregistered until sixteen months later than the ostensible dates of the affidavits)? What is meant by "eight affidavits"? Why could Dr. Hoegh speak of only one affidavit—Benson's—in the fall of 1909? If Holand had the original affidavits, what was his motive in retaining them? Has anybody ever seen the *original* affidavits?

We have learned from the foregoing discussion that the affidavits cannot be considered competently attested documents. We have also seen that the only one of the purported affidavits to be made by relatively disinterested parties—the joint statement by Benson and Olson—proves precisely nothing as to the Kensington stone's being inscribed when it was first discovered. The important thing is, however, that the affidavits have ever since 1910 been seriously offered by Holand as one of the very mainstays of his argument. If the affidavits were not come by the manner described by Holand, they constitute, all considerations of their probative value apart, a humbug and a fraud. The time has therefore come to demand that Mr. Holand make an unequivocal statement on the "affidavits."

It should be clearly understood that the authenticity of a questioned artifact is not the sort of thing that can be established through affidavits, however phrased or attested. Only science can give the answer, through the application of research methods that have won general acceptance in the branches of science concerned. If the contradictory and very late affidavits of Olof Ohman and Nils Flaten are to be taken seriously, they show, at worst, that two men voluntarily committed a legal fraud or were somehow persuaded to execute the documents contrary to their own inclinations; or, at best, that Ohman and Flaten were personally innocent of complicity in a hoax. In no other way do the affidavits authenticate the rune stone itself.

CHAPTER VII

The Stone and the Geologists

It has been shown in previous chapters that the evidence relied upon by Mr. Holand to establish the thing that he desires above all to establish, namely, that the Kensington stone was already inscribed when found under the roots of a poplar tree, suffers from liabilities of great magnitude. It would seem, however, that the stone itself is palpable enough. Surely, so concrete an object as a slab of stone, which can be seen, measured, weighed at leisure by responsible persons, cannot be the subject of conflicting reports as to its physical aspects? Surely the Kensington stone, conceived in its basic role of mineralogical specimen, is sufficiently unambiguous that one could expect uniform reports on it from geological experts? One would indeed think so. But such is not the case.

Professor Winchell and Dr. Upham of the Minnesota Historical Society were both geologists of note, and they both were keenly interested in the Kensington stone. Both of them published articles on the stone, of which Winchell's became the famous MHS Report (discussed in Chapter X). Holand reports that the stone was in the keeping of the MHS for "about two years";[1] there can be no question, at any rate, that Upham and Winchell had ample opportunity to form responsible and precise opinions on the petrological aspects of the stone.

59

After reconnoitering the Ohman farm and remarking on the numerous rocks and boulders found in the area, "sometimes . . . found in numbers near the bases of the hills and in the swamps," Winchell reported that of these boulders, "five in a hundred may be compared with the rock of the rune stone, being some of the various forms of graywacke."[2]

Defining the character of the stone more precisely, Winchell wrote as follows:

> The interior of the stone is dark or dark gray. On close inspection it can be seen to contain many grains of quartz which are roundish, showing a sedimentary detrital origin. In a thin-section, prepared for microscopic examination, it shows not only rounded quartz grains but also feldspar grains, and a finer matrix consisting chiefly of quartz and biotite. The dark color of the stone is due to much biotite, mainly, but also to an isotropic green mineral (chlorite?), magnetite, and hematite. The quartz has become mainly re-formed by secondary growths. There is a crypto-gneissic elongation prevalent in the mica, and also to some extent in the larger quartzes.
>
> The weathered surface is somewhat lighter, and yet it is firm and wholly intact. It is evident that the surface color has been acquired since the Glacial period, and therefore that some 7,000 or 8,000 years may have elapsed since its face was first exposed to the elements. The reverse of the inscribed side is more altered by weathering and carries evident older glacial striations.[3]

With the foregoing mineralogical analysis of the stone, there seems no reason to quarrel. The situation is very different, however, where statistics of a simpler order are involved. For example, when Upham, writing in 1910 for *Magazine of History*, describes the stone he says that it weighs 230 pounds, is 30 inches in length, 16 inches wide, and 6 to 7 inches thick.[4] But Winchell's official report that same year to the MHS makes the stone (230 pounds in weight and) 36 inches in length; width is 15, thickness $5\frac{1}{2}$.[5] The Kensington stone we know today is described by Professor Johannes Brøndsted as being (in 1948) $29\frac{1}{2}$ inches in length, and by Jansson as weighing 202 pounds.[6] The author's examination of the stone in 1953 was made under conditions that did not permit of weighing the stone, but the circumstances of Brøndsted's investigation are such that his statistics are accepted as accurate.

This poses a problem. How did the geologists Upham and Winchell, the Museum Committee's two petrographical experts, arrive at descriptions, on so easily ascertainable a matter as the weight and dimensions of the stone, that differed from each other and differed still more markedly from present-day descriptions of the stone? The difference between 29½ and 30 (or even 31) inches for the length is trifling; the difference between 36 and 30 is a cause for comment, as is the difference between 202 and 230 pounds.

A photograph[7] antedating at least the carving of Mr. Holand's initial "H" on the lower left-hand edge of the Kensington stone in 1908, indicates, as nearly as can be established by a study of later photographs, together with the author's personal inspection of the stone in 1953, that that stone is identical with the one now preserved. Must one fall back upon the ridiculous assumption that Upham and Winchell worked with grossly inadequate instruments? Or did one of them, or both of them, while having the genuine stone before them—assuming it was the genuine stone—uncritically accept statistics given them, statistics pertaining to some other stone not now available for comparison?

Holand himself, writing in 1910, gave the weight of the stone as 230 pounds, the length as 30 inches, thus agreeing with Upham rather than the MHS.[8] But on May 19, 1910, Holand wrote to Winchell (letter in MHS Archive): "Is not the bevel on the inscribed side?" The bevel is a matter of some moment in discussions as to whether the stone, after being placed upright in 1362, as assumed, would ultimately have fallen forward or backward. Holand's inquiry is very curious for a man who had at that time known the stone during a period of thirty-three months. For the bevel to which he refers is not on the inscribed front, but on the back of the stone (Fig. 2).

Do these several ambiguities stem from two separate "Kensington" stones? Does this have a bearing on the conflict in the dates of the discovery: August versus November 8; on the location of the find: hillside or swamp; on the distance from Flaten's house: 500 feet or 1241? Whatever the true explanation may be, one thing is clear: The widely relied upon expertness of the MHS geologists is open to some doubt. By 1956, Holand appeared to be preparing an alibi for his own statement as to the weight: "It was weighed and measured [by the MHS] and reported to be 36 inches long . . . and weighed 230 pounds."[9] But he makes no attempt to harmonize discrepancies.

Since, in spite of these uncertainties regarding the stone, there is no real proof of a substitution or alternation of stones, one is not privileged to drop the investigation at this point. On the assumption, therefore, that we are discussing one and the same stone throughout, we proceed to a consideration of the physical appearance of the inscription on the Kensington stone. As all readers of Holand's works are aware, this is one of Holand's key points. He relies heavily upon the evidence of the geologists to establish that the inscription actually was carved in 1362, as it claims, rather than at some time during the nineteenth century. This is a topic upon which a philological technique—that of textual analysis—can augment the findings, or apparent findings, of natural science. In other words, it will be helpful to check on what the geologists have actually said on this point. Their primary spokesman is Professor Winchell. In the MHS Report of 1910, Winchell, convinced of the authenticity of the inscription, made statements which, while they were seemingly based on strict scientific reasoning, he considered as establishing for it a considerable age. Winchell wrote as follows:

The first impression derived from the inscription is that it is of recent date, and not 548 years old. The edges and angles of the chiseling are sharp, and show no apparent alteration by weathering. The powder of the stone when crushed is nearly white. None of this powder is preserved in the runes on the face of the stone, and it is necessary therefore to allow it some years of age, but it is quite impossible to draw a decisive inference of the age of the inscription from that alone. The edge of the stone differs in this respect from the face, since most of the rune letters show the white powder formed by crushing the stone. This difference was said to be due to the fact that the runes on the edge had been filled with mud and had been cleaned out by scraping them with an iron nail. Indeed in the runes in some places on the edge can be seen with a pocket magnifier small quantities of fresh metallic iron evidently derived from that process.[10]

Referring to the calcite deposit that covers a portion of the face of the stone, Winchell asserts it to be plain "that it has had approximately as long direct exposure to the elements as the rest of that surface. . . . Marble slabs in graveyards in New England are more deeply disintegrated than this calcite, when they stand above the surface of the ground."[11]

Winchell adds: "The immediate surface of the calcite, especially the edges formed by cutting the runes, is smoothed by recent friction of some kind, much more than the surface of the graywacke; and this is attributable to wearing away when the stone served as a stepping stone at the granary."[12]

It should be noted in passing that, although the stepping stone version is a stock feature of the story[13] it has been emphatically denied by Ohman's sons, Arthur and John Ohman, that the Kensington stone was ever used as a stepping stone.[14] If that is true, the "recent friction" is of some other origin, concerning which this book draws no conclusions (see note 12).

Noting that the calcite on the stone shows no "fine white powder of natural disintegration," Winchell asserts that:

. . . it is evident that either the calcite has but recently been exposed or has been protected from the weather. If the slab was separated from its neighbor 548 years ago, it must have lain with its face side down during most of that period, and if separated earlier it must have been covered by drift clay. If it was so separated fifteen or thirty years ago, it may have lain with its face side up and probably would show no more weathering than it now evinces. In short, there is no possible natural way to preserve that calcite scale from a general disintegration for 548 years except to bury it beneath the surface. If it were not thus buried and still is intact, it must have been exposed and the inscription must have been made less than a hundred years ago, and probably less than thirty years ago.[15]

At the same time Winchell quotes Professor W. O. Hotchkiss, state geologist of Wisconsin, as estimating that "the time since the runes were inscribed is 'at least 50 to 100 years.' "[16] Winchell has just pointed out, however, as regards his own calculations as to the weathering of graywacke, that such "figures are but rough estimates . . . and to a certain degree they are subject to the

errors of the personal equation of the person who gives them."[17]
Perhaps "36 inches" and "230 pounds" were rough estimates
similarly liable to subjective error.

Professor Winchell, to summarize, concluded that there were
two alternate possibilities. The inscription showed a degree of
weathering that would comport with one of two possibilities: an
inscription that was medieval, and on a stone that had lain face
down through the years, or an inscription which had been exposed to the elements for a short period of years. In the latter
case, the degree of intactness pointed to an age of "fifteen or
thirty years,"[18] and again, "probably less than 30 years."[19] Furthermore, his "first impression derived from the inscription is
that it is of recent date, and not 548 years old."[20] There is perfect
harmony between Winchell's firsthand impression of modernity
and his corroboration of this possibility through the aid of geological techniques, including the use of a microscope. This is
further reiterated in that portion of the MHS Report which
summarizes the findings: "Owing to the easy disintegration of
calcite in the weather, it is evident that the inscription is either
recent or the stone was so placed (or was overturned) as to pro-
tect the inscription from the weather."[21]

If Winchell arbitrarily ruled out the first possibility in favor of
the second, he clearly did so on the basis of nongeological evidence derived from other sources: He was taken in by the story
about the roots of the tree,[22] and, unfamiliar with Scandinavian
philology, he accepted Holand's arguments on the runes and
language of the inscription.[23] Thus supported, Winchell's conclusion has in turn been extensively quoted as *geological* evidence in
favor of the stone's antiquity. It should be made clear that we
are not insisting that Winchell's estimates were accurate. We
are merely clarifying his own statements on the age of the inscription.

By strict geological reasoning, then, the minimum age of the
Kensington inscription by Winchell's estimate would not be 500
years, but 15. Discovered in 1898, the inscription was demonstrably at least a dozen years old by 1910 (under the constant
assumption that Winchell was examining the right stone). By
1910, likewise, Ohman had sat on his farm for 20 years (since

1890), Flaten on his for 26 years (since 1884). It is quite gratuitous to conclude from this chronology that the Kensington inscription is, therefore, nothing other than a product of the fourteenth century.

There is an unclear intimation in Winchell's discussion that the runes on the side of the stone gave greater evidence of modernity than those on the face, on which his estimate of age in the main seems to be based.

The powder of the stone when crushed is nearly white. None of this powder is preserved in the runes on the face of the stone, and it is necessary therefore to allow it some years of age, but it is quite impossible to draw a decisive inference of the age of the inscription from that alone. The edge of the stone differs in this respect from the face, since most of the rune letters show the white powder formed by crushing the stone. This difference was said to be due to the fact that the runes on the edge had been filled with mud and had been cleaned out by scraping them with an iron nail. Indeed in the runes in some places on the edge can be seen with a pocket magnifier small quantities of fresh metallic iron evidently derived from that process.[24]

The phrase "was said to be due" reveals that Winchell—after discovering the minute particles of iron—accepted the explanation supplied him, even though other explanations might have been possible.[25] Professor Brøndsted, too, reported (in 1949) that approximately a hundred of the runes had been "scraped, pricked, or chopped with iron"[26] subsequent to the original carving, so that the patina had disappeared and the runes in question had become deeper. No chronology of "improvements" can be worked out from these statements, nor does Winchell's observation establish that the edge portion of the inscription is more recent than the face portion.

We remember that Professor Hotchkiss considered fifty years as the minimum estimate of the age of the inscription (as of 1909). Hotchkiss cannot be cross-examined as to this; one can only point to Winchell's warning that estimates as to weathering are but estimates, after all. It is not necessary, however, to leave the last word with the men who investigated the problem during the heat of controversy back in 1909–10. Permission has been granted to quote from a letter written in 1954 by Dr. R. H.

Landon, Plant Physiologist of the University of Minnesota and member of the Editorial Board of the Minnesota Archaeological Society. Landon, whose professional training included geology and petrology, writes that he has never been antagonistic to the pretensions of the Kensington stone and "would be happy were it shown to be genuine." Landon states that he had three replicas of the Kensington stone made just before World War II by an artificer of the Minnesota Historical Society, in the course of which work the stone was thoroughly coated with engine oil. In cleaning the stone afterwards,

... several gallons of petroleum ether were used with the result that the Stone was cleaner than it had ever been. The oil softened any adherent material and the ether carried it away. A careful inspection of the inscription, including use of microscope, showed a complete absence of any trace of weathering or patination. . . . The cuts were as fresh as if they had been made the day before. The elements and soil solution would surely have dulled the freshly exposed graywacke even tho it is a comparatively resistant stone.[27]

The author, who first saw the Kensington stone in 1953, was amazed at how new and fresh it looked fifty-five years after its discovery.[28] Professor Gould reported in 1910 that the runes "were the work of a careful workman who had plenty of time and good tools."[29] Professor Hægstad reported the runes to have been "clearly written as though they were written yesterday."[30] J. J. Skørdalsvold, a supporter of the stone, writes: "The inscription is so clear, the edges so sharp, that one at first sight is inclined to assume that the work was performed recently and not 551 years ago."[31] Skørdalsvold remarks that even the calcareous deposit on a portion of the stone is "hard and fresh." Professor Flom spoke in 1910, of the "smooth surface of the stone which gives it the appearance of having been shaped and chiselled in recent times . . . and the perfectly distinct runes themselves; so different from the characters of genuine old inscriptions."[32] Observing that about ten of the runes are carved into the calcite, Flom remarks that though the calcite has rotted, the pattern of decomposition has not affected the inscription:

Through the decaying and wearing away of the stone portions of the inscriptions of many an old runestone have been effaced and its text often left fragmentary. But our Kensington rune-master was more fortunate; the stone went on decaying, pieces falling off (observe the piece, three inches long, near the upper left hand corner, and observe the depressions elsewhere), but by some miraculous influence the disintegrating process failed to affect the runic characters; they were to be left unmarred, so that nothing in the account left by these intrepid explorers might be spoiled![33]

These reports are perfectly in keeping with what an early examiner of the stone reported in 1899. *The Chicago Tribune* for March 1, 1899, reports the following on the basis of an interview with Professor Curme: "Suspicion attaches to the engraving itself. A close study shows it was done by a skilled workman, and yet there seems to be a studied attempt to disguise this fact. The letters are well formed and symmetrical and most of the lines are clear cut, but as a whole the letters have a careless and unfinished appearance."[34]

Curme's views are summarized at greater length in *The Daily Inter Ocean* of the same date, from which is quoted the following:

The letters were evidently cut by some one not a novice, for although they have an irregular appearance a close observation shows that the lines are almost as true as those on a modern tombstone, though the roughness caused by the implement used in cutting has not been smoothed and covered as in the inscriptions of today.

The most positive proof that the inscription is not of the ancient origin claimed by its discoverers is the fact that the crevices which form the letters are of a lighter color than the outer surface of the stone; this could hardly be the case if the stone had been buried for the 600 years that must have elapsed provided the inscription is authentic.

Professor Curme is in doubt about 1362 being the exact date of the stone. The last line of the inscription was cut through a portion of the cement surrounding the base, and the letters and figures cannot be clearly distinguished, the cement having been chipped away. This cement also throws a doubt upon the origin of the tablet, for if it was placed there by the Norsemen mentioned in its story they must necessarily have waited a week for it to dry before the last line could have been cut through it.[35]

Even Mr. Holand writes in 1910: "After 11½ years' exposure to the elements, these characters upon the edge of the stone still appear white and fresh as if cut today."[36] It is indeed unfortunate that Mr. Holand has never drawn the proper inference from an observation which is so signally in accord with what many others have remarked in the Kensington inscription.

In the Royal Library at Copenhagen there is a letter to Professor Wimmer from the geologist, John F. Steward, a member of the Chicago Academy of Sciences.[37] Dated October 15, 1899, the letter is accompanied by four photographs of the stone that are not known in other sources and must have been made by Steward or at his direction. Unusually clear, they seem to depict the stone we have today, despite Steward's curious statement that its weight is "about 100 pounds" (he gives the length accurately enough as 75 cm).[38] Apparently unknown and nowhere quoted, so far as can be learned, by historians or runologists (see note 35), Steward's report contains a startling remark on the carving of the inscription. According to him, the runic grooves were cut with a "diamond pointed tool." All other commentators have assumed the carving to have been performed with steel chisels—Brøndsted speaks of the three chisels that were used, in his own opinion or that of Mr John Howard Benson, sculptor of Newport, Rhode Island.[39]

It will be seen that the foregoing reports, though issuing independently from different schools of thought and from twelve different observers over a period of fifty-four years, are far from irreconcilable. Their joint testimony is that no great antiquity need be posited for the inscription on anything approaching geological grounds.

An inference drawn by Holand from the weight of the stone—whether 230 pounds or 202—is that under any circumstances the stone could not have been handled by one man. To quote Holand: "The stone was found in plain view of Nils Flaten's house, and as it was too heavy to be carried, the inscription must have been chiselled on the spot where it was found. But any such 'forger' would certainly have been seen by Flaten who had lived there since 1884. . . . Completely mystified, Olof Ohman hauled home his stone and dumped it down by the granary door, fortunately with the inscribed face down."[40]

A major idiosyncrasy of this stone was that it could be *hauled* in only one direction. However, why need one assume with Holand that the "forger" could have had no assistant(s)? To quote again from Holand, who, in turn, quotes from an interview in the *Minneapolis Star* given to Mr. Jay Edgerton by the sculptor, John K. Daniels:

The rune stone (Mr. Daniels explains) is fascinating to a man who works in stone because of the highly individual characteristics of its carver—or carvers. There may have been two of them. If the stone is the work of one man, then certainly he was ambidexterous. He could work with equal facility with both his left and right hands. Daniels explains that the chiseling on the stone is what a sculptor would describe as "one stroke" work. It was done with a hammer and chisel mostly working from right to left—although towards the end of the inscription the strokes are from left to right. He says that the inscription was put on quickly with sure deft strokes by a person thoroughly familiar with carving runes. The whole job may have taken about two hours.[41]

Dr. Martin Allwood has told us that, to his knowledge, the English-language rune stone found on his property at Mullsjö, Sweden, in 1953, was carved in fifty-three minutes.[42] The very creditably carved sixty or so characters (including separation marks) contained in this inscription—shallowly carved, it is true—were not carved "by a person thoroughly familiar with carving runes." Dr. S. A. Hallbäck, Provincial Antiquary at Vänersborg, Sweden, has recently reported that a rune stone carved by him during his school days was completed in the space of an hour.[43] These details by Allwood and Hallbäck would roughly corroborate the estimate by Mr. Daniels that (once the stone had been prepared and the message drawn up), two skilled stone masons, or even one ambidexterous person of energy and skill, could have carved the Kensington stone in two hours.

As a humorous commentary on this discussion we append a quotation from Professor A. D. Fraser's article, "The Norsemen in Canada": "To me, as a student of archaeology, the most convincing point in its favor is the condition of the stone. This is a prosaic and mechanical consideration that would escape the notice of the philologist."[44] Professor Fraser adduces no source for so curious a misconception.

CHAPTER VIII

Some Historical
and Geographical
Details

Apart from dendrological fancies and petrological contentions, a favorite aspect of Mr. Holand's rune stone story is that "we know" that an expedition was sent into American waters in 1355 by the king of Norway and Sweden, with the expedition returning to Scandinavia in 1364. Through skillful combinations this expedition is made identical with a purported penetration into Minnesota in 1362 by a party of "8 Swedes and 22 Norwegians." In proof of this hypothesis, Holand cites a document at either end of that mightly trek. One is the Kensington rune stone, which Holand's principal geological expert considers to have been at least fifteen years old by the year 1910.[1] The other is a late Danish version of a medieval document, discovered by a famous historian, that selfsame Gustav Storm who so distressed Holand by denouncing the Kensington stone as "a clumsy fraud."[2] As the Kensington stone, being itself considerably in need of proof, is not of such nature that it can be used to prove shaky contentions about anything, we shall here comment only on the other item, the existence of which seems established.

Dated 1354, the document as published by Storm and translated by Holand, reads as follows:

Magnus, by the Grace of God, King of Norway, Sweden and Skaane, sends to all men who see or hear this letter good health and happiness.

We desire to make known to you that you [Paul Knutson] are to take the men who shall go in the Knorr [the royal trading vessel] whether they be named or not named, from my bodyguard . . . and also from among the retainers of other men whom you may wish to take on the voyage, and that Paul Knutson, who shall be the commandant upon the Knorr, shall have full authority to select the men whom he thinks are best suited to accompany him, whether as officers or men. We ask that you accept this our command with a right good will for the cause, inasmuch as we do it for the honor of God and for the sake of our soul and for the sake of our predecessors, who in Greenland established Christianity and have maintained it to this time, and *we will not now let it perish in our days.* Know this for truth, that whoever defies this our command shall meet with our serious displeasure and thereupon receive full punishment.

Executed in Bergen, Monday after Simon and Judah's day [October 28th] in the six and XXX year of our rule [1354]. By Orm Østenson, our regent, sealed.[3] [Italics supplied. Foregoing brackets by Holand.]

The original letter perished in the Copenhagen fire of 1728 and is known only through a sixteenth century copy. On the basis of that, taking the intention for the deed, Professor Storm assumed that Paul Knutson headed an expedition to Greenland to keep Christianity from perishing in that most distant outpost of Christian faith and Scandinavian culture.[4] It had been reported by a party of seventeen Greenlanders who were driven ashore on Iceland in 1347, and who traveled the following year to Bergen, Norway, that the Greenlandic settlements were in a process of disintegration.[5]

If there is no way of proving that Paul did not in fact make such an expedition, there is equally little proof that he did. Following Storm, several other historians have concluded in favor of such an expedition, none of them on the slightest showing of evidence. Even Holand is forced to admit: "The documents and libraries of the Scandinavian countries have very little to tell, however, of what happened to Paul Knutson's expedition."[6] For "very little" one should substitute "nothing whatever." The burden of proof is on those who claim the expedition took place. What is of great importance, however, is that

Gustav Storm, as will be shown in a later chapter, is the man who probably did most to stir up the controversy over Norse voyages to America that raged during the latter years of the nineteenth century. His controversial monograph, *Studies Over the Vinland Voyages*, appeared in Copenhagen in 1888 (it also appeared separately) and reached this country by about 1889.[7] It was reviewed and argued over at length in the Scandinavian language newspapers of the United States.[8] Nor was this the only writing by Storm on the Vinland question. The Library of Congress Catalog reveals that an English version of the work was published in Copenhagen in 1889 under the title *Studies on the Vinland Voyages*. In 1893 there appeared at Christiania a separate printing of Storm's contribution to a geographical yearbook. The translated title of this is *Columbus in Iceland and the Discoveries of our Forefathers in the Northwesterly Atlantic*.[9] And that same year the J. Andersson Publishing Company of Chicago brought out an American editon of *Christofer Columbus og Amerikas opdagelse, af dr. Gustav Storm*.

In particular, Storm's contention that the Scandinavian voyagers never reached the territorial limits of what is now the United States, aroused acrimonious discussion and brought forth rebuttals. And what has that to do with the Kensington stone? Mr. Holand's own comments should illustrate this. He is speaking of Halvdan Koht (born 1873), biographer of Henrik Ibsen and currently the dean of Norwegian historians:

> Professor Koht is professor in history and is one of the leading investigators in Norway. He recently made an extensive trip through America and thus overcame the supercilious disdain which is a common European attitude towards American scholarship. After my address in Christiania he told me in private conversation that if the Kensington stone was *in situ* in 1890, it was in all probability genuine. The significance of this date (1890) lies in the fact that in that year (or 1889) appeared Professor Storm's *Studier over Vinlandsreiserne*, where the fact is brought out for the first time that in the very year of the inscription there was a Norse expedition in American waters.[10]

This incautious admission of 1911, with its vast perspective of possibilities for an anti-Storm hoax, at Kensington, represents, so far as has been learned, Holand's first and last reference to the dangerous surmise by Halvdan Koht.

As to the possibilities of an important royal expedition to Greenland from Scandinavia in the middle of the fourteenth century, there is very little to discuss. Being reduced to pure conjecture, one finds as many factors militating against the likelihood of the expedition as those which favor it, indeed, many more. Much of the reign of King Magnus Smek (1336–74) of Sweden and Norway was a period of bad finances, political turmoil, and dynastic treachery in a joint monarchy harried by the Black Death (1349–51) and by Magnus' enemies: Denmark, Russia, the unforgiving Swedish religious leader St. Birgitta, by whom Magnus was charged with misgovernment and gross immorality; and ultimately, by the Pope himself, who, after severe threats in 1355, finally excommunicated Magnus in 1358.[11] His son Erik, calling himself King of Sweden, proclaimed war on him in 1356; Erik died in 1359, but Magnus' troubles did not die with him. The years 1365–71 he passed in prison. There is no reason to doubt his zeal in the interests of spreading the Faith (in spite of the excommunication), but that does not prove that the Paul Knutson expedition ever got under way. Magnus' regent in Norway, Orm Østenson (or Øysteinsson), keeper of the royal seal, had to abandon the former post upon Haakon's accession to the Norwegian throne in 1355; thereafter Orm's authority was more circumscribed. Before long he fell into disfavor; in 1358 he was imprisoned, and in 1359 or 1360, executed for treason, with the confiscation of most of his property. The letter ostensibly signed by him in the name of King Magnus is vaguely formulated, and perhaps not accurately dated. All this renders the matter of the expedition highly questionable.

The chief difficulties with regard to the putative expedition are, however, more geographical than historical. It is true that the distinguished geographer, Professor Richard Hennig of Düsseldorf, in page after page of highly rhetorical German, repeatedly pokes scorn at anyone who ventures to assail the Kensington stone.[12] An extended scrutiny of his principal article, however, reveals very few insights into questions that involve the geography of North America. It reveals, furthermore, very little scholarly independence of Holand, who in one way or another contrives to be his authority at almost every point. One has the impression that present day America is even more remote and unfamiliar to Hennig than the Minnesota wilderness of 1362: He naively quotes American newspapers as scientific authorities, asserts that philology is powerless to cope with the Kensington problem,[13] swallows everything about poplar roots and the weathering of the stone, and parrots Holand's ridiculous assertion that O. E. Hagen, who taught a few years at the University of South Dakota, was one of America's greatest Scandinavian philologists.[14] In short, Hennig is but little beyond Holand translated into the German. Holand, in turn, cites Hennig as an independent authority.[15] One wonders whether there is objective truth in Hennig's assertion of 1938: "The majority of European geographers today, as I have ascertained, inclines to acknowledge the authenticity of the Kensington stone and to draw from this the necessary historical consequences. Among most historians and ethnologists as well, the same willingness seems apparent."[16]

A European geographer of the first rank who thinks very differently about the Kensington voyage is the Italian geographer Roberto Almagià, president of the Academy of Rome. Professor Almagià, far from indulging in historical fancies, speaks out of thorough familiarity with the voyaging habits of the ancient Norsemen, who were essentially sea-farers, not overland explorers. He puts his finger on the geographical kernel of the matter: "An expedition of this nature, the purpose of which, furthermore, is not apparent, if carried out in the manner supposed by Holand, could be conceived of only if it had been preceded and prepared by a long series of more limited but repeated reconnaissances towards the interior, concerning which there is not the slightest evidence."[17] In other words, Almagià very reasonably assumes that men of the caliber we must suppose for the purposes of a royal expedition would behave like canny, trained explorers rather than like wandering nomads or a pack of fools, clutching at every straw in order to execute a purpose, or shifting series of purposes which have no demonstrable reality outside of Mr. Holand's imagination. Concerning this last point, nothing is so illuminating as a reading, in sequence, of Holand's own self-contradictory suppositions as they have developed, decade by decade. Carefully read, Holand is the best refutation of Holand.[18]

The fantastic difficulties entailed in a journey by canoe from Hudson Bay to Kensington, Minnesota, are aptly narrated by Dr. Quaife, who discusses Holand's theory that the hypothetical explorers left Hudson Bay by the Nelson River, proceeded to Lake Winnipeg, from there via the Red River of the North to either one of two lakes named Cormorant in Minnesota, and thence, by means unknown, proceeded either twenty or eighty miles—both distances guaranteed by Holand—by unknown routes only to wind up in a lake or swamp at Kensington:

We may now consider the problems involved in the ascent, by the explorers, of the Nelson River. The very roadstead where the vessel must lie for a year is one of the most dangerous places for shipping in the world. Into the trumpet-like river mouth, seven miles wide at its outer extremity, sweeps a twelve-foot tide, bearing during two-thirds of the year the ice masses of Hudson Bay. The river itself is commonly ice-locked until July, and the period when boats may proceed from York Factory to the interior is limited to three months. . . . Lake Winnipeg, fifth in size in America, assembles the rainfall of almost half-a-million square miles of country, and by the Nelson River discharges it into Hudson Bay. The mighty flood, ranging from 50 000 to 150,000 cubic feet a second, makes the seven-hundred-foot descent from the lake to the bay in a series of chutes and rapids, interspersed with stretches of level water, or lakes. The current divides and re-divides; while the lakes are plentifully bestrewn with islands to bewilder the explorer. Although the ascent of the river may be physically possible, so arduous and dangerous is the task that not even the natives will undertake it, and in almost two hundred years of occupancy of the region by the Hudson's Bay Company, with constant necessity of travel between York Factory and the interior, there seems to be no single record of any ascent of the Nelson River by trader or explorer.[19]

Quaife goes on to tell of a descent of the Nelson in 1883 by O. J. Klotz, whose party were told by natives when they set out from Norway House that they " 'would never return alive.' " "The downward voyage, in a canoe manned by experienced paddlers, entailed forty-seven portages."[20]

"The downward voyage. . . ." What must the upward voyage have entailed, against the mighty current, through a maze of lakes, rivers, marshes, past hundreds of confusing islands and hazardous portages, in an area where game is scarce and, because of the swampy nature of the terrain, all but impossible to track down? Anyone who believes that Quaife has exaggerated this should read the chapter in Eric Sevareid's *Not so Wild a Dream*, that deals with the attempt in 1929 by Sevareid and a friend, probably influenced by the Kensington rune stone, to paddle the estimated 2200 miles from Minnesota to Hudson Bay via Lake Winnipeg and the Red River of the North.[21] This, let it be noted, was a descent, not an ascent.

Holand attempts to counter this by pointing to Norse voyages into the Arctic wastes and survivals even of single individuals in the distant North.[22] What has this to do with the problem of ascending the Nelson River, much less making it to Minnesota? It is well known that the Eskimos have survived in the Arctic for centuries.[23] Arctic conditions, however, are very different. One must assume that Paul Knutson and company did not ascend the Nelson on skis or snowshoes or by means of dogsled, for according to Holand, they must have abandoned their seagoing vessels at the mouth of the Nelson and thereafter become marvelously skilled in the use of Indian canoes. And perhaps the Indians who taught them the art of constructing and navigating canoes were of a more amicable disposition than those who scalped ten of the explorers somewhere in Minnesota. But would not these new-found friends then have warned Captain Paul Knutson against so insane, so fruitless a project as the ascent of the Nelson? The alternative left us is to suppose that the Scandinavians mastered this new navigational technique by themselves, then proceeded to demonstrate their prowess at it by the most difficult test of all.

But this is only the beginning of the things one must suppose in order to bring the explorers as far as Kensington. Holand supposed for several years that they made the trip from Hudson Bay to Minnesota in exactly fourteen days. When the absurdity of this became manifest, he decided that the correct elapse of time was forty-one days.[24] When this reversal of the figure 14 was shown to have fatal implications for the supposed date 1362,[25] he took refuge in the assumption that the phrase "14 days' journey" meant, not a journey of fourteen days' duration, but an arbitrary measure of distance, a day's journey being taken to mean a fixed unit of 80 miles, whether on land or on sea. Holand arrives at this neat figure of 80 miles through a manipulation of an estimate by Professor William Hovgaard that a day's sail among the Norsemen meant an average of 150 miles. Holand halves this so as to conform to a working day rather than to the 24-hour period probably envisioned—if that theory is correct— by Scandinavian mariners who, on the high seas, sailed day and night; and then, for good measure, he adds 5 miles to arrive at 80.[26] Holand argues in effect, that no matter how long it took these explorers to get themselves bottled up (in Nils Flaten's swamp) at Kensington, they would have known almost to the mile how great a distance they had covered, and rendered this in explicit terms that would have done credit to a modern surveying party. Of all of Mr. Holand's unsupported conjectures, this is perhaps the most fantastic. It is interesting that Knutson and company came to Minnesota by the most efficient route, almost as straight as an arrow to the mark, negotiating it in a mere 1100 miles, or again, 1500 miles, of travel, more or less, although Eric Sevareid, proceeding in the other direction, with a general knowledge of where he was going, calls the total distance 2200 miles. But bearing in mind the countless blind alleys so vividly chronicled by Sevareid, one surmises that the wanderers—and that they must have wandered randomly is shown by the character of the locality in which they assertedly wound up—might well have travelled 5000 miles, or even much farther, poking into this lake and that, trying this river and that, but constantly on the go, and constantly able to calculate true distance, almost as though able to measure it on a Rand-McNally globe of the world. Without a logging device or pedometer, without a chronometer, likely enough without a compass—this, one dare not assert with assurance—and more important than all this, in totally unknown territory without knowledge of the geodetic relationship between their destination and their goal, they were yet able from this single voyage to calculate true distance covered—*i.e.*, the distance they *should* have covered—quite as though they had mapped it by air. If this is to be taken as true, then the Paul Knutson expedition performed a far more brilliant geographical exploit than Mr. Holand seems to realize. Not to speak of the fact that many of the lakes of Minnesota were likely covered with ice by the time the travellers, after thousands of miles and months of the conscientious exploration which, according to Holand, was by now the object of their journey, got to Minnesota. If the explorers had started by July 1st—it is doubtful that they could have started earlier[27]—they might conceivably have reached Kensington by what is now Thanksgiving or Christmas time.

There are times when even Mr. Holand seems to doubt his grandiose structure of unproved hypotheses. Reacting to Quaife's strictures, he asks plaintively: "Does all this prove, however, beyond the possibility of a doubt, that the Kensington inscription is a flagrant falsehood?"[28] It does not. The existence, or non-existence of the Knutson voyage has no probative value one way or the other for the Kensington stone. What does seem likely is the intimation by Professor Koht, Helge Gjessing, and others, that Gustav Storm's uncorroborated theory of 1888 about a voyage by Paul Knutson may have something to do with the discovery of a rune stone among Scandinavian-Americans ten years later.

After all this, it seems almost petty to go into Mr. Holand's various allegations as to skerries and mooring holes found here and there in Minnesota along the route that his explorers assertedly took. Lest it be asserted by him that such assertions cannot be met, it should here be pointed out that glaciated Minnesota has not for nothing been called the "Land of ten thousand lakes." Endless rocky islets—the definition of a skerry —can be found there, as Holand himself has demonstrated at no little length. If Holand requires a set of skerries at a distance of twenty miles from Kensington, in conformity to his definition of an Old Scandinavian "day's journey" as precisely that distance, he is able to find them. If a newer theory of what is involved in a "day's journey" calls for skerries at a distance of sixty–seven miles, Holand finds them without fail. If the concept of a "day's journey" should in the future expand to one hundred miles, or contract to six miles, Holand will again find the skerries, whether on dry land, submerged, or protruding from the water.

All this was predicted by Professor Flom back in 1910.[29] Minnesota is one state in which it is pointless to locate anything as imprecise as "two skerries." Accordingly, there is nothing to discuss, beyond recording the opinion that the reference in the inscription to "2 skerries" within a day's journey of the present-day Ohman farm was an apt and humorous touch, well in keeping with a supposition that the entire inscription is part of a modern hoax.

Likewise frequently met with in Minnesota are the type of man-made holes in rock which Mr. Holand likes to term "mooring holes" from 1362. Local reconnoitering has resulted in the conclusion that the majority of these have been drilled by farmers in preparation for abandoned attempts at black powder blasting.[30] Several such holes—not mentioned by Holand—are plainly visible on the Flaten and Ohman properties today.[31] The depth of these holes will necessarily vary, and this gives Holand an opportunity to claim the deeper of them for ancient mooring holes. According to an opinion supplied by Mr. W. Babcock of the curatorial staff of the Minnesota Historical Society, many of the holes of this nature have been drilled by surveyors as section marks.[32] To this there should be very little to add. But once again, Holand has girded himself to meet the criticism.

Changing some of the details of his previous hypotheses, Holand has written a chapter on "Mooring Stone and Camp Sites" in his *Explorations Before Columbus*. He states that "In the interior part of America, no mooring stones are known to have existed, except in Minnesota, where ten have been found."[33] Whereupon, out of the surely several hundred mineralogical specimens that would fit the definition of a mooring stone, Holand accepts only the ten that conform to the route which he has chosen for Captain Paul Knutson and his company, "from Hawley in the northwestern part of Minnesota to Sauk Centre in the central part."[34] This is historical methodology with a vengeance. Holand "proves" the age of these mooring-holes by the testimony of old settlers and by allegations as to the patina of the chiselled portion of the stone. In view of what has been shown in the previous two chapters of the present book with regard to testimonial and geological evidence submitted by

Holand, there is no reason for dwelling further on material of that kind.

It is worthy of note, however, that Holand has enlarged somewhat the number of the Kensington party, who now—presumably after the slaughter of ten of their group, and after leaving ten men at Hudson Bay—number 20 men (*i.e.*, there were 40 to begin with, not 30 as claimed in the inscription); even the size and weight of their boat is given (because 20 men would need a boat of these dimensions): 27 feet long and weighing 1500 pounds. "It is, of course, possible that two boats were used."[35] Or ten. Or none. As to the canoes which would have been required for the portaging conditions of so much of the journey from Hudson Bay to the swampy lake at Kensington, these have vanished from the picture entirely.[36]

CHAPTER IX

Mr. Holand as Investigator

Sven B. F. Jansson, the Swedish runologist, writes: "If one were to discuss the [Kensington] question fully, one would be compelled to write a book thicker than any of Holand's."[1] "Mr. Holand . . . is really the main part of the Kensington stone," declared C. N. Gould in 1910.[2] This is substantially in accord with Holand's own estimate of his indispensability to the Kensington stone. Writing to Winchell in 1910, he says: "Inasmuch as your answer [in the MHS Report] to the linguistic objections is in the main a copy from my dissertation, I think it proper that you make suitable acknowledgment."[3] A bit later, Holand refers to "the assistance you have received (free of charge) from me who am the only one yet able to prove the language authentic, which most critics seem to think a very difficult job."[4]

It is unfortunate that an attack on the credentials of the Kensington stone must in part take the form of an attack on the credentials of Mr. Holand, but the reasons for that are solely of Mr. Holand's making. It is admitted by everybody, including Mr. Holand, that the Minnesota petroglyph would have died a natural death long ago had he not resuscitated it in 1907 and kept rallying to its defense ever since.

Holand has given us at least two mutually contradictory accounts of the opening phase of his discovery. They are quoted with italics supplied:

A. *At the time [1899] I had no faith in the alleged runestone; but having made a study of runes for many years, I finally found opportunity to visit the place of discovery.* . . . I therefore procured the stone and made a minute and prolonged study of it. . . . It weighs about 230 pounds.[5]

B. At the time the stone was found and rejected, I was a student at the University of Wisconsin, absorbed in the writing of my Master's thesis on The Age and Home of the Elder Edda. *I, therefore, knew nothing about the Kensington Stone. But nine years later I accidentally came in contact with it.* At that time I was writing a history of the Norwegian settlements in America. In order to get material for this work, it was necessary to visit all these settlements and get the facts from the old pioneers. One of the last settlements I visited was Kensington, a very small Scandinavian community. As I went from house to house inquiring about past experiences, almost the only thing I heard was the story of this runic stone. As I had studied runes and Old Norse in the university and knew a little about these things, my curiosity was aroused, and I went to see Mr. Ohman. He showed me the stone and told me that certain scholars in Norway or Sweden said it was a forgery. As I had read the works of several of them and held them in highest esteem, I did not doubt their verdict. But this neatly engraved stone was a work of art, and I thought it would be an interesting souvenir of my history-hunting years. Ohman did not care for the stone, and the result of my visit was that he gave it to me.[6]

Perhaps it is immaterial to ascertain which of these two conflicting stories is true, and which false. Perhaps it is not even fair. Holand made neither of them under oath, as an affidavit or otherwise. And Holand has intimated, in one of his rejoinders to Dr. Quaife, that only that portion of a man's testimony which is made under oath need be considered strictly valid.[7] This allows much latitude to persons whose interests are served by deviations from truth. In spite of this, Holand apparently expects to be believed in his reporting of facts, and even his conjectures and theories must be respected as though they were facts. Holand deals sternly with those of his critics who make the slightest blunder in reporting on what Holand himself considers facts.[8] But since he has written so voluminously, making it all but im-

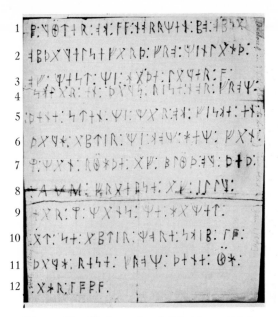

Fig. 10. The Hedberg sketch. Numbers added

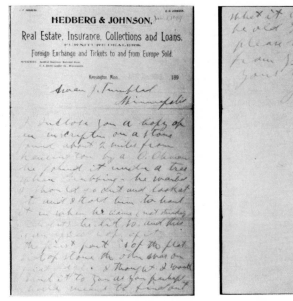
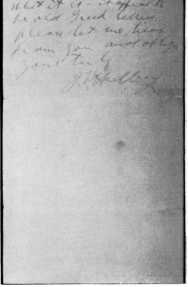

Fig. 11. The Hedberg letter

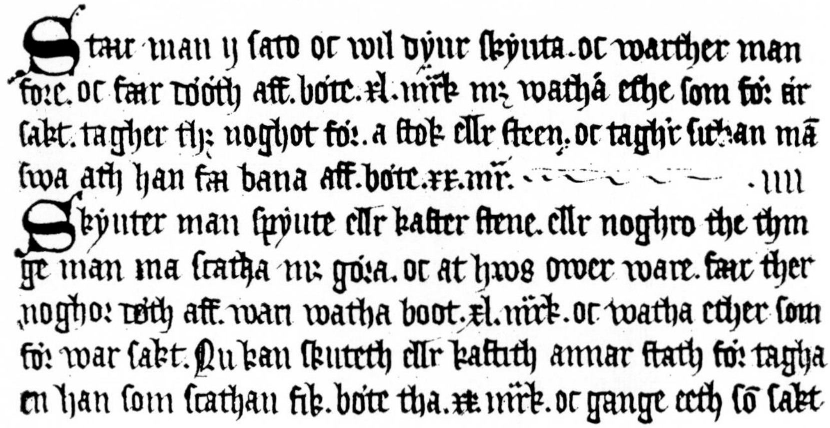

Stair man y sato oc wil dyur skyuta. oc warther man
fore. oc faar wooth aff. bote. xl. mrk m: watha ethe som for: ar
sakt. tagher th: noghot for. a stok ellr steen. oc taghir sithan mā
swa ath han far bana aff. bote. xx. mr. IIII
Skyuter man skyute ellr kaster stene. ellr noghro the thm
ge man ma scatha m: gora. oc at hwos ower ware. faar ther
noghor woth aff. wan watha boot. xl. mrk. oc watha ether som
for war sakt. Nu kan skuteth ellr kastith annar stath for: tagha
en han som scathan fik. bote tha. xx. mrk. oc gange eeth so sakt

Fig. 12. *Magnus Eriksons Statslag*

? Swedes and Norwegians on a journey of discovery from Vineland
? west--we camped ? ? one day's journey north from
this stone--we fished one day--after we came home we found ? men
red with blood and dead-- A U M (?) Save us from evil (?)--Have ?
men at the ocean to look after our ships ? days' journey
from this island (?) .
Year ?

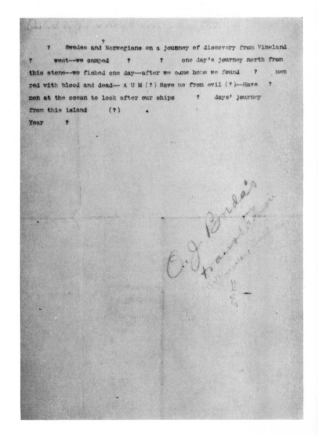

Fig. 13
Professor Breda's
translation

Ett märkligt fornfynd i Minnesota.

Fig. 14

Sketch and article in *Svenska Amerikanska Posten*, February 28, 1899.

Farmaren O. Ohman hittade sistlidne november månad under ett gammalt träd å sin farm i närheten af Kensington, Douglas County, Minnesota, en med runskrift försedd sten, 30 tum lång, 15 tum bred och 6 tum i tjocklek vägande 215 lbs. Ofvanstående bild visar inskriptionerna såväl som stenens utseende och platsen, der den påträffades. Mr. Ohman gjorde en afskrift af de å stenen inristade figurerna eller runorna och sände afskriften genom J. P. Hedberg i Kensington till SVENSKA AMERIKANSKA POSTEN. Vi sände den derpå till Minnesotas universitet, der professor O. J. Breda undersökte densamma och kom till den slutsatsen, att det var en blandad runskrift, men trodde dock, att det hela var ett skämt af någon, som förstått runskrift och ville drifva med de lärde professorerna. Emellertid sändes en liknande afskrift till professor Curme vid universitetet i Evanston, Illinois, och han bad om att få sig stenen tillsänd, hvilket också skedde. Professor Breda öfversatte runorna sålunda (tankstrecken äro ord han icke förstod, då de icke äro riktiga runor):

"Svenskar och — nordmän på upptäcktsresa från Vinland vesterut — Vi slogo läger — en dagsresa norr om denna sten. Vi fiskade en dag. Efter det vi kommo hem funno vi — män röda af blod och döda. A V M räddade från — har — män vid hafvet för att se efter våra skepp — dagsresa från denna ö. År —".

Professor Curme öfversätter inskriptionerna sålunda.

"Ett sällskap nordbor är ute på upptäcktsresa vesterut från Vinland. Vi hade ett läger jemte två båtar en dagsresa från denna sten. Vi gå ut dagligen och fiska. En dag vi kommo hem, funno vi en man röd af blod och död. Ave (farväl). Frälsa från eld. Har man någonsin haft en sådan kamrat som vi haft. Vi äro på väg för att se efter våra skepp, fjorton dagsresor från denna ö."

Professor Breda påstår, att det är bevis i sjelfva inskriptionen på att den icke är äkta. Det vigtigaste af dessa bevis är att runskriften synes vara en blandning af svenska och norska i nutida grammatisk form och med ett eller annat engelskt ord emellan. Det är icke fornnordisk runskrift, säger han. Professor Curme är af alldeles motsatt åsigt. Han anser, att på den tid, då stenen upprestes

på det ställe, der den nu påträffats, var detta stranden af Superiorsjön, hvilken då för omkring 500 år sedan var betydligt större än nu, hvarigenom det icke alls är otroligt, att platsen ifråga vid den tiden var en ö. Efter en noggrann undersökning af denna runsten, kommer den att fotograferas och dessa fotografier skola sedan sändas till kännare på detta område de både här i landet och i Europa. Bland dessa föreslår prof. Breda såsom de förnämsta auktoriteter. L. V. A. Wimmer i Köpenhamn och Sophus Bugge i Kristiania. En fornnordisk forskare vid namn Carl Dilge i Chicago är öfvertygad om att stenen är äkta. Han meddelar, att Dr. D. B. Freeman, 400 Drexel Boulevard, Chicago, har i sig ett armband förfärdigadt af nordmän, hvilket också upphittats i Minnesota.

H. M. Wagner i Starbuck, Minn., anser att den funna runstenen är äkta. Han tror dock icke att stenen ursprungligen upprests, der den nu blifvit funnen, ty det är mera sannolikt, menar han, att stenen upprests längre österut, förmodligen å någon ö i de stora sjöarne, och sedan hitförts af indianer, hvilka betraktade det kurlösa stenblocket såsom någonting öfvernaturligt och heligt samt att den öfverlemnats i vården af deras medicinmän.

Professor Curme vid Northwestern University i Evanston, Ill., har noga undersökt inristningarne och lemnat en ny öfversättning, som skiljer sig något från hans första försök, ehuru han medgifver, att en del ord och figurer äro obegripliga. Den nya öfversättningen lyder:

"Åtta göter (i Sverige) och tjugutvå norrmän äro ute på en upptäcksexpedition från Vinlandet i vestern. Vi hade ett läger jemte två båtar en dagsresa norr om denna sten. Vi voro ute och fiskade en dag efter vi hemkommo funno vi en man röd med blod och död farväl (eller ave); frälstes från ondo har någon en sådan kamrat (man) som vi haft. Gå fram vår väg att efterse våra skepp fjorton dagsresor från denna ö; år 1362 (eller 1462)."

Professor Curme anser, att professor Breda misstydt flera af de vigtigaste meningarne af dessa runor.

Under alla omständigheter kan man dock med skäl anse fyndet såsom ett ytterst märkligt sådant, och det skall blifva intressant att se, hvad Europas lärde komma att säga derom.

Indskrift paa Fagaden.

Fig. 15
Runic sketch in *Skandi-
naven*, February 24, 1899.

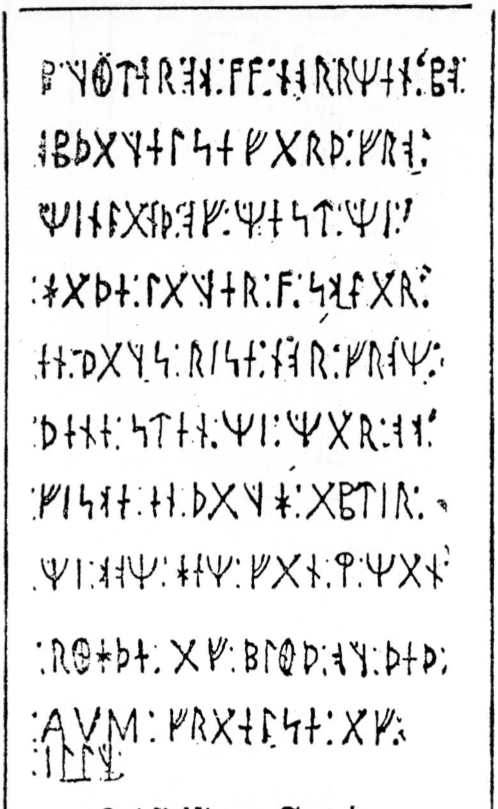

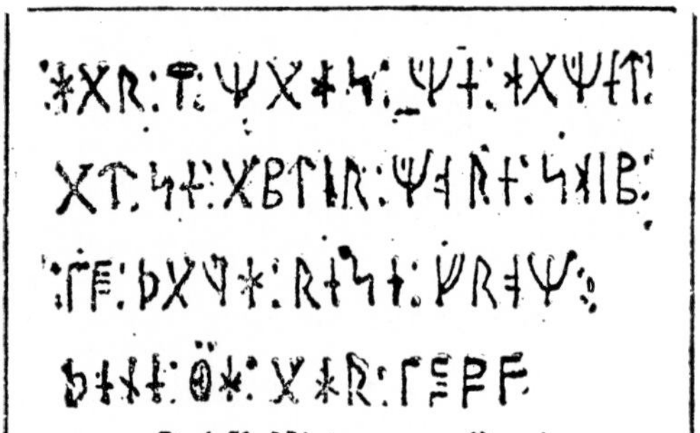

Indskrift paa en Kant.

THE SUPPOSED
RUNIC STONE

INSCRIPTION ON FACE OF STONE.

Fig. 16

Runic sketch in Chicago *Tribune*, February 21, 1899.

INSCRIPTION ON EDGE OF STONE

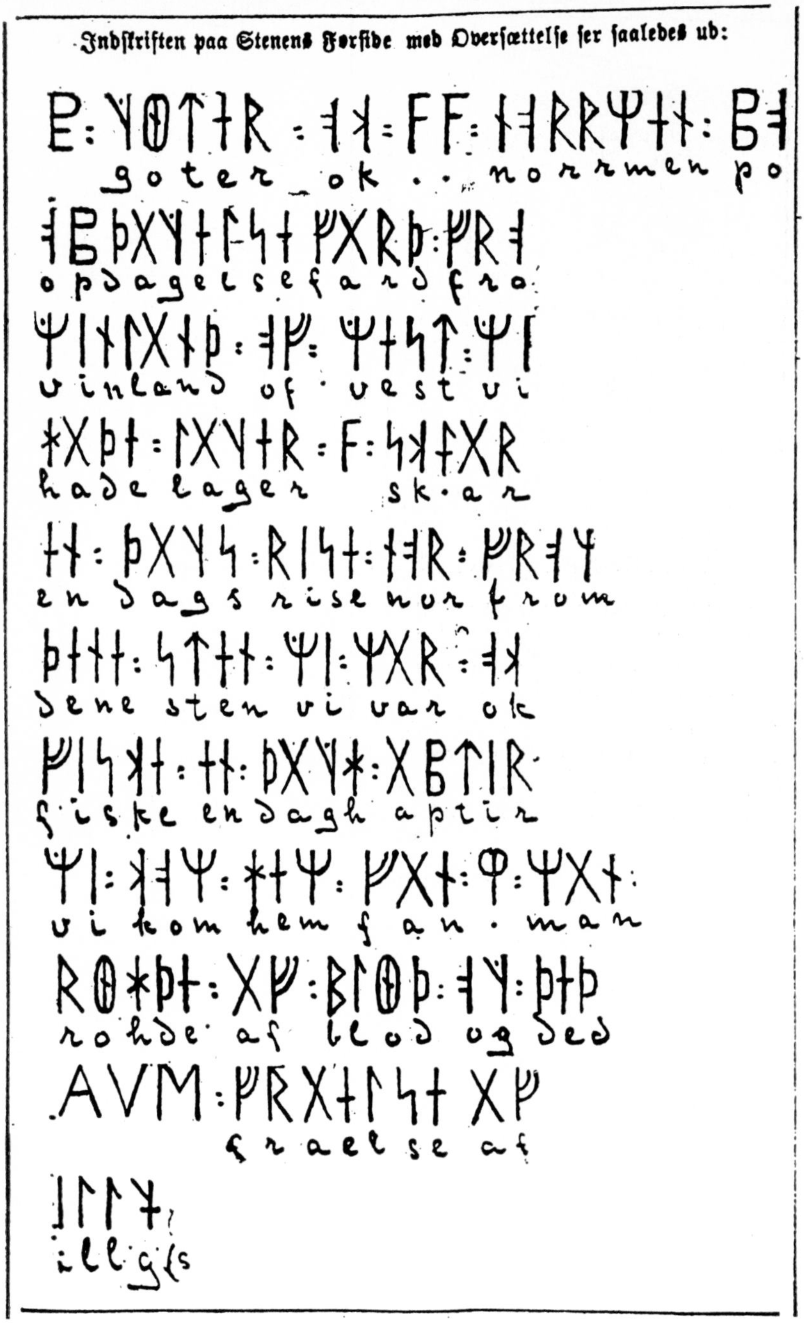

goter ok .. norrmen po

opdagelsefardfro

vinland of vest vi

hade lager sk·ar

en dags rise nor from

dene sten vi var ok

fiske en dagh aptir

vi kom hem fan·man

rohde af blod og ded

fraelse af

illg(s

Fig. 17. Runic sketch in *Skandinaven*, March 10, 1899. Face view

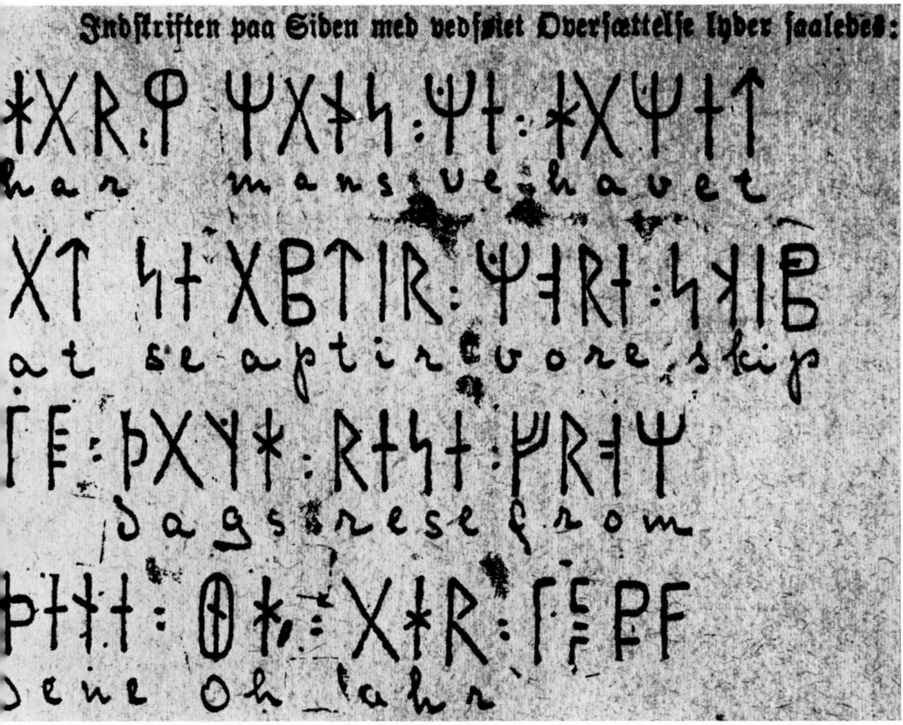
Indskriften paa Siden med vedføiet Oversættelse lyder saaledes:
har mans ve havet
at se aptir vore skip
dagsrese from
dene Oh lahr

Fig. 18. The same. Side view

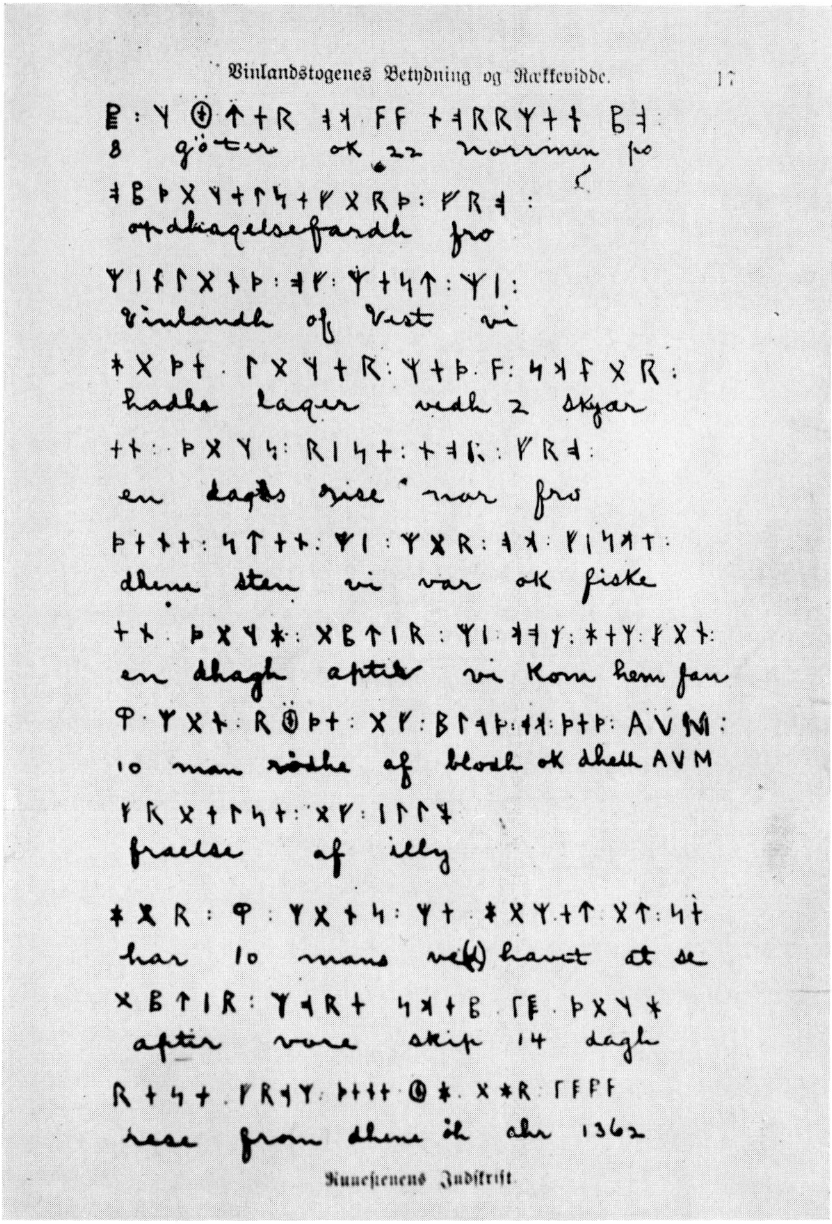

8 göter ok 22 normen po

opdakagelsefardh fro

vinlandh of vest vi

hadhe lager wedh 2 skyar

en dags rise nor fro

dhene sten vi var ok fiske

en dhagh aptir vi kom hem fan

10 man rödhe af blodh ok dhødh AVM

fraelse af illy

har 10 mans vedh havet at se

aftir vore skip 14 dagh

rese from dhene il ahr 1362

Runestenens Indskrift

Fig. 19 Runic sketch in Holand's immigrant history.

possible to collate his numerous assertions, and since the arguments in favor of the Kensington stone are almost exclusively Holand-made rather than natural, it is difficult for his critics to avoid giving offense in this way. However, the purpose of the present chapter is not to attack Holand indirectly through an onslaught on his Kensington stone, but to establish outright—if previous chapters have not already shown it—that Holand is not an investigator upon whom one can rely for competent, impartial, and accurate presentation of the rune stone matter.

Very early in the game, Holand, the purported linguistic authority, showed his unfamiliarity with, and indifference towards, ordinary linguistic terminology. Thus, writing to Professor Winchell in 1911 with regard to Professor Flom's linguistic criticisms of the MHS Report—which, as we have seen, owed its linguistics to Holand—he says: "His [Flom's] remark about the 'science of Semasiology'—whatever that may be—is quite beyond me. . . . I prefer to be ignorant with Vigfusson than wise with Flom."[9] Had Holand felt even a modicum of curiosity about linguistics he could have looked up the, to him, unfamiliar word in the dictionary. But Holand preferred, as he says, to be ignorant.

Referring in an essay of 1910 to an Old Icelandic passage on the launching of boats, Holand is literally unable to distinguish between the nominative, dative, and accusative usage of nouns. Here is the almost unbelievable quotation from Holand's manuscript, uncritically accepted by Winchell and printed in the MHS Report: "For instance, in the Vinland Saga (A.M. 552) we read '*Lata their i* haf *fram tveñ̃ṇụm̃ skipụm̃ thegar their eru bunir.*' (See Vigfussons Grammar page 123 line [blotted] 23) haf is here nominative in [form?] and should be dative while tveñ̃ñum ski*pum* is dative and should be accusative."[10]

Now, any sentence in Old Icelandic reading *Láta þeir i haf fram tvennum skipum þegar þeir eru búnir* can only mean: 'They launch, *i.e.*, put to sea with two ships as soon as they are ready.' In such a sentence, *haf* is an accusative, and not nominative, nor should it be by the rules of Old Norse-Old Icelandic grammar, as every beginner in the language is required to learn. The first semester student of Icelandic is also taught the instrumental use of the dative in certain instances where English uses the accusative; *tvennum skipum* is such an instrumental dative, analogous to such English usage as 'to fight with a sword' in the sense by 'by means of.' But Winchell knew this no more than Holand.

Holand's ignorance of the elements of Old Icelandic is parallelled by his innocence of Latin, that indispensable adjunct to research into medieval sources. As late as 1932, in trying to demonstrate the existence of the letter Ø in the Danish *Nestved Obituarium* of the fourteenth century, he writes: "Ø[*bit*] Dom[*inus*] *Jacobus*, etc. (see Fig. 11 above for illustration). For some reason, the Ø was used as a symbol or abbreviation of *obit* (death). This was probably less due to a mistake in spelling than to the thought that, as Ø was the last letter of the alphabet, it better symbolized death than did O."[11]

Obit is, of course, a verb, not a noun. Furthermore these are Latin words, not Danish, and there is no letter ø in the Latin alphabet, in which the final letter is z. And finally, some brief training in palaeography would have demonstrated to Holand that the curlicue dipping into his alleged Ø (*Ô*), was not a symbol of vowel modification but a typical example of scribal shorthand—the abbreviation for -*bit*.

L. M. Larson was quick to point out Holand's concatenation of errors: "It would be difficult to pack a greater number of misconceptions into a single sentence than Mr. Holand has done in this case."[12]

It is not to be supposed that Holand was incapable of response to this criticism. His answer deserves to be quoted:

I acknowledge with thanks Professor Larson's correction that ö was not the last letter of the Danish-Latin alphabet in the fourteenth century. While it appears as a separate letter variously marked to indicate different sounds between *e* and *o*, it was considered as a form of *o* until much later. I have given numerous examples from the fourteenth century showing a close similarity in form to the *ö* in the inscription, as Professor Larson admits.[13]

This "answer" gives perfect insight into a basic feature of Holand's methodology, which is disingenuously to "misunderstand" every criticism that cannot be answered on its own

terms—in this case the Latin word *obit*, which Holand dismisses
from the discussion. Furthermore, in his book, four years later,
the claim about ∅ remains in the discussion, quite as if it had
never been questioned.[14] Holand is oblivious to evidence.

It can be shown, too, that Holand's philological carelessness
is not limited to ancient languages. In *Westward from Vinland* he
reproduces a letter to himself in modern Swedish by S. Welin,
Director of the Westgothland Museum at Skara.[15] In the nine
lines of the main text of the letter, Holand commits no fewer
than ten gross errors in transcription, chiefly of such kind as a
Norwegian typically makes in writing a composition in Swedish.
This does not purport to be a free composition or a translation,
however, but the direct reproduction of material written by a
Swedish scholar. The text of the letter possesses an inexplicable
feature above and beyond this: Although dated 1928, the orthography is *in part* that prevailing before the Swedish spelling re-
form of 1906 (hvilket, trifvel). These are not included in the
count of ten errors, since we do not have access to the original
letter.

A persistent aspect of Holand's methodology is to cite books
and documents that lie remote from the investigative resources
of most readers, drawing from these works conclusions as un-
warranted as they are recondite. One example will serve for
many. At one point Holand purports to demonstrate the modernity of the Danish language by the year 1350; this he does by
quoting a passage from Brandt's *Gammeldansk Læsebog*. The
quotation concerns Africa and is from the Danish *Lucidarius*, a
popular medieval compendium of knowledge.[16] But the fact is,
the passage proves very little about any given point in 1350, for
as Brandt clearly indicates, the *Lucidarius* is only known to us
through a late copy from the period 1450–1500. This is quite as
though writers some hundreds of years hence were to prove an
example of English usage in the year 1825—say, the use of the
word "smog"—by triumphantly quoting from a work written in
1950. And it will illustrate Holand's incapacity to guide us in the
exacting discipline of textual criticism. Yet when caught up in
one of his contradictions by a responsible investigator, Holand
disposes of the point with a sarcasm (" 'Little things affect little

minds,' " quoted from Disraeli to dispose of Quaife's trenchant criticisms);[17] or he brazens it out by "misunderstanding" the point at issue, as with *obit;* or he ignores the issue completely, as with the affidavits.

How Holand treats his critics is seen in his attacks on Quaife, Holvik, and Moltke. Holand's characterization of Quaife's arguments from 1934 is as disingenuous as it is untrue: ". . . the body of evidence which Mr. Quaife cites . . . demands the instant and absolute rejection of even the consideration of any other data, geological, runological, or linguistic, which may be adduced in favor of the inscription."[18] And again: "He says not a word—and thinks not a word should be said—about the vast runological learning a presumptive forger would require to falsify this inscription. . . ."[19]

This is inaccurate since Quaife, in the article under attack by Holand, merely limits *himself* to the historical aspects, which alone he regards himself as competent to judge. To quote Quaife: "The laborious effort to demonstrate the validity of the runic record on historical grounds ends, therefore, in utter failure . . . . the runologists may continue their study of the inscription entirely free from any supposition that an historical presumption favoring its authenticity has been established."[20]

Quaife's article of 1947 on the Kensington stone is one of the most devastatingly specific refutations of Holand's fancies that has ever been advanced. Holand's answer to this is largely a strategy of bland evasions, topped off with allegations of personal bias: ". . . Mr. Quaife is more concerned with impugning the scholarship and, indeed, the integrity of those whose opinions on the Kensington stone differ from his than in any objective evaluation of the arguments for and against the stone's authenticity. . . . 'Little things affect little minds.' "[21]

It is solely out of "little things" that Holand has evolved his detailed theory as to the Knutson expedition. If one is not privileged to examine scrupulously these and other little things, the entire study of history as a serious discipline becomes impossible.

A worse technique is applied to J. A. Holvik, with the purpose of discrediting both Holvik and the Danish runologist, Erik Moltke, at a single stroke. To quote: "A graver charge is

Moltke's statement that 'Ohman owned antiquarian books [. .]. that shed no little light on the peculiar inscription.' Moltke knows that this is not true because his co-worker, John A. Holvik, investigated and reported on these alleged runic books."[22] And after explaining this, Holand adds: "Since Holvik was selected for this job, partly because he was known as an unbeliever in the authenticity of the Kensington inscription, Moltke's claim must be dismissed as unfounded. Moreover, because he knew of Holvik's report, it having been printed in the official committee report, and again in my first book on the Kensington stone, his statement must further be labeled reckless."[23]

Even for Holand, this is an audacious, a breathtaking statement. His pretended conclusion as to fraud by Moltke—in collaboration with Holvik—has been drawn through false association of two entirely unrelated facts. The first is that Professor Holvik, during his student days in 1909, was asked to study Sven Fogelblad's (the itinerant parson and schoolmaster— see Chapter XVI) copy of the Swedish grammar by Almquist (which had been borrowed by Ohman from Fogelblad), in order to determine whether it was a source of the Kensington inscription. Holvik reported his opinion that it was not, and one may agree with that conclusion even today (there is, to be sure, a runic alphabet in the volume, which is still preserved at St. Paul).[24] But what has that to do with Moltke's, or Holvik's, investigation of the Ohman library today? Are these gentlemen, or is anybody else, debarred from discussing the encyclopedia by Rosander,[25] the Swedish history by Montelius,[26] and the telltale scrapbook[27]—or the Almquist grammar either, for that matter— because the last named was pronounced unimportant in 1909?

The second element in Holand's false equation is that, forty years afterwards, Professor Holvik communicated to various scholars and the public his opinions concerning certain volumes associated with Ohman and, as he believed, with the Kensington stone. These were the books mentioned in the previous paragraph. Moltke's prediction regarding them has been amply confirmed and documented point for point in the present volume. In short, the Almquist grammar is Holand's red herring.

There is one area in which it is hopeless to argue with Mr. Holand, and that is the field of linguistics. He has sufficient respect for acknowledged scholars in this subject to quote (or misquote) them when it suits his purpose. His deference does not extend to the rules of evidence whereby, and alone whereby, responsible investigative techniques can serve the aims of science. His insistent aim is merely to prove the genuineness of the unfortunate Kensington document. Holand tries at one point to sum up the Kensington problem in a single sentence: "It has become an either-or problem; either the inscription was made by Ohman or it is authentic."[28] In other words, according to Holand, if science cannot prove that one certain person, Olof Ohman, drew up the Kensington text and carved it on a stone, then science must acknowledge that the inscription is genuine. This is sheer nonsense. Suppose that a carved rock should be discovered tomorrow, bearing a message in English, or Choctaw, or Esperanto, and purportedly left by visitors from Mars. Several hoaxers are suspected, but nothing can be proved against them. By Holand's logic, the inscription would therefore be genuine.

Holand has frequently quoted Professor Einarsson as linguistic authority for his own contentions, and that Einarsson twenty-four years ago expresssed himself charitably on Holand's work has been seen from the quotation in Chapter IV, above. But it is time to supply a corrective to Holand's rosy claims, drawn from that same review by Einarsson: "On reading his linguistic commentary, the first impression is astonishment over the wealth of material quoted and the wide scholarship displayed in the footnotes. But very soon one is not a little surprised at the extraordinary way in which the author sometimes uses his sources both primary and secondary."[29] After some documentation, Einarsson states: "Grammatical discrimination seems not to be his strong point, as may often be seen in his use of grammatical authorities."[30] Showing by some examples what he means, Einarsson adds: "Another misunderstanding, if not misrepresentation, is seen in the discussion of the noun *opdagelese*. . . ."[31] And again: "I believe this discussion of Holand's linguistic commentary shows that his statements have to be taken with a grain of salt. I should not be surprised if more errors were not to be found in his quotations of Norwegian and Swedish sources which I have not had at hand and have thus been unable to control."[32] Professor Einarsson's charitable concluding assumption is that "Holand is a historian, not a linguist. . . ."[33]

At about that same time, the distinguished Canadian historian, W. S. Wallace, was writing: "His [Mr. Holand's] book is difficult to characterize. While using the language of impartial history, he is in reality a special pleader: he reminds one of the lawyer who seeks to squeeze out of the evidence every ounce of weight that he can in favor of his client."[34] It is thus the opinion of these two experts, both of them relied upon by Holand as witnesses for the defense, that Holand is not the authority he would have his readers believe.

One is frequently puzzled over the source of some of Holand's citations. In *Explorations*, for example, Holand quotes two paragraphs by Professor Curme purporting to show that Curme, despite his linguist's skepticism, regarded the inscription as 600 years old from a geological point of view. The supporting footnote locates this reference in *Skandinaven* for May 3, 1899. According to the Librarian of Luther College where the country's largest collection of Norwegian-American newspapers is found, there is no article on the rune stone for that date.[35]

Turning to the theories of Mr. Holand, one must characterize his "methodology" as an isolated, piece-meal examination of each individual word and rune without reference to corporate incongruities. Every natural language, and every natural system of writing (excluding code systems and artificially constructed languages), indeed every cultural form ever known belongs to a consistent, definable, slowly developing system. Changes in language, just as with changes in art, take place gradually. There are times when Mr. Holand seems to understand this. Thus, arguing with L. M. Larson and Stefan Einarsson about the traditional shape of spears, he refers to "well-established national customs."[36] And earlier, referring to the form of numerals, more particularly the runic symbol for the numeral 14, he had declared: "It is reasonable to suppose that the runemaster would use the simpler form, which every one would be familiar with, rather than introduce a new sign."[37]

But only when it will suit his purpose for the moment does Holand accept the fact that there are traceable norms in cultural expression and that such norms constitute invaluable indices for or against the genuineness of a disputed artifact. Holand has a habit of twisting runes and word forms in accommodation to the requirement at hand. He adds or subtracts letters; converts them into other letters; turns runic symbols backward at random, then asserting that "this is the same symbol, only reversed"; adds or subtracts dots, and raises or lowers cross-bars without warning. Thus, Holand confidently asserts in his recent book: "The carver of the Kensington stone has forgotten the correct form of runic K and has substituted the Latin K [reversed!]; likewise, his a is different and his y is upside down. . . . Finally he needed some *umlauts*, and for these there were no runic archetypes. He was therefore obliged to introduce several new signs shown above."[38]

In other words, the runecarver of Kensington was an innovator of distinction, exercising his creative genius in the face of death itself. But a bit later in explaining a totally contrary feature of the inscription, namely its *archaic* features, in this case the rune for *n* which had been extinct for 250 years, Holand assures us: "But round about in the woods and fields of most parts of southern Sweden could be seen dignified memorials from former days, and here he could get his alphabet. . . . It therefore seems reasonable that the carver of the stone would use the more common form."[39]

It also seems that Mr. Holand changes the ground rules on every play. He carefully shows us how the pioneer runecarver, seven years from home, was forgetting his mother tongue and spoke uncertainly, or at least wrote with uncertain spelling and a jumble of lacerated verb forms. Nevertheless, the inscription was carved " 'with sure deft strokes by a person throughly familiar with carving runes.' "[40] And even if, after years of wandering, the runecarver had forgotten the "quaint characters"[41] of the runic system, so that he literally had to invent new symbols (a distinguished epigraphical feat in itself) yet for some reason he remembered the long extinct rune for *n* from his native West Gothland.[42] And although the runic system "had become obsolete and was of interest only as an antiquarian curiosity,"[43] the explorer of 1362 nevertheless chose it as the means of communicating most effectively with future generations in the uninhabited wilderness of North America.

One of Holand's favorite arguments concerns the umlauted o, written with two dots, thus: ö. Holand is desperately eager to show that this letter—ö—existed in Scandinavia in the fourteenth century. Now, such a writing may actually have existed here and there, through accident, error, or scribal idiosyncrasy, as striking exceptions to the general system then prevailing for marking the modification of a vowel. But the arguments and "examples" that Holand uses are almost uniformly misleading, erroneous, or downright false. We shall take several examples. Attempting to establish this ö, Holand cites the great grammarian Axel Kock, and adds: "In the 14th century the letter *ö* was in a transitory form. Manuscripts of that period show no less than ten ways of writing this letter, and there are some writers who use two or three forms on the same page without any difference in sound. The most common forms were *o* with one dot above, *o* with an oblique bisecting line and a circumflex above, and *o* with a cross in the middle."[44]

In other words, one finds, says Holand, Ȯ , Ø̂ , and ⊕ . But this has no evidential connection with the ö, a circle with two dots above it, that he is pretending at this point to document. And nothing else but ö will do. In actuality, Holand is merely speaking of a sound (phonetic [ø]), formerly spelled in various ways but nowadays represented in standard Swedish orthography by the letter ö. Holand has simply confused the sound with the letter. Holand's phrase "the letter *ö*" should therefore be translated alternately as "the letter now written as *ö*," and as "the sound nowadays represented by the symbol *ö*."

The passage by Kock cited by Holand to prove his allegations as to ö makes exactly two mentions of this letter. One is to state that since 1526, ö has been used with frequency in Swedish printed books.[45] The other points out that modern, printed editions of Old Swedish texts have standardized the spelling of the symbol as either ö or ø.[46] This is called "normalization," and represents a practice called forth by editorial convenience, even necessity, under recognized rules which every careful editor specifies in his introduction. Readers must check on these in each individual case before propounding conclusions as to the orthography of such original manuscripts as are concerned.

Adolf Noreen, in his article on ö in *Nordisk Familjebok* (also cited by Holand), indicates substantially the same thing as Kock. Sam Jansson's (not be be confused with Sven B. F. Jansson, the runologist) thorough discussion of Swedish palaeography in *Nordisk Kultur*, XXVIII, has thirty-one photographic reproductions, of which thirty show manuscript writings from the period 1164–1545.[47] Many examples of ø are found here, but not one example of the form ö. Holand is fond of citing umlauted vowels with two dots from the great palaeographic atlas by the Danish scholar, Kr. Kaalund.[48] What Holand overlooks or ignores (among other things) is that one must distinguish between the appearance of the original manuscripts as photographically reproduced in Kaalund, and the latter's standardized transliterations of these in the parallel printed texts, in which ö with two dots appears in abundance.

While on the subject of Kaalund, it must be pointed out that Holand has made at least two incorrect references to Kaalund on page 168 of *Westward*, where footnotes 16 and 17 are supposed to document certain umlauts in manuscripts reproduced by Kaalund. No date is here stated for the Kaalund volume, but references to Kaalund on pages 166, 169, and 170, respectively, all refer to the volume of Kaalund's *Palaeografisk Atlas* which was published in 1903, and no other volume or date is given for the reference on page 168. But the volume of 1903 does not contain the references made by Holand. After much research it was discovered that the references belong in a different volume entirely, namely a new series of reproductions published by Kaalund in 1907, and that the anonymous references have no pertinence to Holand's contentions.[49]

Similarly devious is Holand's treatment of asserted double dots used for umlaut in a Swedish legal manuscript from 1387,

Magnus Eriksons Statslag, a portion of which is reproduced by
him on that same page 168 of *Westward*. The caption to Holand's
reproduction describes the Swedish text as "SHOWING
NUMEROUS DOTTED *ö*'s, *ä*'s and *y*'s." And the accompanying discussion by Holand is aimed at persuading the reader to
accept examples of the single dot above a vowel as *bona fide*
examples of double dots, which "must also have been frequently
used," even though Holand has none to show. Fig. 12 was
photographed from the same source as that used by Holand,
namely, Hans Hildebrand, *Svenska Skriftprof*. It clearly shows
a number of instances in which *a*, *o*, or *y* is provided with a
dot, thus: å, ȯ, ẏ. In the case of *a* and *o*, the dot is provided with
a tiny tail, thus: ͬ. This tail gives it the appearance of an
elevated comma and is quite usual in manuscripts of this sort.
But note that there is no single example of *two dots* above a
vowel. In the instances in which the passage really does exhibit
two dots above a word, these are *not* umlauts but marks of abbreviation, *i.e.*, they represent omitted elements of spelling, something very typical of the semi-shorthand employed by medieval
scribes; see, for example, the word *mᵣ̈k* in line 2; *mᵣ̈* in line 5; *mᵣ̈k*
in line 7 and again in line 9. If Mr. Holand thinks these abbreviation marks above an *r* can be passed off as examples of vowel
umlaut, he is mistaken.

The point of our discussion is not whether ö, for example,
could or could not occur in the writings of ancient Sweden. The
point is rather to demonstrate the nature of what passes for
scholarly evidence in the writings of Mr. Holand. For the ostensible point of Holand's lengthy effort to document the ö is its
putative connection with the Kensington stone. But since the
ö—an o with two dots—if it existed at all, was a profound rarity,
a maverick character, so to speak, on fourteenth century parchment, its presence in a *runic* carving from the same period is ten
times more inexplicable. Not even Holand pretends that the ö
(actually, ꝋ) is anything but a borrowing from non-runic modes
of writing, the difference between Holand's argument and our
own being that he would place his borrowing some hundreds of
years earlier than could possibly have been the case. See, for
example, *Westward from Vinland*, pages 174–75, where he re-

produces Noreen's table of Dalecarlian runes, showing late ö-runes for 1726, 1773, and 1832, respectively. In his haste to make these medieval, Holand has on the page previous falsely labelled the latter two of these runic sets as "Runic Alphabets of the Middle Ages."

The runes of Kensington are not medieval, and their connection with printed books is clear enough. That is a topic to which we shall return in Chapter XIII.

Holand is similarly devious in his treatment of the letter *j*, citing in asserted proof of its use as a consonant in the fourteenth and fifteenth centuries, the authority of the great Swedish philologist, Adolf Noreen. In so doing, he allows us to believe that Noreen's encyclopedia article adduced by him as reference is specifically an article on "consonantal J." It is no such thing. Furthermore, Noreen actually writes in the article (translated, with italics supplied): "In Swedish manuscripts from the 14th cent. or even earlier the symbol *j* is not unusual, f. ex. in the Law of Uppland (especially for the preposition *i* [*as a vowel*]), the Law of Gotland (especially at the end of words [*as a vowel*]), etc. This early distinction between *i* and *j* is however *merely graphic, without reference to its function as a vowel or consonant.*"[50]

Inversely, as Noreen goes on to remark, right down to the time of Charles XII (d. 1718), Swedish books customarily employed the letter *i* for the sound of *j*. Mr. Holand's disclaimer that "it is immaterial how it [he clearly means the Kensington symbol for *j*— ᚠ] was used"[51] does not obviate the falsity of his reference to Noreen. Furthermore, this discussion by Noreen is concerned with manuscripts and books in the Latin alphabet, modified for writing and printing Swedish, and has nothing whatever to do with *runes*. Or has Holand abandoned his contention that the Kensington inscription is written in runes?

Holand distracts and wearies the reader's critical faculties through an accumulation of *irrelevant* "examples." Thus, in discussing consonantal *j*, Holand blithely asserts that the Kensington rune for *j* is found twenty-two times "in cursive form" in a letter by Queen Margaret from 1370.[52] In proof of this, he shows the reader the symbol ᛈ (for *I* in the word *Idher* 'you'). Three fallacies are here involved: (1) the letter shows not a consonant, but a vowel, the vowel *i*, capitalized as I, (2) the vowel occurs in an example of European cursive writing, and is *not* a rune or the transliteration of a rune, and (3) irrespective of all else, the runes for *j* and *I* are not more alike than P and F, or X and Z. Holand's argument amounts to this: A horse and a cow are identical. But make the horse smaller, give it horns, alter the tail and change the whinny to a moo. Behold, a horse is a cow, Q.E.D.

But to publish *all* of Holand's blunders or misstatements is not necessary here. He knows quite well what his philological disquisitions are worth. In 1932, he commences one of his chapters with the assertion: "The language of the inscription, being the principal means by which the writer reveals himself, presents one of the best fields for testing its authenticity."[53] Twenty-four years later he seems to regret that early, unfortunate admission: "It would greatly simplify the solution of the question concerning the authenticity of the inscription if the critics would lay aside their philological calipers for a while and take a good look at the circumstances surrounding the finding of the stone."[54] An exceedingly fruitful suggestion, this one, as earlier chapters in the present book have shown.

With consummate skill, Holand breaks down and distributes related portions of a given set of arguments throughout widely separated areas of text, so that the reader often fails to note discrepancies. Thus, in one place we read: "There were none who had the knowledge, skill and time to sit *for days* [italics supplied] carving ancient inscriptions on rocks which could bring them no profit."[55] But twelve pages later, in a passage that quotes an interview with the sculptor John K. Daniels, we are told with Holand's evident approval: "The whole job may have taken *about two hours*."[56] (Italics supplied.)

Occasionally Holand forgets to allow time for the obliteration of one's recollection of his argument when its converse is required for a different purpose later on. The unconscious humor of the following passage speaks for itself:

The stone was found in plain view of Nils Flaten's house, and as it was too heavy to be carried, the inscription must have been chiselled on the spot where it was found. But any such "forger" would certainly have been seen by Flaten who had lived there since 1884. And what could have been the motive for such a laborious forgery? Completely mystified, Olof Ohman hauled home his stone and dumped it down by the granary door, fortunately with the inscribed face down.[57]

As previously stated, the major idiosyncrasy of the stone was that it could be hauled in only *one* direction.

The Douglas County historian, a lawyer accustomed to precise terminology, nevertheless repeatedly used the phrase "Professor Holand" in speaking to this writer in 1953.[58] The article on the stone in *Records of the Past* is attributed to "Prof. Hjalmar Rued Holand."[59] It is perfectly true that the title of "professor" has been employed without discrimination in this country. But it is another matter when, in a letter to Winchell of August 6, 1911, Holand speaks of securing "without much delay the eventual chair of Old Norse at Minnesota University. I turned down such an opportunity at Columbia eleven years ago."[60] In other words, Holand states that he was offered a *professorship* at Columbia University around 1900. Mr. Holand's evident high regard for the coveted status of professor did not extend, however, to any specific holder of an academic post whose views differed from his own. Regarding Professor Flom he wrote to Winchell on August 17, 1911: ". . . taking out the egotistic bombast and the errors it is a most futile sally."[61] Of Marius Hægstad at Christiania University he published: "During my extended visits to the different seats of learning in the Scandinavian countries I met only one philologist who would go on record as being convinced that the inscription was a forgery. This was Marius Haegstad . . . his objections are so elementary and so deficient in knowledge of the Swedish literature of the XIV century that it belittle the discussion to consider them seriously."[62] Two pages before he had spoken airily of the European linguistic authorities as "men of ability but little experience in this line of study."[63]

What one chiefly criticizes in Mr. Holand is not his naïveté, nor yet his arrogance towards men of learning, but rather his complete lack of respect for the purposes and function of scientific inquiry itself. What, then, is the reason for Holand's interest in the Kensington stone?

We have Holand's own admission that his major interest was the promotional value of history. In the concluding paragraph of a three-page letter to Winchell on January 11, 1910, he had written with respect to negotiations then going forward between himself and the Minnesota Historical Society concerning purchase of the stone by the Society: "The $5000 which I ask is therefore not so much a price upon the stone itself as a compensation for my contribution to American history."[64] On April 10, Holand raised his price to $6000, claiming he could obtain several times as much abroad; but the bargain was never consummated.[65]

Olof Ohman's claim to ownership is not a definite matter of record. Quaife was informed by Holand in 1914 that he had purchased the stone from Ohman for $25.[66] During the recent lawsuit over the stone at Alexandria, its value was tentatively established by the court in setting bond at $25,000, according to newspaper reports. The suit, which has never been fought through, was begun by three citizens, and the heirs of seven others, who claimed that they purchased the stone at one time of Holand for $2500.[67] Holand has counterclaimed that the money was instead a free scholarship with which to travel abroad.

Mr. Holand, as a professional promoter, does not incur blame for his quite natural financial interest in the Kensington stone; but his pretenses to responsible scholarship are peculiarly illuminated by the foregoing.

CHAPTER X

The Report of the Minnesota Historical Society

The discussion, in Chapter VIII, of the Kensington rune stone in its historical aspects, did not dwell on the attitude of historical bodies or other learned societies towards the disputed stone and its inscription. It is known, however, that the problem was discussed at a public meeting held by the Chicago Historical Society on February 3, 1910.[1] Mr. Holand spoke for the stone at this meeting, and Professors Gould and Flom spoke against it. It is also known that the problem was discussed at a formal meeting of the Illinois State Historical Society held at Springfield on May 6, 1910, at which time Professor Flom delivered the negative report which subsequently was printed in *Transactions of the Illinois State Historical Society for the Year 1910*.[2] In April, 1910, the Philological Society of the University of Illinois appointed a committee of seven faculty members, all of them chosen for their knowledge of Old Norse, who examined the problem and, after a study of Flom's report, unanimously pronounced the Kensington stone a recent forgery.[3] Professor Jansson pointed out in 1949 that, inasmuch as Mr. Holand had never labored to bring this matter to attention, the adverse verdict of the Illinois committee of linguists had long since been forgotten.[4] There is one investigation, however, to which Holand has referred early and late. That is the official investigation of the Minnesota Historical Society, made in 1909–10, presented at a meeting of the Society's Executive Council on May 9, 1910 and published in December of that same year. The results of that investigation were highly favorable to the authenticity of the rune stone.

In 1910, the Minnesota Historical Society published an official "Preliminary Report to the Minnesota Historical Society by its Musuem [*sic*] Committee."[5] This committee consisted of Professor Winchell, Dr. Upham, E. C. Mitchell (1836–1911), antiquarian and clergyman; O. D. Wheeler (1852–1925), advertising manager of a railroad and earlier an assistant to Major J. W. Powell in the survey of the Colorado River, 1874–79 (on Powell's survey of Grand Canyon see Chapter VII); F. I. Schaefer (1869–1943), Catholic historian and rector of the St. Paul Seminary. Sixty-six pages in length, the Report was reissued in unaltered form, in 1915. Included in the Report[6] is a bibliography of the Kensington discussion, arranged chronologically and extending from February 22, 1899 through September, 1910. Conspicuously absent from this bibliography is the very complete condemnation of the stone by Professor C. N. Gould of the University of Chicago, whose name is mentioned elsewhere in the Report.[7] Addressed to Dr. Upham of the MHS, who had solicited a formal opinion, Gould's systematic exposition goes so thoroughly to the heart of the Kensington matter that, had it been printed at the time, much future scholarly labor might have been spared. Dated March 19, 1910, Gould's paper is preserved among Upham's papers in the MHS archive at St. Paul.

From documents preserved in the same files it is established that the MHS bibliography was compiled by Hjalmar Holand. Holand states in an accompanying letter to Upham of October 2, 1910: "I have included only such articles as are of importance to a full study of the subject."[8] In other respects, as well, Mr. Holand's share in the MHS report was very large. One reason for this is obvious. None of the five gentlemen who officially constituted the Museum Committee pretended to the slightest familiarity with any of the Scandinavian languages. The Committee nevertheless made important linguistic pronouncements on the Kensington inscription, including the following: "1. It cannot be the work of some unlettered amateur of the present day. . . .

The linguistic internal evidences of the genuineness of the stone coincide with and confirm the indications that come from the finding of the stone and its attendant condition."[9]

In conclusion, the Committee unanimously resolved on April 21, 1910, "That this Committee renders a favorable opinion of the authenticity of the Kensington rune stone, provided, that the references to Scandinavian literature given in this Committee's written report and accompanying papers be verified by a competent specialist in the Scandinavian languages, to be selected by this Committee, and that he approve the conclusions of this report."[10] The council of the MHS, at its May 9, 1910, meeting, voted to receive and print the report and resolution of its Museum Committee "with a statement that the council and Society reserve their conclusion until more agreement of opinions for or against the rune inscription may be attained."[11] Selected as linguistic expert was Professor Gisle Bothne of the University of Minnesota. On July 19, 1910, Professor Bothne declined the nomination. In a letter to Professor Winchell he made his attitude towards the controversy quite clear: "I have examined your report carefully, have visited Kensington and neighborhood, and have read most of the papers and articles relating to the rune stone. . . . But what has been testified to about the finding of the stone is not convincing, and I do not consider the Kensington stone authentic. It seems to me that the stone should be brought to Norway to be examined by expert runologists, and, in my opinion, nothing else will dispose of the matter."[12] Bothne also failed to approve the stone in his capacity as member of a committee of three appointed by Det Norske Selskab of Minneapolis.[13]

These negative opinions may have soured the Museum Committee on linguistic experts, for although Holand several times proffered his services in this regard, no "competent specialist in the Scandinavian languages" was ever appointed, and the committee report was printed. The Archive preserves a letter to Winchell from Professor A. Louis Elmquist of Northwestern, suggesting that it would be cheaper to bring the great Swedish runologist, von Friesen, to Minnesota, but in 1911 the stone was brought to Norway by Mr. Holand, and there it was examined by Professor Hægstad, who promptly labelled it a modern product.

The MHS archives contain the handwritten original report prepared in the meantime by Professor Winchell of the Museum Committee, together with a typed copy. The latter bears the pencilled annotation: "Partly verified in Madison, Wis., April 29, (1910)." This verification apparently concerned text references, including passages in Brandt's *Læsebog*, of which Holand has made a great deal. Obviously made by a man—Winchell—who had no conception of what he was doing, these verifications are quite without value, as was illustrated by checking the very first reference selected by us for verification. For example: On page 263 of the MHS Report, a certain verb form, *hawdhe*, 'had,' is postulated as Swedish of the year 1200, and attributed to Brandt, page 39, line 1. First of all, one discovers that "p. 39" is an error for page 38; secondly, the phrase as quoted by the MHS Report contains two mistakes in spelling; third, last, and most important, the passage proves nothing for the year 1200, inasmuch as the MS from which the edition was prepared (after being strained through two intermediaries) is stated by the editor himself on page 36 to be from the year *1350*, no copy from 1200 being extant. As will be seen, the bizarre philological materials through which non-linquist Winchell was attempting to wade, had been supplied him by Holand.

At about this same time, as we have already noted, the Scandinavian specialist, Professor A. L. Elmquist of Northwestern University, was urging caution with respect to the Kensington stone. This did not prevent the authorization of the report for printing under the date of 1910. In the light of this, Dr. Upham's undated letter earlier in the year to his colleague Professor Winchell takes on a peculiar interest. After reporting that nearly all the experts had condemned the stone, and after listing M. Olsen, H. Gjessing, O. Breda, G. Bothne, J. Olson, R. B.

Anderson, G. Curme, S. W. Cutting, C. N. Gould, and G. Flom,
Upham states that the facts "indicate that very probably a
fraud has been attempted . . . accounts of a poplar tree . . . may
be a part of the deception."[14] He urges Winchell to investigate
both Ohman and Holand.

Couched in a similar vein is Professor Andrew Fossum's letter
to the Committee on March 7, 1910: "I would suggest that a
very keen lawyer be employed to examine Öhman, to find out if
he knows of any fraud in this connection."[15] This shrewd suggestion was never carried out. Fossum added: "It would be well
to find out what people have lived with Öhman or with his neighbors in the past years. What was their occupation, did they have
books and read, what kind of books, etc."

Professor Winchell, however, believed in the stone. In a letter
to Holand of April 30, 1911, a full year later, he states: "You
must understand that while I personally think the stone is valid
and vindicated, I wish to have unanimous consent to our action
in the Committee and also in the Executive Council."[16]

The action referred to is authorization of a financial agreement with Holand respecting the stone. The agreement provided, among other things, that the stone was to be sent to
Europe in the company of Holand and another "messenger," to
be selected by the Society. The journey was to take place in
1911, and final decision on purchase of the stone was to be
made by January 1, 1912.[17] Holand had written in a letter to
Winchell of January 19, 1911: ". . . so far our side is steadily
on the ascendency . . . it is up to us of the faithful . . ."[18] Until
his death in 1914, Winchell stoutly adhered to the stone's
authenticity.[19]

It was noted in Chapter VII, that the geologists of the MHS
had formed certain odd notions of the stone: 230 pounds, 30
inches long, or possibly 36. But there is criticism more significant than the charge of carelessness to level at the official report
on the Kensington stone. That report is manifestly a partisan
document. For example, although the MHS Committee had
formally solicited the opinion of the Swedish runologist, von
Friesen, no mention of his negative finding may be found in the

MHS Report. What most invalidates its character of impartial verdict, however, is the evidence of numerous changes and excisions to which the report was subjected before it was published. These were largely at the insistence of Holand and made in several of the dozens of handwritten communications on the stone addressed by him to Winchell or Upham and still extant in the St. Paul archives. In consequence of this, the official MHS Report was in many places altered, as the archives today show. Since both the handwritten manuscript of the MHS Report and the typewritten version prepared for the printer are preserved, one may compare the two documents with one another, with the printed MHS Report, and with the letters which urge the excisions and emendations.

For example, Holand's twelve-page manuscript of May 19, 1910, to Professor Winchell, corrects the report at length and in no fewer than forty places. These "Notes," as Holand called them, were accompanied by a letter in which he stated in part (page 1): "In harmony with your request I have taken the liberty of making a number of suggestions and amendations [*sic.*] which will be found in accompanying notes. . . . [page 2] Inasmuch as your answer to the linguistic objections is *in the main a copy from my dissertation*, I think it proper that you make suitable acknowledgement."[20] (Italics supplied.) On page 3 he refers to "the assistance you have received (free of charge) from me who am the only one yet able to prove the language authentic, which most critics seem to think a very difficult job."

A letter from Holand to Winchell on October 2, 1910, is accompanied by a manuscript called "Remarks on Report." Regarding page E of this document Holand writes: "I would strongly recommend the omission of any reference here to Dalecarlian system of Runes. That is a wrong track entirely."[21] The reference to Dalecarlian runes remained in the report, however, which had already been approved.

It will be enlightening to quote some typical examples of Holand's "directions" to Winchell:

[Page] 47 line 10: Everything after "Gothland" and up to "Stockholm" must go out. The language of the island of Gothland (Sw. Gotland) was quite different from that of the inscription and it could not be proven genuine if we bring in the island of Gothland. [Page 4 of Holand's letter.]

Page 61 lines 12 and 13. This last sentence should be omitted as it is irrelevant and confusing. [Page 8.]

Page 62 last two lines. Everything written in ink in these two lines must be omitted as it shows a serious misconception of the dialects of Visby or of Dalarna. [Page 8.]

Page 70. No. 21. . . . Strike this paragraph and write . . . [Page 11.]

And so on, for 11 pages in all.

In the handwritten manuscript by Winchell we have a report on the highly controversial Kensington problem, compiled on behalf of the Museum Committee after a lengthy study of the problem. In the published version we see the report after its modification at the behest of an interested outside party, which modification is uniformly in the direction of *favoring* the genuineness of the Kensington inscription. This published MHS Report, in turn, has been repeatedly cited by that same interested party as an unbiased and "scientific" presentation of the facts, although the very Library of Congress printed card for the MHS Report lists Holand as part author of it.

As previously stated, the members of the Museum Committee were, one and all, totally unversed in the elements of the Scandinavian languages, and there is something pathetic in this attempt by Winchell to compile a dissertation on Scandinavian linguistics and runes, when he could not read even an elementary Scandinavian text. As late as 1913, Winchell was compelled—in Scandinavian Minnesota—to wait from some time in October until November 24th before he could learn the substance of an article on the Kensington question by Helge Gjessing.[22] For this very reason, caution was indicated in 1910. Nearly all of the philological opinion which had been solicited was unfavorable to the cause of the Kensington stone. It was natural and proper for the Committee to solicit likewise the opinion of Mr. Holand as representing the opposite camp. And it was not improper for Mr. Holand to believe in the stone or to argue in its defense. For the Committee to allow Holand to make, or remake its report, was, on the other hand, distinctly out of order in a responsible scholarly proceeding. Apart from the question of scientific propriety, Holand's qualifications as a linguistic expert were plainly not such as to have motivated reliance upon them. On this score Winchell had been warned from several quarters. And when Holand, at as late a stage of the controversy as October 2, 1910, wrote to him: "As I am sure that no such character as þ ever existed, I don't think it is fortunate to agree with Flom that it did," Winchell himself was moved to protest in a marginal note that þ was a recognized runic letter.[23]

On January 19 and 22, 1911, Flom wrote to the Committee pointing out numerous errors in the MHS Report, and on the latter date he urged on Upham the advisability of consulting the German-born Friederich Klaeber (1863–1954) of the University of Minnesota, a specialist in Old English and other older Germanic dialects.[24] But the Committee appears to have avoided Klaeber. In fact, they avoided, so far as can be learned, all the linguists of the nearby campus, once Bothne had expressed his negative opinion. What they obviously wanted at this point was someone who could be counted on to support the stone from a linguistic point of view, and they had learned that, of all people, those with linguistic training were the least likely to do so. Flom's criticism, which was acknowledged in the MHS Report, did not deter the committee from re-publishing the Report, in unaltered form, in 1915.

Nowhere mentioned in the MHS Report is a circumstance that was either unknown to Upham and Winchell or was ignored by them. This was the matter of a whetsone found in the immediate vicinity of the runesite. Ohman called its attention to a local citizen of excellent repute, E. E. Lobeck, and Lobeck reported this to Skørdalsvold, a defender of the rune stone, who in turn mentioned it in one of his articles on the controversy, suggesting that it might cast light on the carving.[25] Ohman presumably meant to imply that this whetstone was the one upon which the runecarver had sharpened his chisels; at any rate, he stated that it was worn with heavy use. The explorers of 1362 would scarcely have thrown away at this point the valuable whetstone that they had carried about for 10,000 miles in order to keep in trim the chisels with which they carved "mooring holes." Unless, of course, out of terror or despair, they were abandoning most or all of their impedimenta at this point. The whetstone, then, was modern, hence potentially an important clue to the commission of a hoax, at least in Ohman's opinion. And a clue concerning which complete silence has been maintained for a full fifty years.

The fact that Olof Ohman took the trouble to point out the whetstone during a discussion of the runic carving should certainly have prompted an investigation of the possibility of its connection with the carving and of Ohman's motive in mentioning the matter, inasmuch as self-incriminating admissions are often made by way of unconscious confession. Ohman's remark may even have been a boldly humorous attempt to give the deadly serious investigators something additional to argue about. It is hoped that Chapter XV, below, will demonstrate that whoever committed the Kensington hoax had a considerable sense of humor. The attempt to interest anybody in so basic an artifact as a (rune-carver's?) whetstone failed, at all events, and all one can record is the incompleteness of the MHS investigation.

Professor Winchell kept a record of his investigative activities in a so-called field book. Most unfortunate is the fact that the field book has disappeared and is not found with the Winchell papers in the MHS Archive. There can be no question that it would contribute a great deal to enlighten us on questions of major importance to the Kensington question. It should be added here that an effort made in 1949 by Professor Holvik to have the entire Kensington matter reinvestigated by the MHS proved unsuccessful.[26]

The foregoing shows that the Report of the Minnesota Historical Society, upon which Holand and so many others have publicly relied, far from being an impartial and dependable résumé of the Kensington problem by investigators competent and willing to make it, was in many respects little more than a formal defense of Holand's own theories.

CHAPTER XI

The Language and the Runes

The arguments marshalled to show that the Kensington inscription can be from the fourteenth century impress by their quantity if nothing else. Expressed in English and repeated over and over in works printed in this country and available for purchase or consultation in libraries, whereas the major counterarguments by critics of the inscription have not thus been available, the defense theories have created a "climate of opinion" favorable to the stone. One might almost think this a matter of politics or public relations, rather than a problem in science and as such subject to very strict rules of demonstration. But here, as with the other aspects of the Kensington story, whether dendrological, geological, or testimonial, a myth has been created and carefully nurtured, a myth conspicuous for one central assertion: that no convincing arguments have been brought, or can be brought, against the genuineness of the language and runes of the inscription. The author and guarantor of this myth is Mr. Holand.[1]

Holand has, to be sure, a host of arguments and "proofs." But many of his citations are unrelated to the matters he is seeking to establish, or if related, they are erroneous, as already demonstrated. Above all, his arguments lack a cohesive structure: They have a random character, are not integrally related to that hard core of ascertained or ascertainable fact upon which alone a scientifically defensible theory can be erected.

Now, human beings do not use language with the exactness required in mathematics. Any study of language is required to take that into account, for as in most fields of research, the methodology employed must be inductive, rather than deductive: New evidence may at any time force the revision of accepted theories. The rules of the game require that favorable evidence be contrasted with unfavorable evidence and a balance struck between them. If strict evidential rules are not adhered to, if a verifiable procedure has not been set up and exactly reported on in a given investigation, its results may properly enjoy no status beyond that of mere opinion. Unsupported opinion does not, or should not, pass for science.

The study of language did not become scientific before the nineteenth century. Its basic materials, its conclusions, its methodological techniques have been built up over several generations of laborious trial and error. At no point does it claim to be infallible. What is important in linquistics, as in every science, is not dogma, a fixed body of "facts" resistant to change, but a *method* of acquiring, arranging, and testing these facts. The method—constantly sustained by man's urge to inquire and not by any particular fact or facts—is of the essence of scientific thought, and whoever would make valid contributions to science, must pay homage to this principle.

Mr. Holand's linguistic method, or methods, have already been criticized at length (Chapter IX) and found notably deficient in both accuracy and pertinence. The present chapter will make no further attempt to deal more than by implication with Holand's multitudinous linguistic asseverations. For these have no fixed point of departure, no overall established doctrine to which they may be referred or in the light of which they may be tested. Reduced to its lowest common denominator, the Kensington inscription as seriously presented by its cardinal apologist is first, last, and foremost, a concatenation of anomalies. Its exceptional character repeatedly alluded to by Holand meets with his full approbation, and he then affects to construe these very oddities as the strongest proofs of authenticity. But Holand's erratic and self-contradictory arguments and methods do not constitute a methodology.

Before turning to some of the specific arguments against the stone it should be noted that the present investigation does not endorse or take responsiblity for all the linguistic arguments that have been proffered in this direction, for these have varied considerably in accuracy, merit, and importance. On the other hand, chiefly because nobody has bothered with every detail, arguments have occasionally been overlooked. The present treatment will lump the more important arguments together under appropriate headings, with no special effort to credit them to particular commentators.

We shall begin by transliterating the inscription as accurately as can be done, considering that there is a certain amount of room for difference of opinion. The transliteration is Exhibit A below. B is the same text, rendered into the most likely equivalent in Old Swedish.[2] C and D are, respectively, the nearest equivalences in modern Swedish and modern Danish.[3]

A	B
8: göter: ok: 22: norrmen: po:	atta gøtar ok twer ok tiughu normæn pa
o: opdagelsefard: fro:	faerþum fra
vinland: of: vest: vi:	vinlandi væster vi
hade: läger: ved: 2: skjar: en:	hafdhum lægher viþ twem skæriom en
dags: rise: norr: fro: deno: sten:	daghsfærþ nor fra þessom steni
vi: var: ok: fiske: en: dagh: äptir:	vi varum a fiski en dagh æptir
vi: kom: hem: fan: 10: man: röde:	vi komum hem funnum tio mæn røþe
af: blod: og: ded: AVM:	af bloþi ok døþe AVM
fräelse: af: illy:	frælsæ os af illu
har: 10: mans: ve: havet: at: se:	har tio mæn viþ hafinu at sea
äptir: vore: skip: 14: dagh: rise:	æptir varum skipum fiughurtan daghsfærþir
from: deno: öh: ahr: 1362:	fra þessi ö ar A. D. MCCCLXII

C	D
8 göter och 22 norrmän på	8 gøter og 22 normænd paa
——— upptäcktsfärd från	——— opdagelsefærd fra

Vinland västerut; vi	Vinland vestover. Vi
hade läger vid 2 skär en	havde lejr ved 2 skær en
dagsresa norr om denna sten.	dags rejse nord fra denne sten.
Vi var och fiska(de) en dag; efter	Vi var og fiske en dag. Efter
vi kom hem fann (vi) 10 man röda	vi kom hjem fandt 10 mænd
	røde
av blod och döda. AVM	af blod og døde. A V M
frälse av ondo.	frelse fra ondt.
(Vi) har 10 man vid [ve] havet att se	Har 10 mænd ved havet at se
till våra skepp 14 dagsresor	efter vore skibe 14 dagsrejser
från denna ö. År 1362.	fra denne ø. Aar 1362.

Apart from the obvious unpredictabilities involved in reconstructing a medieval text—a multiplication of those met with in making any kind of translation whatever—there is the additional discrepancy that the style and formulation of the Kensington inscription are so disconcertingly modern in the psychology they reveal that even the possibility of a reconstruction into something genuinely medieval becomes problematical. For example, how would one render a modern newspaper article into Old Swedish?

From text C and the Norwegian version appearing on page 148 below, it becomes apparent to anyone with an ordinary reading knowledge of modern Swedish and Norwegian how some writers have considered the Kensington inscription modern Norwegian: Instead of Swedish, the adjectival endings in *rödhe* and *vore* (Sw. *röda* and *våra*), and the spellings *rise* and *vedh* (Sw. *resa*, and *vid*), not to speak of the preposition *og* (Sw. *och*), are indeed reminiscent of Danish and Norwegian. The word *opdagelse-fard*, too, is almost pure Dano-Norwegian. We cannot overlook the factor, often suggested, of certain dialects from northerly districts in Sweden which may help explain idiosyncrasies in the inscription. But after all, the inscription was found in the midst of a community of Swedes and Norwegians in Minnesota in which a mixture of the two languages is the commonest thing in the world, and there is no special problem involved here (Professor Flom observed in 1910 that Ohman's language, for example, revealed Norwegian influence).[4] In Chapter XIII will be listed the reasons for considering the text essentially modern Swedish with attempts made to give it an archaic cast. Chapter XII will indicate reasons for deriving the word *opdagelse* 'discovery' (which is modern and not medieval) from heated newspaper discussions and reviews during the 1890's of Gustav Storm's Norwegian writings on Norse voyages of exploration.[5]

Texts A and B give an indication of the grammatical discrepancies between the message of Kensington and a hypothetical reconstruction of the same text in proper Swedish of the mid-fourteenth century. What this comparison can give most readers no indication of, however, is an equally serious discrepancy which belongs under the heading of style. Considered as a runic message, it is quite the most remarkable inscription in history, thoroughly modern in its circumstantiality, its wealth of detail. Genuine old inscriptions are extremely laconic in their formulation. The occasional lengthy inscriptions found on Swedish stones served a different purpose, were carved under very different circumstances in the homeland, in the midst of leisure and prosperity. And even these are so frequently baffling in their cryptic brevity that they cannot satisfactorily be interpreted. Not so the wondrously explicit Kensington inscription, almost every line of which breathes a strictly modern attitude. The very fact that it uses not a single abbreviation of any kind (AVM is a special problem, considered in Chapter XV) alone brands it as a deviate from runic tradition. Consider likewise the amazing fact that alone of historical markers and memorial stones—it purports to be both—it bears not a single personal name, neither that of the man who carved the runes nor that of the one who commanded the carving to be done and/or was commander of the expedition. Compare this with two typical runic messages of accepted genuineness. One is from Sweden, eleventh century, the other from the northernmost outpost of the Scandinavian colony, off the eastern coast of Greenland, fourteenth century:

A. Gundkel erected this stone after Gunnar, his father, son of Hrothi. Helgi laid him, his brother, in a stone sarcophagus at Bath in England.[6]

B. Erling Sighvatsson and Bjarni Thórtharson and Eindrithi Jónsson
on the Saturday before minor Rogation Day (April 25) piled this
cairn and cleared . . .[7]

As a linguistic record in Old Swedish, the Kensington inscription amazes through its consistent use of singular verbs for the
plural. This has been "explained" as unusually early influence
from the oral language, and Mr. Holand has gone to great
length to turn up ancient examples of this usage. But as Professor Jansson remarks, a demonstration of isolated and occasional
examples of singular verbs in plural situations carry no weight
whatever as contrasted with the overwhelming preponderance of
plural usage (where appropriate) in all Swedish writings from
the earliest times down almost to the very present.[8] To which
might be added that a runic inscription—late representative of a
conservative tradition—was probably the least likely of all
documents to reflect oral influence. The fourteenth century
Greenlandic rune stone just referred to certainly did not. As a
matter of fact, the Kensington school of thought is at this point
involved in a very deep contradiction from the point of view of
both linguistic methodology and ordinary logic. The use of singular verbs for the plural was a great rarity, particularly in
Swedish formal documents, during the Middle Ages. By the
nineteenth century it had made much greater headway, even
if it still was not appropriate to formal documents (in Norway this
process proceeded much faster and was officially adopted during the 1860's). Now comes the Kensington document, containing *nothing* but singular verb forms. All other arguments aside,
can this possibly constitute a reason for us to consider it ancient,
rather than strictly modern? In short, the six verb forms found
in the inscription: (*vi*) *hade, var, fiske, kom, fann, har*, might be
expected to read (*vi*) *hafdhum (hafðom, hafþom), varum, (fis-
kadho?), komum, funnum, havum*.

Professor Assar Janzén, in his review of Holand's *Explorations*
declares:

The language represented in the Kensington Stone is strange in many
ways. One of the most striking features is that plural subjects consistently are accompanied by singular predicates. This fact alone refutes
the idea that the stone was carved in the 14th century. In order to sur-

mount this obstacle Holand has developed the hypothesis, later adopted
by Thalbitzer and others, that the language of the inscription reflects
the *spoken* language of the 14th century, which could be assumed to be
more advanced than that of the written sources preserved today. This
statement could perhaps fool some people, but Holand does not know
that the dialects of West-Gothland, from where he assumes that the
runer came, still today preserve the plural forms of the verb. He will
have to find another birthplace for his runer. Hälsingland, where Olof
Ohman, the probable runer of ca. 1890, was born, is a better proposal.
The end-vowel -*e* in *rise*, 'journey' belongs to this dialect, while in West-
Gothland the word is *resa*.[9]

Old Swedish requires the use of special forms for the dative
case. *Ve(d) havet* is modern; correct would be *vidh, viþ hafinu*
'by the sea.' Similarly one expects *vidh tvem skæriom*[10] 'near two
skerries' or something very close to this, in place of *ved* ᚠ (2)
skjar, and *fra þessom steni*[11] 'from this stone' instead of *fro þeno
sten*, and *fra þessi ø*[12] 'from this island' instead of *from þeno öh*.
The spelling cannot in every case be predicted with exactitude,
but these are reasonable and normal expectations based on our
knowledge of Old Swedish grammar, expectations which the
anachronisms on the Kensington stone consistently flaunt. The
forms on the stone are all modern forms from which the flec-
tional distinctions have vanished. Compare this fact with an
observation by Professor Jansson: "One must remember that
this inscription is considered by its adherents to have been
carved not only during the age of Old Swedish, but during the
period known as Older, *Classic* Old Swedish. This period has
been termed Classic Old Swedish because the sources for that
period show no obvious tendencies towards a dissolution of the
inflectional patterns. *The only source which consistently shows
such a dissolution is—the Kensington stone.*"[13]

Although the inscription reveals other remarkable grammatical features, the reader is referred to the various technical
treatises for a fuller coverage of this point. Meantime, attention
is called to the vocabulary of the carving, which evidences at
least two striking anachronisms. One is the word *opdagelsefard*
'voyage of discovery'; the other, is the phrase alternately rendered as *dags rise* and *dagh rise* 'day's journey.' The element
opdagelse 'discovery,' is Dano-Norwegian of fairly recent origin.

The word *uppdaga* 'to find,' is recorded in that sense in Sweden beginning in the nineteenth century. A passive form *uppdagas* is recorded for the eighteenth century in the meaning of 'to grow light, dawn.'[14] The word and the complex of meanings around it entered Scandinavia from Low German at a late date. The word *opdagelse* (for Sw. *upptäckt* 'discovery') has never been recorded in Swedish sources for any period.[15] It is not found in Older Danish or in Middle Dutch or in Middle Low German. It is in every sense a modern word. Furthermore, the term 'voyage of discovery' is a modern concept. There is no record whatever of such a term's being used by Scandinavian explorers in former times. At least two verb phrases are known in Old Icelandic to describe the exploring activity. One is *leita landit* 'to search out the land.' The other is *kanna landit* 'to explore the land,' ('to get to know the land'). *Landaleit* and *landaleitan* are nouns used for what we now call 'discovery of new lands'; similarly the noun *landafundr*. The Icelandic phraseology helps illustrate the absurdity of an early *opdagelse* in this connection.

The other anachronism is the *dags rise; dagh rise*.[16] The Old Swedish forms would most certainly have been *daghs færdh* or *daghs ledh*, words well known in such connections. The modern Swedish *dagsresa* 'day's journey,' is first recorded for 1599, hence it may (or may not) have been in use some years earlier.[17] For it to be genuine and convincing in a message from 1362, we should have to assume that the Kensington explorer used it precisely because it was a standard and well understood phrase. But this is rendered impossible by the fact that the word *resa* in OSw. meant 'to raise,' *i.e.*, was a transitive verb. The intransitive verb *resa* 'to travel,' and the noun *resa* 'journey,' are of later origin, apparently from Middle Low German. In OIcel., too, the verb *reisa* is transitive: *reisa ferð* 'to start on a journey.' Common travel terms in OIcel. applicable to maritime travel were *dag-roðr* 'day's row(ing),' and *dag-sigling* 'day's sail.'[18] Once more, a modern term has mistakenly been used on the Kensington stone.

An assumption frequently made by Europeans that *rise* 'journey,' in the inscription derives from English influence (the word 'rise') does not, for semantic reasons, recommend itself as a probability. A more likely connection will be discussed in Chapter XIII. It may possibly be otherwise with the word *ded* in the phrase *röde af blod og ded*, but if so, the contamination from English is almost certainly intentional rather than naïve. It would thus be a humorous, semi-cryptic rendering of 'red and dead,' an explanation which allows harmony between the semantic and phonetic considerations. As to the humorous aspect of hoaxes, see Chapter XV.

There will be occasion to discuss the spelling of the inscription in Chapter XIII. Suffice it here to remark on the word *norrmen* 'Norwegians' (Sw. *norrmän*), the two r's of which are a suspicious modernism: OSw. *norþmæn, normæn.*

The rune forms, likewise, present convincing evidence that the Kensington document is a late creation. Of the twenty-two runes it exhibits, half are very odd. To briefly consider a few points:

The rune for *j* had disappeared some hundreds of years before 1362. In trying to demonstrate a *j* for the fourteenth century, Holand has confused the consonant *j* with a scribal (and printed) form of the vowel *i*, that is, an *i* written with a long tail. Its phonetic use shows that it was used as a vowel, not as a consonant. Holand's mistaken examples prove the truth of our assertion.[19] Holand is quite regularly unable to differentiate between orthography and phonology.[20] The Kensington *j* reveals very late influence.

The Kensington form of the rune for *n* had passed out of existence by the year 1100. Its archaic form contrasts strangely with the modernized symbols that accompany it. One of these is the rune ⊕. The sporadic use of ö as a runic symbol for (printed) ö in Dalecarlia clearly represents a very late and contaminated tradition, influenced by printed sources. Ö signifies a phonetic modification of *O*. The Kensington stone uses a symbol for *ö* (⊕) which is not related to its symbol for *o* (⊣). This lack of organic relationship between the symbols as the outgrowth of a need can be explained in only two possible ways: Either the symbol (of the umlauted *o* with a superimposed *x*) on the stone was pure invention, or it was borrowed. If invention, it is an over-compensated form, for either an umlauted *o* or an *o* with just the superimposed *x* would do the trick. Late Dalecarlian alphabets (1726, 1773, 1826) reproduced in Holand's books show Ö for *ö;* one of them shows ⊕ for *o*.[21] The umlauted *o* with the superimposed *x* is a neat blend. In most of these late alphabets, just as with the Kensington runes, the symbol for *o* (usually φ) is unrelated to that for *ö*, where this occurs at all. While the runemaster was at it, he went one step further and used dots to make a symbol that appears to stand for *u, ü,* or *y*. That, too, is similar to late Dalecarlian runes. But as will be shown, additional explanations are possible, and no all-embracing or exclusive hypothesis is required. One wonders whether this *u/y* or *ü/ÿ* is not a deliberate ambiguity, similar to the letter *u/y* in the Syasy/Suasu hoax of 1867, discussed in Chapter XV. At all events, this rune is uncertain in its purports.

The symbols used on the Kensington "rune stone" for *a, g,* and *k* are odd, if we are to consider them in the light of known runic tradition. The "rune" for *a* on the Kensington stone is a Latin X with a hook projecting from the right arm, thus Ж . The X itself is a pronounced innovation, being totally unrelated to runic symbols for *a;* the hook is an absurdity, for it serves no conceivable function and has no known antecedents. As the whim of a subliterate nineteenth century antiquarian the hook is highly appropriate to the whimsical Minnesota carving. The symbol for *k* is suspicious in being a reverse *k* from our Latin alphabet and very like the Ж of archaic Greek; while the "rune" for *g*, instead of being a near relative of that for *k*, something we should expect in any inscription comprising genuine runes, has gone its own way, exactly as has the *g* rune found in late Dalecarlian alphabets.

If the Kensington stone was carved just for fun, as one can well believe, the idiosyncrasies mentioned above, along with the other odd features it exhibits, are eminently in place. But if it were a genuine, tragic message from the fourteenth century, carved in anguish and terror by lonely Northmen hoping to leave for posterity some record of the disaster that had befallen them, its divagations from traditions of runic writing then prevailing would certainly be minimal.[22] Its purpose above all would have been to communicate to all who could read. And one does not thus communicate in symbols selected quite at random. Like all other modes of writing, and indeed like all other types of cultural behavior, runic inscriptions follow conservative patterns and constitute a definable tradition. "Runological" innovations as basic as those found on the Kensington stone could not possibly be explained as fourteenth century products except under one hypothesis: The supposed party of explorers from 1362 had come into contact with a new, thriving civilization in the North American wilderness—one that spoke nineteenth century Scandinavian, was familiar with modern printed books, and had observed the tables of early Greek alphabets (cf. the reverse *k* noted above) available in encyclopedias and Bible helps of our era.

The analysis must turn now to the numerals. These are plainly spurious, for while they have a "runic" appearance, they are based entirely on the so-called *Arabic system of notation*. Now Arabic numerals were certainly known to some people in Scandinavia by 1362,[23] although we do not find them on rune stones— not even on the Kensington stone. There are ways of writing numerals in runes, but the system was unsophisticated and ill adapted for writing the comparatively large numerals involved in dates. Earlier rune stones often dated themselves as belonging to the reign of some monarch; in the very few stones, late ones, on which dates were used at all, the date was either cumbrously written out, or carved in the Roman style.[24]

What is on the Kensington monument is a triply fantastic phenomenon: a self-dating numeral which (a) is not written out or given in Roman style; which (b) is written in faulty runes; and which (c) though written in would-be *runes*, is based on the *Arabic*. This is quite as if English, or Swedish, were to be written in the Greek, Russian, or Hebrew alphabet. It can be done, of course—for amusement. Arabic notation is obviously inseparable from the Arabic numerals; everywhere in the Western world that the system is used, the numerals are used with it. The genius of the Hindu-Arabic system, as we know, is the use of the decimal and of "place value" for the digits. This radical innovation was first introduced into Europe by the Arabs. But on the Kensington stone we find the miracle of miracles, Arabic reckoning translated into runic. And wrongly translated, besides, for runic ciphering had its own mode of representation, which the stone fails to follow.

From a runological point of view, the only correct numerals on the stone are those for 8 and 2. On the basis of the rune for 2 (ᚠ), the Kensington runemaster erroneously concluded, as most modern Europeans and Americans would, that two such symbols in sequence would make 22. In runic writing, however, the net result of such a sequence cannot be 22, for the concept of the place value of zero is wanting. If anything, therefore, the resultant value is 4. Arabic reckoning could no more mix with runic than with Roman. This point alone discredits the entire inscription. Holand's discussion of decimals in *Westward from Vinland*[25] adroitly eludes the point, which is that the Arabic system of decimal notation with place value for the digits (whereby, for example, 1 can come to stand for a value of ten, as in the number 11; or for a hundred, as in 150; or a thousand, as in 1362) has not the remotest connection with the runic system. And, indeed, Holand's entire argument is negated by his own examples from Ole Worm's *Fasti Danici*, which plainly controverts any assumptions as to the identity of the two systems.[26]

Inasmuch as Holand adduces credible evidence that his earlier book, *The Kensington Stone*, was used "for a number of years" as "a topic of study in [a] seminar devoted to Methods of Historical Research" at Yale University,[27] it will be pertinent to insert a remark on methodology. It should be clear that, in comparing one document or set of symbols with another, the only admissible practice is to set forth what is actually found in the two variant exhibits. In the following table, the comparison has been shorn of the incrustation of fiction with which Holand has overlaid it, so that the representation of the Kensington numerals differs at several points from Holand's. Here are the numerals as they appear in *Fasti Danici*, on the Kensington stone, and in Holand's purported version of the Kensington numerals:[28]

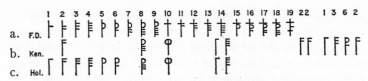

a. Numerals in *Fasti Danici*.   b. Numerals on the Kensington Stone.
c. Holand's version of the Kensington numerals.

It is seen that the Kensington stone does not use the numeral
1 (instead, the word *en*, 'one' is written out), 3, 4, 5, 6. It does
show the numerals 22 and 1362, both omitted by Holand.
(Holand's apparent reduction of 22 and 1362 to their component
ciphers 2, 1, 3, and 6 cannot be admitted, any more than the
Roman numerals I, III, VI, II could be admitted as the analytic
equivalent of the Roman date MCCCLXII; two radically different systems of notation are involved.) The numerals 2, 8, 10,
14 are common to the Kensington stone and Holand's representation of them. Only the Kensington numerals for 2 and 8 are in
any way similar to the corresponding numerals in *Fasti Danici*.

What is the origin of the Kensington numerals? Their superficial similarity to runic numerals remind us of Ohman's remarks
to Professor Winchell that every Swede and Norwegian knew
something about runes, but not how to use them.[29] The runecarver doubtless had some memory of late runic calendars, but
did not understand or remember the principle employed in them
(viz., that they do not follow the decimal system).[30] Of course,
the symbol ᛎ for 10 can be explained as a cipher with superimposed 1, that is, a digraph for 10. This symbol has apparently
been practiced on the cover of one of Ohman's few books.[31]

To sum up, from the point of view of medieval studies, this
"veritable neolithic record"[32] as the writer Stewart Holbrook
has recently called our great American equivalent of the Piltdown skull, has liabilities of such magnitude that one regrets,
not its fitting demise in 1899, but its artificial resuscitation in
1907. The point can be driven home by means of a parallel. The
Kensington chronicle, if genuine, would be contemporary with
Geoffrey Chaucer (*ca.* 1340–1400), author of *Canterbury Tales*.

How much faith would one place in an alleged new Chaucerian manuscript which (1) by its own uncorroborated evidence claimed to reverse all accepted notions of British colonial history; which (2) had turned up in the year 1898 in the midst of an English-speaking settlement in, say, South America; which (3) employed a bizarre, nondescript alphabet derived from widely differing periods of history; which (4) was written in a type of English whose structure, spellings, and very misspellings, though diluted with quasi-archaic features, were unmistakably those of nineteenth century English conversational style; which (5), purporting to use Roman numerals, rendered the numeral 22 by IIII (II–II) instead of XXII, and gave for the date 1362 the symbols IIIIVIII (I–III–VI–II) instead of MCCCDXII? The document would be dismissed at once as an absurd forgery. A close parallel to this is found in the case of the Kensington stone.

Having spoken thus severely, one should nevertheless admit to a certain respect for the preposterous inscription and its waggish, modern, and anonymous author. Both have been underestimated. The Kensingtonian school of thought has carefully nurtured a legend in which Olof Ohman, the farmer on whose land the stone was assertedly found, figured as a dull-witted rustic ("Poor Ohman! etc."),[33] whereas firsthand testimony, based on inquiry among persons who knew and liked Ohman, makes it appear that he was anything but dull-witted. As for the *historiola* on the stone, Holand has with apparent seriousness pronounced it "free from all premeditated ingenuities."[34] This is a contention which, like many of Holand's claims, deserves to be pondered at length. In this matter, as in many others, Holand's sure instinct for the weaknesses of the Kensington narrative can help guide us to the real truth.[35]

CHAPTER XII

Related Cultural Factors

No decade could have been more propitious than the 1890's to the manufacture of a rune stone among the transplanted Scandinavians. In 1874, Professor Rasmus B. Anderson (1846–1936) of the University of Wisconsin (who from 1883–88 was American Minister to Denmark) published at Chicago his *America Not Discovered by Columbus.*[1] This was a small book that called attention to the prior claims of the early Norsemen to be called the first discoverers of America. The Danish translation appeared at Copenhagen in 1886, and in a famous monograph on the Vinland voyages by Gustav Storm the following year, the latter took issue with Anderson. Referred to in Chapter VIII, Storm's monograph, in translation, was called *Studies into the Vinland Voyages.*[2] Anderson answered Storm in a pamphlet that received wide distribution. Anderson and his pupil and successor, Professor Julius E. Olson (1858–1944), both published newspaper articles which were read by thousands of people in the Middle West and elsewhere.[3]

Storm—says Julius E. Olson—was the first to assert that Northmen in the eleventh century had never been within the present boundaries of the United States. Such an assertion created tremendous ill-will in Scandinavian-American circles. Olson himself wrote a long review of Storm's work and published it in

Norden, Chicago. Throughout 1890 and 1891 the controversy was in full swing, a circumstance that led Olson to posit 1891 as the year in which the Kensington stone was carved. Professor E. N. Horsford of Harvard, an engineer, presently sent the newspapers review copies of his own elaborate work, the *Landfall of Leif Erikson,*[4] and it, too, was widely reviewed.

It should be noted that in eighty pages of text, Storm used the word *opdagelse* 'discovery,' no fewer than twenty-eight times, either as a simplex or as an element of a compound such as *opdagelsesrejse* 'voyage of discovery.' The word and the phrase, 'voyage of discovery,' were duly repeated by the journalists. Not only Olson, but also Helge Gjessing surmised influence from Storm: ". . . it is possible that the inscription owes its existence to Prof. Storm's treatise. . . ."[5] Iverslie's article of Aug. 17, 1912, seeks to refute this point: "Storm's essay of 81 pages appeared in the beginning of 1888, and in April of the same year a copy of it arrived at the Smithsonian Institute, safely embalmed in the 'Yearbook for Northern Archaeology,' a heavy volume of probably a thousand pages. It seems that the essay was never published separately, and was never for sale by booksellers in this country."[6]

This, of course, has nothing to do with the problem, as shown in Chapter VIII. Storm's views reached the daily press and caused the stir which Olson has documented. Evidence of a similar kind is a contemporary work on the Norse voyages by the famed Swedish-American editor, J. A. Enander, *The Northmen in America.*[7] The famed Columbian Exposition at Chicago[8] contributed not a little towards stimulating the Vinland controversy; there is no need to show that any specific person in Douglas County, Minnesota, had toiled through a thousand page work on archaeology. An exact replica of the famed Viking ship of Gokstad was sailed to America for the Chicago World's Fair. Leaving Norstein, near Bergen, on April 30, 1893, it arrived at Newfoundland on May 27.[9] The ship is still on exhibit in Chicago's Lincoln Park, where it was moved years ago.

In a famed book printed at Copenhagen in 1837 and often quoted by American writers of later decades, the word "Opdagelsesreiser" appears as part of the Danish title. This was C. C.

Rafn's *Antiqvitates Americanae*.[10] Though pro-Kensingtonians have gone to great lengths to establish a medieval origin for the suspect word, *opdagelsefard*, on the Kensington stone, in view of the historical controversy which was raging during the 1880's and 1890's, a far more probable explanation recommends itself: It was borrowed from the newspapers of the day. Let it be emphasized that the controversy was not merely academic in nature, but was carried on at the popular level through the columns of the press. In any hoax pertaining to Norse discoveries and perpetrated during the 1890's, references to a voyage of discovery would be found in an appropriate cultural context.

The nineteenth century was receptive to the notion of the universality of cultural materials. Viktor Rydberg's famous Swedish work, *Teutonic Mythology*, was translated into English by Professor Rasmus B. Anderson.[11] In dealing with the traditional materials of Scandinavian prehistory, this work inevitably discusses the widely known legend of the Scandinavian god Odin's emigration from Asia to Scandinavia. In 1869, E. Hildebrand published a Swedish translation of a famous Norwegian book, *Nordisk Mytologi*.[12] This work makes reference to a supposed connection between Odin and "the Indian Buddha," and states that the influence of Buddhism had not necessarily been limited to Scandinavia: "According to legend a tribe in Guatemala alleges descent from a foreign military leader Votan (Humboldt, *Vues des Cordillères*, 1816, I, 208); whether this, as some believe, is our Odin, concerning whom the saga may have been transmitted through the early voyages of Scandinavians to America, is an investigation too distant from our present subject."[13]

This fanciful and romantic possibility is echoed in the commentary to Rasmus B. Anderson's English translation of *Snorre's Edda*, published at Chicago in 1880: "According to Humboldt, a race in Guatemala, Mexico, claim to be descended from Votan (Vues des Cordilleres, 1817, I, 208). This suggests the question whether Odin's name may not have been brought to America by the Norse discoverers in the 10th and 11th centuries, and adopted by some of the native races."[14]

Rasmus B. Anderson was one of the best known Scandinavian-Americans of his day and his works and his views were widely circulated, as Chapter XI has indicated. However legendary and uncertain, the notion of Scandinavian cultural influence in early Central or South America must have stimulated the imagination of many Scandinavian-Americans, with resultant arguments and discussions. One interested enough in ancient lore to carve a runic monument to alleged Nordic exploits in Minnesota would not have turned a deaf ear to such discussions. Now, in the *Wisconsin Magazine of History*, Professor Anderson attributes to Ohman's acquaintance and distant relative by marriage, Andrew Anderson, the statement that A. von Humboldt's *Cosmos* (presumably in an English translation available by 1878) was part of Olof Ohman's favorite reading.[15] There is reason to believe that the good professor may himself have been the victim of a little hoax, for the account given to him by Andrew Anderson has many aspects of the cock-and-bull story. Nevertheless, R. B. Anderson's article is evidence that somebody in rural Minnesota knew about Humboldt and considered his writings pertinent to the Kensington matter. For our purposes, it is immaterial whether that somebody was Olof Ohman, Andrew Anderson, or any other Minnesota Scandinavian.

It is time to note that the latter part of the nineteenth century was the age of Ignatius Donnelly (1831–1901). At first a lawyer in his native Philadelphia, Donnelly came to Minnesota in 1857, served as lieutenant-governor of the state (1860–63) and as a member of Congress (1863–69). He was later a state legislator. Donnelly was a leader in the Farmers' Alliance and the Populist Party. Generally known as "the Sage of Nininger," he was a fabulous humorist, who for a quarter of a century, beginning in 1871, travelled about Minnesota lecturing on humor. His influence from the political rostrum and lecture platform was very wide. But as an author, Donnelly exerted national and even international influence.

In "Ignatius Donnelly and His Faded Metropolis" (on Donnelly and his community of Nininger) R. L. Harmon writes: "Here he penned books that set civilization agog, that thrilled and startled thinkers into new channels of scientific speculation, and that shook the literary world to its foundation. Here he worked by the light of kerosene lamps and penciled through two tons of paper. Here he achieved at once world-wide renown and obloquy, the praise of many critics and the derision of many others, the violent denunciation of political enemies, the confidence and adoration of the common people."[16]

The most famous of Donnelly's numerous books is *The Great Cryptogram*.[17] Published in 1888, this volume, with its 998 pages, is a monumental exposition of the theory that Francis Bacon wrote the plays ordinarily attributed to William Shakespeare. Taking for his starting point the contention that Shakespeare's family was too undistinguished, his education too deficient, and the living conditions of his native town too utterly primitive for Shakespeare to have exhibited the qualities of a genius, Donnelly goes on to find a likelier author and finds none more probable than the scientific philosopher, statesman, and man of affairs, Baron Verulam, Viscount St. Albans, ordinarily known as Francis Bacon. Bacon's interest in cryptic writing and secret codes being well known, Donnelly projects this utilitarian preoccupation with code writing as an adjunct to Elizabethan politics into the poetic sphere and attributes to the drily logical and much pressed statesman not only Shakespeare's vast dramatic production but likewise the construction of an elaborate code which, properly interpreted, would uncover his anonymity. The code is a gigantic cryptogram, the key to which is found in the words of the plays themselves when properly arranged and interpreted in sequence. It is obvious that if Bacon wrote the plays *and* the asserted cryptogram secretly and in his spare time, at that, he was a far greater genius than most people have supposed even Shakespeare to have been. However, it is often seen that the more irrational a given theory, the more it appeals to the romantically inclined, and Donnelly's book achieved tremendous popularity.

Donnelly had already acquired worldwide fame with his book *Atlantis*.[18] First published in 1882, this volume, according to the publisher, has sold, in its numerous editions, "well over one million" copies. Donnelly's presentation in *Atlantis* of the lost continent theory was so convincing that even Prime Minister Gladstone was induced to seek a Parliamentary appropriation for the purpose of sending an expedition to trace the outlines of submerged Atlantis—the money was not granted. However, the Atlantis theory aroused at least some interest at Kensington, for a clipping on the subject is found in a certain scrapbook—described in Chapter XV—which was the common property or the successive property, of the itinerant clergyman, Sven Fogelblad, and the farmer, Olof Ohman. And on dipping into *Atlantis* one finds a variety of discussions which conceivably have pertinence for the Kensington question. There is a reference, for example, to the explorations of Alexander von Humboldt (author of *Cosmos*, see above) and to the latter's conjectures about Vikings in Central America.[19] Donnelly likewise mentions the several "Odins of the Goths,"[20] along with the supposition by the Sanskrit scholar Sir William Jones that "Odin and Buddha are probably the same person."[21] "Goths," to the number of eight, are clearly mentioned in the Kensington inscription; as a matter of fact, they enjoy the place of honor at the very beginning of the little history of "viking" penetration into *North* America. Buddha, too, figures in the scrapbook that existed very close to where the rune stone was uncovered. As to the euhemerized Odin—the hero king who became a god of the "Goths," or Swedes—it is quite regularly stated that he is the god of poetry and of runes; this is stated, for example, on a page devoted to runes in a history of Sweden by Oskar Montelius[22] (see Fig. 30) which comprised one of the few books in Olof Ohman's library (see below). Although Odin is not mentioned in the inscription, the runes are there beyond question. Some of these are rather ambiguous in their purports, and there are three Latin characters that may be even more so (treated in Chapter XV). The magical and secret tendency of many runes is discussed both in Montelius and in another, even more important, book found together with it at Kensington, which will be examined in the following chapter.

At least one of Ignatius Donnelly's works must have been known to many Scandinavian immigrants in their own tongue, if not in English. The Library of Congress Catalog shows that Donnelly's novel, *Cæsar's Column: A Story of the Twentieth Century*, published at Chicago in 1890,[23] was within the space of two years translated into Norwegian and brought out by the publisher of the original version. Interestingly enough, the Norwegian edition was translated from the *twenty-ninth* English language edition. A further index of Donnelly's popularity was the appearance in 1891 of a Swedish edition, also published at Chicago, by the Swedish Book Company.

For the sake of completeness it should be mentioned that Donnelly, in 1883, published another book with the Scandinavian title *Ragnarok*.[24] In addition to various mentions of Vinland, *Ragnarok* makes mention of Ygdrasil, the sacred tree of the Scandinavians, and its identity with, on the one hand, the tree of the Aztecs, and on the other, the tree of Hindoo legends.[25] This book, as well, speaks of the "ancient runes of mighty Odin"[26] and the "golden tablets" (inscribed with these runes) "found in the grass."[27] In *Ragnarok*, Donnelly affirms his conviction that the Middle West was the ancient center of a great civilization.[28] There is one other point of interest in *Ragnarok*. That is a picture of the great comet of August, 1862, helping to illustrate Donnelly's thesis that legends of dragons and of fiery destruction that are so widespread in the world have their origin in the various comets that man has observed since the dawn of history.[29] The month of August, 1862, was of more than ordinary importance in the history of Minnesota (see Chapter XV, below), and it is possible that the Kensington inscription makes cryptic reference to this in its date of "1362." At all events, Donnelly was well known in Minnesota, and influence from *Atlantis*, at least, can be demonstrated near the Kensington rune site. Furthermore, there is reason to believe that the Kensington inscription reveals ambiguities, including one or two cryptograms, that are appropriate to a hoax.

"Combinations" of the sort described above, were not limited to Scandinavians, and they can be shown to have existed in contexts of a different sort entirely. For example, whoever studies the place names of Grand Canyon National Park will be interested in many of these. Along with such ordinary and predictable types of identifications as Fossil Bay, Powell's Plateau,[30] and Great Thumb Point, one notes the following and more romantic names: Holy Grail Temple, Jupiter Temple, Freya Castle, Wotan's Throne (Wotan=Odin), Buddha Temple, Shiva

Temple, Hindu Amphitheatre, Walhalla Plateau. According to
P. P. Patraw, Superintendent of the Park, these names were
given by the First U. S. Survey party in 1880, were retained by
the U. S. Board on Geographic Names, were printed in Capt.
C. E. Dutton's *Tertiary History of the Grand Canyon District* in
1882, and have appeared generally on maps ever since.[31] How
many citizens of Douglas County, Minnesota (besides O. D.
Wheeler of the MHS Museum Committee)[32] had visited Grand
Canyon or studied maps of it is quite beside the point. The
point is merely that such designations as "Buddha Temple"
and "Wotan's Throne" were in keeping with the temper and
interests of the time. The Kensington carving itself is an appropriate monument to the same temper and interests.

Strange though it may seem, that early writer of science-fiction
thrillers, Jules Verne, contributed to an interest in runes through
his famous book of 1864, *Voyage au centre de la terre*, which has
been examined in the Boston edition of 1874, *A Journey to the
Centre of the Earth*[33] as well as the recent New York edition, *A
Trip to the Center of the Earth*, to which Vilhjalmur Stefansson
has written an introduction.[34] In the earlier edition there is a
discussion of runes and the solving of a runic cryptogram on
pages 12–26. To quote a pertinent passage: " 'It is a Runic manuscript, the language of the original population of Iceland,
invented by Odin himself,' cried my uncle, angry at my ignorance."[35] The use of runes, the association of runes with cryptic
writing, and the almost inevitable reference to Odin as inventor
of the runic "language" are as typical of the age that gave them
birth as are the writings of Ignatius Donnelly or the nomen-
clature of the Grand Canyon.

There was opportunity in the nineteenth century for an interested Scandinavian to acquire an elementary acquaintance with
runic characters in the United States, even if he had not done so
in his homeland. One typical example concerns the Norwegian
immigrant Peter Iverslie, born in 1844, who seems to have
favored the stone. In a letter dated in 1911 he declared: "When
20 years old I copied an article containing the said runic system
as well as several series of runes and two runic inscriptions from
Magazin for Ungdommen, owned by the treasurer of the school

district where I first taught English school. I believe the article must have dated from the thirties or forties of the last century."[36]

If it were necessary to refute the notion that Minnesotans could know nothing of runes, this quotation would suffice. Since most commentators agree that the language of the Kensington inscription is mainly Swedish, it is pertinent to observe that an elementary knowledge of runes was not too uncommon in Sweden and that this knowledge had been fostered by government action from the seventeenth century on. Ljungström's little work on *The Art of Reading Runes*, 1866, was issued in a new edition in 1875, of which the Swedish government distributed 2000 copies to the country's school teachers.[37] Olof Ohman, for example, told Professor Winchell that he had studied runes in school: "Every school boy, and every Swede and Norwegian, knows something about runes, but not how to use them."[38] Ohman's observation—as repeated by Winchell, who considered Ohman innocent of fraud—deserves attention, and although Ohman could not fully have been aware of this, the observation applies with equal force to the Kensington inscription. For the inscription was itself made by a person who knew "something about runes," but not how to use them.

It was not at all unusual for the Scandinavian language newspapers to reprint Scandinavian classics for their subscribers. In the fall of 1897, for example, *Skandinaven* of Chicago began to publish Norwegian translations of the *Vinland Sagas* and *Heimskringla*. Similarly reproduced was *Sveriges historia*, by Oskar Montelius. This was the first volume of a famous six-volume work on Swedish history of which Montelius was general editor.[39] First printed in 1877, the book was reproduced—page by page and drawing by drawing—and distributed as a supplement to subscribers by *Svenska Amerikanska Posten* of Minneapolis from November 16, 1897 to February 15, 1898.[40] A copy of this reproduced text was owned by Olof Ohman. What is of interest is the fact that discussions of runic alphabets and drawings of rune stones appear in a number of places in the volume, especially pages 212–23 and 353–59. The so-called younger runes appear on page 353 of Montelius; the following page, to sample the illustrations, carries a full-page illustration of a certain mound called

Inglingehög at Ingelstad near Växiö in the Swedish province of Småland. Interestingly enough, the drawing of a mound with an upright rune stone on the sloping surface reminds one of the knoll on Ohman's farm as it might be presumed to look (from the swamp) after the addition of a standing rune stone. Greenland runes mixed with Latin expressions are discussed on page 290; the "Norse" tower at Newport, Rhode Island, is described on page 292, and the preceding page contains a drawing of it (Fig. 348). Montelius considered it a genuine relic of Norse explorations of perhaps the twelfth century. Along with the discussion of the Newport tower is a mention of Columbus and reference to a voyage from Greenland to Vinland in the year 1347. It is not too far a cry from these discussions in Montelius to the discovery, some years later, of a runic carving at Kensington that contained Latin letters, mention of Vinland, and the date 1362.

Professor Montelius describes the famous and puzzling runic inscription from Rök, Sweden: "The longest memorial inscription that is found on a fixed monument, whether in Sweden or any other land, is read on a great stone which had been walled up in the tower of Rök Church in Östergötland, but in the year 1862 was taken out of the wall and set up in the churchyard."[41]

As stated, a copy of this very Montelius volume is extant on the Ohman farm. The word "Supplement" (which is Swedish as well as English) appears printed on an uneven page. The book was borrowed by Professor Holvik, who had the MHS microfilm certain portions of it. The volume (bound in leather by a local shoemaker) bears Olof Ohman's signature and the date "Kensington 1898." On page 220 there is mention of the well-known Skåäng inscription, "Kuth hialbi salu hans," 'God help his soul,' a phrase commonly found on rune stones carved by or at the behest of Christians. In the bottom margin of this page are two lines of handwriting which have been erased but in which one can read "sten" and "Kensingtonstene[n]." On the back cover of this Montelius volume is inscribed "J. P. Hedberg." Hedberg's name will recur in Chapter XIV.

CHAPTER XIII

A Certain Printed Book

It has been previously noted that Professor Flom, back in 1910, tried unsuccessfully to solve the origin of the Kensington inscription on the basis of modern dialect research.[1] More recently, the Danish runologist K. M. Nielsen, has similarly asserted the probability that the mystery can be solved through dialectology. "A satisfactory solution of how the alphabet of the Kensington stone can have come about in modern time is not possible with the help of the existing literature. It does not seem to have been created from literary sources . . . ."[2]

It can now be shown that this view is unduly pessimistic, and that a book existed in the immediate vicinity of the Kensington runesite which casts extraordinary light on the language of the inscription. The possibility of literary influence had been suspected back in 1910 by Professor Fossum. ". . . what . . . books did they . . . read?"[3] And Professor C. N. Gould anticipated such a discovery in his article of that same year: "Such books would therefore be easy of access and it would not be strange for a Swede in America to have, or formerly to have had, such a book in his hands."[4]

If Gould had had the opportunity of examining, say, the little book collection of Olof Ohman, as Hjalmar Holand (by his own account) had done in 1907,[5] his surmise would doubtless have received even more explicit expression. But Gould, unlike Holand, did not know about Ohman's ownership of Carl Rosander, *Den Kunskapsrike Skolmästaren* (The Well-Informed Schoolmaster).[6] This was a one-volume compendium of popular knowledge first issued at Stockholm in 1864 and subsequently reissued in a number of editions in Sweden and the United States, including Chicago editions of 1893 and 1902–5. The various editions, and in particular the Chicago edition of 1893, which was distributed as a premium to all full-year subscribers to *Svenska-Amerikanaren*, must have been fairly well known in Swedish America of the 1890's. The existence, on the Ohman farm, of an edition of the Rosander book, was confirmed several years ago by Professor Holvik.

Olof Ohman, however, did not have to wait until 1893 to grow familiar with Rosander, for his edition was the Stockholm edition of 1881–82.[7] The flyleaf bears his signature at Kensington, March 2, 1891 (see Fig. 21). In other words, Olof Ohman had owned this book as long as he had owned the farm upon which he excavated a rune stone seven years later. In view of this, one is not surprised at the insight of Holand's bold remark in 1936: "Why couldn't [the forger] have followed any ordinary textbook on runes and Old Swedish syntax?"[8]

One is struck instantly by the much-finger-marked pages 61–64 of the Rosander volume, which are devoted to a treatise on the history of the Swedish language (Figs. 22–25). Very little beyond these four pages is required to penetrate the orthographic rationale of the Kensington inscription. After some preliminary information on the secret and magical character of early runes, there is a depiction of the younger runic alphabet or futhark of 16 characters, together with their early names, the meaning of these, and the transliterated value of the runes. These runes are then referred to as "Uppsala runes," as a variation on which are mentioned the well-known reverse runes found in many inscriptions (the Kensington rune for *g* is a reverse rune). Hereafter there is reference in Rosander to the practice of "stinging" the runes, *i.e.*, providing them with a dot in order to modify their respective phonetic values and thus increase the range of the runic alphabet (a number of stung runes are found in the Kensington inscription). Rosander then states that the stung runes, by enlarging the runerow of 16 characters, provided an alphabet nearly as large as the Latin alphabet. The Kensington inscription employs 22 characters. A bit further on in Rosander we learn that most runic stones are tombstones, but that certain of them commemorate a praiseworthy undertaking. The Kensington stone ostensibly performs both functions. It is then stated that many of the rune stones give evidence of the Christian belief (the AVM of the Kensington inscription is accepted by nearly all commentators as a reference to the Virgin Mary),[9] and that the greatest concentration of runic inscriptions took place from 900 to 1300. The date 1362 would then not appear unreasonable for an outlying inscription, or so a falsifier might reason.

In Rosander there follows a remark of importance and one which is repeated with emphasis in his subsequent discussion, namely that no definite conclusions can be arrived at regarding the Old Swedish language as a whole, inasmuch as the runecarvers often showed great ignorance of proper spelling, so that we must be cautious in judging the inscriptions. The spellings of the Kensington inscription are very strange, as its critics have repeatedly pointed out.

Rosander goes on to state that Old Swedish, as the language in use from 1000 to 1300 is designated, was gradually enriched with new glosses, especially new compounds. One thinks immediately of *opdagelsefard* 'voyage of discovery,' that *hapax legomenon* for which the Kensington stone is our sole "medieval" authority. Religious teachers, states Rosander, brought in foreign words from English, German, etc., and such words can nowadays scarcely be distinguished from "genuine Swedish" words (it is not inconceivable that one explanation of the curious word *from* in the Kensington inscription may be found in the hoaxer's misunderstanding, and consequent misapplication, of this "rule").

A statement concerning the rune þ and its equivalence to "D" is found in Rosander, page 61. Quite prominent in the Kensington inscription, the symbol þ has been discussed pro and con at great length. In the present book, þ in the inscription is consistently rendered as *d*, not only because this spelling is appropriate to O.Sw. *dagh* and *-land*, but because the Kensington runecarver almost certainly could not pronounce þ (Engl. *th*) himself.

Still according to Rosander, the sound represented by modern Swedish *å* (for which English long *o*, without the off-glide, is an approximate equivalent) was first written with the letters *a* or *o* and later with *aa* (in the Kensington inscription with the rune ᛆ). The sound of Sw. *ä*, says Rosander, was designated by the letter *e*, and that of *ö* by the letter *ø;* but the orthography was "very indefinite and various" (the Kensington stone has *norrmen* and *vest* as contrasted with *läger* and *äptir*, while *fräelse* shows both *ä* and *e;* the rune for *ö* in the inscription combines the forms *ö* and *ø* into a single symbol, ᚯ).

The uncertain status of O.Sw. spelling, says Rosander, is shown by the fact that so short a word as *efter* 'after,' is found in no fewer than 28 different spellings; of the nine sample variants which he lists, *aptir* and *eptir* most clearly approximate the *äptir* of the Kensington stone, which thus appears as a compromise between them. Seen in the light of this, the much disputed word *of* on the stone is less uniquely inexplicable than many have supposed. Sometimes vowels and consonants are doubled purposely, states Rosander, and he lists as examples *naat* 'night,' *flerre* 'several,' and *manss* 'man's.' This last word is clearly a genitive singular but is not indicated as such for the guidance of the ungrammatical. Could one find a more apt explanation for the otherwise irrational use of the oft discussed *mans* in line 10 of the Kensington inscription?

Once again Rosander emphasizes that the Swedish language pursued a wavering course, and this particularly during the period of *Middle Swedish*, 1300–1523, so that finally a "total confusion of tongues" prevailed. Specific dating of the various phenomena is not given, and the modern runic fabricator simply had to take his chances. For the word *allir* 'all,' to quote Rosander, Middle Swedish begins to write *alle;* in short, the masc. pl. adj. ending *-ir* is transformed into *-e;* and this very ending appropriately appears in our inscription in the word *röþe* 'red,' used as a masc. pl., as well as in the pl. possessive adj. *vore*. Rosander explains that under Danish influence after the Treaty of Kalmar (1397), that is, during the fifteenth century, Swedish *k*, *p*, *t* were gradually modified to *g*, *f*, *d*, as in *tage* for *taka* 'take,' and *skifta* for *skipta* 'exchange, divide' (the Kensington stone, which purports to antedate the Kalmar Union by a generation, shows both the "survival" form *äptir* and an "advanced" form *og*). *Skip* 'ship(s)' in this period became *skep* (modern Sw. *skepp*), says Rosander (properly enough, the Kensington stone shows the conservative vowel *i* in *skip*, though this word itself is an error for the more probable *skipom;* the conservatism in the first syllable of the Kensington version of the word failed to carry through to the d. pl. ending which, anticipating linguistic developments of a later generation, was here suppressed).

Continuing with Rosander: O.Sw. *vin* 'friend,' gradually became *væn* (Sw. *vän*), and *siga* 'to speak,' developed into *sæga* (Sw. *säga*); in this connection one thinks of the word *rise* 'journey,' of the Kensington inscription and of Sw. [*dags*] *resa* ['day's] journey.' From Danish, asserts Rosander, was borrowed the ending *-else* (*opdagelsefard* was the runecarver's Kensingtonian answer to this challenge). From German was borrowed the habit of marking a long vowel, either by writing it double, as in *troo* 'faith, to believe,' *reen* 'pure,' or by adding an *h*, *åhr* 'year,' *fahra* 'travel (the modern Sw. forms of these words are, respectively, *tro*, *ren*, *år*, *fara*). It should surprise no one, therefore, that the "runic" monument of Kensington exhibits the forms *öh* 'island' (Sw. *ö*) and *ahr* 'year' (Sw. *år*, cf. *fahra* above). *H* was likewise used at the end of a word, and Rosander's examples of this development are *jagh* 'I' (Sw. *jag*), and *dagh* 'day' (Sw. *dag*), as an exact parallel to which last-named word the Kensington inscription twice uses *dagh* in the same meaning. Rosander once again refers to the highly varied orthography that resulted from the influence of foreign languages. By the end of the Middle Swedish period, he asserts, there was indiscriminate mixing of the spellings *ok*, *oc*, *og*, *och* 'and' (Sw. *och*). True to form, the Kensington inscription has both *ok* and *og* in the same meaning.

With the advent of Modern Swedish in 1523, a number of reforms took place, writes Rosander: ". . . the vowels *a*, *ä*, and *ö*, which were already known, were taken into use instead of *aa*, *æ*, and *ø* . . ." (with singular appropriateness, as we have already seen, the Kensington inscription of "1362" effects a brilliant synthesis by combining into one extraordinary runic character the phonetically equivalent symbols *ö* and *ø*, whose chronologies, according to Rosander, overlapped, in that *ø* as an orthographic device was slated for extinction by 1523, whereas the spelling *ö* was already known during the Middle Swedish period of 1300–1523). Rosander is of course referring to manuscripts and books, not to the runic alphabet. And the Kensington inscription certainly owes most of its rationale to printed books. The accuracy of Rosander's statement on the early use of *ö* is open to serious question, as Chapters IX and XI have shown. But runecarvers at Kensington would have small knowledge of this. Their chief authority was too obviously Rosander.

One of the features of Middle Swedish retained even beyond 1523, likewise according to Rosander, was the custom of distinguishing a long vowel either by doubling it or by adding an *h*, as seen above, *e.g.*, *rööd* or *röhd* 'red' (Sw. *röd*). It is scarcely surprising, therefore, that this very word should turn up in the Kensington message, in the (pl.) spelling *röde;* and an interesting alternate version of the text, to which reference will be made in the next section of this paper, shows it with the spelling *röhde*.

Let whoever will now dismiss these observations as reflections of happenstance similarities rather than of a series of logical or quasi-logical deductions drawn by a nineteenth century lay runecarver from the apparent linguistic prescriptions of Rosander, together with the carver's selective presentation of them in the Kensington inscription. Coming back to our definition of the language of that inscription as nineteenth century oral Swedish archaicized, the language in question is nowhere more clearly explained than in the linguistic petrifacts resulting from a self-taught man's application—or misapplication—of information gleaned from a highly limited source. No longer need we cherish the myth of a learned hermit in the wilderness, a philologer of vast erudition who, anticipating the results of twentieth century research, composed a runic inscription so unassailable that it "has baffled philologists for a half century."[10]

The Rosander volume can help us a bit further. It contains

next to no consecutive material in Old Swedish which might have stood model to a whole sentence or phrase in the Kensington inscription. But there is one significant exception. On page 64 of Rosander are reproduced four versions of the Lord's Prayer in Swedish as they appeared in Church handbooks from, respectively, 1300, 1500, 1527, 1646. The concluding exhortation, "but deliver us from evil," immediately strikes the attention. The 1646 (and modern) version reads: "Utan fräls oss ifrån ondo." The 1527 version was: "Utan frels oss från onda"; in 1500 the prayer was: "Wtan frälsa oss aaff ondho." But the version from 1300 reads: "Utan frælsæ os af illu." The ninth line of the Kensington inscription reads: *"fräelse: af: illu* [or *illy*]."* Much has been written about *"AVM fräelse af illy [illu, illü,* etc.]" and its putative derivation and meaning. Comparing the phrase found on the Kensington stone with the parallel in Rosander, it is obvious that we need look no further.

There is only one final observation to make. For forty-six years—from 1908 to 1954—Mr. Holand maintained profound silence regarding Carl Rosander's book. By 1954, when the name Rosander had reached the public ear, this self-imposed silence was no longer possible. Holand therefore wrote in the Norwegian language newspaper *Decorah-Posten* (translated): "That is just balderdash. I have this book here on my desk. It is not an encyclopedia, but a textbook to assist those who had to be satisfied with the scanty instruction they received at an ambulatory school. The book is called 'The Well-Informed Schoolmaster.' "[11] Not an encyclopedia but a textbook, and that should dispose of the matter at once, thinks Holand.

In 1956, Holand referred once more to Rosander, and decided—with strict avoidance of any discussion of the material devoted to Swedish linguistic history—that the book "would be of no help in writing the Kensington inscription . . ."[12] Most interesting of all is the manner in which Holand flaunts his lofty unconcern with bibliographical trifles: He calls the popular encyclopedist *"Knut* Rosander."[13]

CHAPTER XIV

Rival Versions
of the Inscription

The first notice of the Kensington stone to reach the outside world was from a letter by a resident of Kensington to the Swedish-American publisher, Swan J. Turnblad of Minneapolis (Fig. 11). Dated January 1, 1899, it reads as follows:

I Inclose you a Copy of an inscription on a stone found about 2 miles from Kensington by a O. Ohman he found it under a tree when Grubbing—he wanted I should go out and look at it and I told him to haul it in when he came (not thinking much of it) he did so and this is an excest Copy of it the first part is of th flat side of stone th other was on flat edge I thought I would send it to you as you perhaps have means to find out what it is—it appears to be old Greek letters please let me hear from you and oblige yours truly J. P. Hedberg[1]

Despite its deceptive naïveté, this letter, with its studied casualness, is clever. For along with its runes, the Kensington stone does exhibit several characters very similar to those of archaic Greek and other ancient alphabets, illustrations of which are commonly found in encyclopedias, dictionaries, and Bible aids of wide distribution. Although hitherto ignored by linguists, the reference to "old Greek letters" was in all likelihood an important, original aspect of the entire hoax.

Hedberg was at this time in the real estate business at Kensington. The following April he was one of the group of men who excavated on the Ohman premises in the spring of 1899, searching for "Viking remains" near the runesite. A number of years later he was interrogated (by mail) by Professor Winchell regarding the rune stone and the sketch. It will be noted shortly that Hedberg was devious in his reply to Winchell. From this one deduces that he had a certain role to play in the runic mystification, and that his reference to "old Greek letters" was thus a humorous—and entirely successful—attempt to throw investigators off the track. In view of this, the Kensington inscription begins to appear in a new light, revealing in spite of everything a bit more sophistication than is usually attributed to it.

Accompanying Hedberg's letter was a pencilled sketch, the purported "excest copy" of the Kensington inscription (Fig. 10). Both the letter and the sketch are with the other Kensington documents in the MHS archive. Filed with them is a typed translation of the inscription made by Professor Breda (Fig. 13). All three of these documents seem to have been received by the MHS on August 18, 1925, apparently the gift of one Rodney West.

The Hedberg sketch, as we shall call it, was casually mentioned twenty-four years ago by the historian Dr. Quaife,[2] who was not familiar with Scandinavian languages nor with runes. No earlier reference to it has been found. The first person to subject it to scrutiny as a philological text was J. A. Holvik, who printed it in the *Concordian*, student newspaper of Concordia College at Moorhead, Minnesota, on November 18, 1949, together with a commentary on its peculiarities. It was thereafter reproduced in *Danske Studier*, accompanying an article on the Kensington stone by E. Moltke and H. Andersen, who tentatively accepted Holvik's conclusions.[3]

For a period of forty-odd years—from 1908 to 1951—Holand breathed never a word about the Hedberg sketch. But after the proddings of Holvik and Moltke-Andersen, beginning in 1949, it was increasingly difficult to ignore the subject. Accordingly, Holand quotes Hedberg's letter to Turnblad in an article in *Danske Studier* in 1951, and, without reproducing the Hedberg sketch or going into details, he dismisses the subject as follows: "Nor is it difficult to show from the copy that it is a copy, not a model, but this is not worth the trouble, since it is hard to imagine that Hedberg and the one who made the drawing were stupid enough to send the sketch to a newspaper if the inscription had been copied from the latter."[4] In 1956, Holand discusses the matter briefly for an an American audience in *Explorations*. And what does he say? He explains that he has never considered the sketch worth the bother of comment.[5] That from a man who has devoted a lifetime to dredging up even the most irrelevant trivia, so long as he could associate them in any way with the Kensington stone. Holand goes so far as print the Hedberg sketch, unobtrusively, under a "cover" name ("Ohman's copy of the inscription from the Kensington Stone"), and in an unrelated portion of the book.[6]

Holvik's contention was that the Hedberg sketch, which purports to be an "excest copy" of the carving on the Kensington stone, in fact differs from the now known Kensington inscription at no fewer than seventeen points: three in punctuation, seven in spelling, and seven in forms, and that some of these differences make it evident that the "copy" is no copy at all, but rather a rough sketch or preliminary draught of the inscription that finally was carved on the stone. If Holvik's contention is shown to be correct, we would have absolute proof that the Kensington inscription is every bit as modern as the evidence from other sources uniformly indicates. Both the letter and sketch were examined by the present author at St. Paul in August, 1953, and found fully identical with the photographs already procured from Professor Holvik and which are reproduced in the accompanying plates (Figs. 10 and 11).

As in other matters, Holand gives variant versions of the story about what Breda received. As late as 1940, Holand wrote: "Late in the fall of 1898 a careful copy of the inscription was sent to O. J. Breda."[7] The effect of this would be to indicate that the divergencies of Breda's interpretation are attributable to his carelessness or inexpertness in reading runes; whereas one might rather attribute them to certain peculiarities of the *not so careful* copy sent to Breda, possibly as an aspect of the hoax.

But in 1956 Holand writes: "Shortly after Hedberg sent his letter [January 1, 1899], Mr. S. A. Sieverts [sic], manager of the bank in Kensington, sent either a copy of the inscription or the stone itself to Professor O. J. Breda. . . ."[8] And the supporting footnote asserts: "There is some doubt as to what was sent to Breda. He says he received a copy of the inscription made by the manager of the bank, S. A. Siverts; but the latter in a letter to me, dated November 22, 1935, says: 'I shipped the stone very carefully packed and by express to Prof. Breda.' "[9]

Why did Holand suppress that information for twenty years? Is it once again because he, to speak in the Holand manner, "considered the matter unimportant," one of the "little things that affect little minds"? If so, why has the matter suddenly become important now? This tactic comports with the assumption that Holand is trying to establish counter-defences against the Hedberg sketch, which has been in existence for fifty-nine years and on file with the MHS for thirty-three years, throughout which period Holand has ignored its existence.

At all events, this late revelation by Holand does not add to the likelihood that Breda, who was not a runological scholar, worked from the stone—any stone—or solely from the stone, particularly in view of Breda's own statement that he worked from a sketch. Whether that sketch was the Ohman-Hedberg sketch, or one made by Siverts, cannot now be determined with complete certainty. But the peculiarities of Breda's interpretation are strong evidence that Breda worked from the Hedberg sketch.

How, then, shall one explain the statement printed in *Svenska Amerikanska Posten* on February 28, 1899, that the Ohman-Hedberg sketch was sent to Breda, whereas the runic text simultaneously printed by *SAP* is not the Ohman-Hedberg sketch?[10] The *SAP* text may indeed have come ultimately from Siverts; it is much closer to the stone than the Hedberg sketch and is convincing as a genuine copy from the stone (Fig. 14). However, one notices that a map reproduced with the sketch bears lettering in English: "Slough," "Place where stone was found." The editor, Turnblad, after sending the Hedberg sketch to Breda, may well have procured another sketch from Siverts (no such sketch is preserved by the MHS, see note 22); but the entire illustrative material reproduced in *SAP* appears to be the work of a staff artist, very probably borrowed from an English-language newspaper.

The Hedberg sketch contains nearly a score of recognizable differences from the inscription of which it purports to be a copy; some of these differences are indeed of such a kind as to invest the sketch with independent status as an original document, not slavishly derived from the accepted Kensington inscription, as a copy should be, but rather a variant of it, both the sketch and the stone being descended from a common ancestor. This experimental version can well have been very close to the unknown original draught of the Kensington carving, despite reasons for considering it not literally the *ur*-version.

Though Hedberg asserts it to be an exact copy of the writing on the stone, this exactness does not consist at any rate in line-by-line adherence to its purported original, as only the first line (after the erasure of four runes) corresponds in that regard. Hedberg's letter avoids stating who had made the copy. The article on the stone printed in *Svenska Amerikanska Posten* (see Fig. 14) on February 28, 1899, states in part (translated): "Mr. Ohman made a copy of the figures on the stone and sent the copy through J. P. Hedberg at Kensington to *Svenska Amerikanska Posten*. We thereupon sent it to the University of Minnesota, where Professor O. J. Breda examined it . . . a similar copy was sent to Professor Curme . . . and he requested that the stone be sent to him, which was done."

Whether the statement as to Ohman is based on specific information given the editors of *SAP*, or whether Ohman's authorship of the sketch was purely an inference drawn from Hedberg's ambiguous statement, one cannot at present tell. The archives preserve a letter from Hedberg to Professor Winchell which contradicts that inference. Written March 12, 1910, it states that Hedberg himself made the sketch he sent to Turnblad, after Ohman had brought the stone to his office: "In the first place the stone was brought in to my office by the finder Olof Ohman. I took quite much interest in the same. I copied the same and sent copy to S. J. Turnblad who sent it to the State University

but Prof. Breda thought it was a fake. . . . While I know very
little about runes I never considered the stone a fake."[11]

If Hedberg really did make the sketch, as he retroactively
claimed, then he did so with a certain knowledge of runes, as
will be demonstrated, and was deliberately misleading Turnblad
in 1899 when he pretended to think the runic symbols were "old
Greek letters." For some of the runes, and some of the spellings
of the Hedberg sketch are materially different from those on the
stone.

If, on the other hand, Hedberg merely accepted the sketch
from Ohman and later claimed authorship of it, he was being un-
truthful eleven years later at a time when it was advantageous
to divert suspicion from Ohman. Whichever version of Hedberg's
story we accept—the statement to Turnblad in 1899 or that
made to Winchell in 1910—he has concealed facts of material
relevancy to the Kensington problem. To that extent, he is involved in a runic hoaxing plot.

Hedberg implies in his letter of 1899 that he knows nothing of
runes himself. This circumstance would require him to copy
blindly letter by letter, and though he as copyist undoubtedly
would make mistakes, certain of the canny variations here seen
are precluded as mere copy errors. They are deliberate experi-
ments along the lines—runological and "old Greek"—already
suggested, and whether they were made by Hedberg, by Ohman,
or by some third party concerning whom the two have maintained silence, is quite immaterial. We know nothing, after all,
of what motivated Hedberg in sending the sketch to Turnblad,
or whether Ohman had anticipated this turn of events.[12]

At first sight, the Kensington inscription (Fig. 1) and the Hedberg sketch seem identical. The varying length of the first eight
lines, in the sketch at least, suggests the indentations of the inscription, and the symbols look the same. The inscription and
the sketch are alike in avoiding hyphens; every line in each ends
with a word. The first line of the sketch shows erasure of the
fragment *op*, by means of which erasure the copyist avoids break-
ing up the word *opdagelsefard*. Looking more closely we find not
merely differences, but differences that clearly show the Hedberg sketch to have been made by a man who understood runes

and was closely familiar with the contents of the inscription. This is proved by the addition in line 4 of the sketch of the letter *m* to the word *fro;* the addition in line 7 of the letter *h* in the m. pl. adj. *röde/röhde* 'red';ᚱᚭᛈᛏ/ᚱᚭᛏᛈᛏ (Rosander: *rööd, röhd*). Two changes of *o* to *e* in *deno/dene* in lines 5, 11; the change of *i* to *e* in *rise/rese*.

Not a single one of these substitutions affects the meaning of the word in question. They are variations merely, acceptable alternate spellings, which preserve the semantic integrity of the original and are at the same time within the degree of orthographical latitude allowed by Rosander.[13] It would require nothing more to demonstate beyond cavil that the Hedberg sketch was an experimental creation, and no copy of the stone. The same fact is demonstrated in line 4 in the spelling *nor* 'north,' for *norr;* and in line 7 by ᛒ ᚱᚭᛈ (*blöd*) for ᛒ ᚱᛁᛈ (*blod*) 'blood.' Speakers of Swedish will assume this to be a dittographic error made by one familiar with Swedish. But the graphic difference between ᚭ and ᛁ is too marked to have been made even as a dittographic error, by one *ignorant* of these symbols. The copyist was quite familiar with their meaning and use. He not only had some conception of runes in general, but a definite grasp of these particular runes.

In line 7 is an erasure that is definitely critical. The heavy ᛏ at the point of erasure replaces the *o* with umlaut and superimposed *x*. (See also the symbols in Chapter XVI, note 12.) This makes capital sense and should dispose at once of any arguments that *ded* on the stone stands for anything but some spelling of the Swedish m. pl. adj.—form-chronology uncertain—for 'dead.' The spelling *ded* was likely enough intended to introduce a deliberate variation, either in keeping with the presumed uncertainties of Middle Swedish spelling as emphasized by Rosander, or humorously, as a bit of English influence to deepen the mystery. Concerning a correction from ᛈᚭᛈ to ᛈᛏᛈ there seem to be only two likely possibilities: Either it was a retroactive improvement, or it was the correction of a mere dittographic error (see the discussion just above). This latter assumption merely puts the intention one step backward in time.

What is important is that whoever copied this word knew the

meaning of the word and the phonetic values of the symbol ⊗. Remember that Hedberg had by implication denied knowing anything of runes, and that both he and Ohman denied knowing the meaning of this particular inscription. The erasure in line 7 contradicts one or both of them.

In line 8 of the sketch we see a word *fraelse* which has not yet received—or from which has been subtracted—the Kensington umlaut; the same applies to *aptir* for *äptir* in line 10. The presumed, ignorant copyist was evidently making great strides at mastering both the rationale of the runic symbols and the numerous lexicographical choices afforded by Old Swedish (see Chapter XIII). The orthographical latitude in which he indulged corroborates and conforms ideally to the orthographical philosophy of experiment revealed by the inscription on the Kensington stone.

There are other differences between the two documents, minor in character. Between *po* and *opdagelsefard* in the sketch there is no symbol, whether ᛁ (-*o*) or otherwise. In line 3 the first symbol in the word ᚤᛁ (*vi*) is not dotted; the runes for *ved* are omitted before the "runic" numeral for "2." This is a typical copying error and confirms the impression gained from the garbled line structure that the Hedberg sketch was not actually the oldest document in the case. In line 5, the same symbol reappears and is not dotted, although the same letter in ᚤᚷᚱ has the dot, as on the stone. Discrepancies of this kind are plausible copying errors. In line 8, the two heavy dots under the word *illy*, whose singly dotted ᚤ already marks it as a variant, are not clearly related to the inscription. In line 9, the sketch has *ve* for *ved*, a perfect example of modern phonetic spelling by a speaker of Swedish who knew the value of these runes.

In general, the pencilling of line 8 shows sign of smearing, since the sheet of paper has been folded along it. A free-hand line with the same or a similar pencil has been drawn under line 8 of the text to effect a division between the text of the face and that of the edge of the Kensington stone. A sentence in Hedberg's first letter (see Fig. 11) clearly implies that the pencilled line was contemporary with the rest of the text: "... the first part is of th flat side of stone th other was on flat edge."

Now, if Hedberg merely took over the sketch from Ohman, as asserted in *Svenska Amerikanska Posten* on February 28, 1899, the *age* of the sketch is uncertain. Hedberg himself would not necessarily have known the time of its commission to paper, an act which to all appearances does not antedate the decision to divide the message into a "face" portion and an "edge" portion. Counting the extensive rearrangement of lines as but a single feature and disregarding the erasures and the dots under *illy*, and disregarding at least five divergencies in punctuation, the Hedberg sketch nevertheless reveals 18 clearly marked differences from the inscription it pretends to copy. How totally implausible the sketch is as a copy made from the stone will appear from a comparison of it with a different sketch, namely the one accompanying the *SAP* article just referred to (Fig. 14). Despite, or rather because of its divergencies from the stone, the *SAP* sketch is a believable copy of the stone. The nature of the Hedberg sketch's differences from the inscription leads to several conclusions regarding it:

A. It cannot literally be the first draft, or *ur*-text, of the Kensington inscription (such a feature as the omission of *ved* in line 3 indicates that it is a copy of something).

B. It is a copy of a message that had taken definite form as to its wording (the wording is identical with that of the inscription, except for the copying error), and even as to the *number of symbols* to be employed (the accidental omission of *ved* reduces this number from 222 to 219).[14]

C. It—or the version from which it was literally copied—reflects certain indecisions as to *spelling* (*röhde; rese; dene; nor; aptir; from;* probably also the erased *död*).

D. The Hedberg sketch is therefore intermediate between the unknown *ur*-text and the final version, that on the stone.

E. It was made by a person completely familiar with these "runes," inasmuch as the confident and purposeful way in which the runes are drawn seems to exclude an uninitiated outsider. A leading handwriting expert who was consulted in this matter indicated, however, that no reliable conclusions could be drawn as to the identity of the author of the sketch or carving of the inscription.[15]

Fig. 20

Rosander, title page

Fig. 21

Rosander, with Ohman's signature

lossningskonsten; *Limrunor* och *Örtrunor*, läkareskickligheten medelst användande af växter; *Hugrunor*, skaldskap och vitterhet; *Meginrunor* eller *Kraftrunor*, insigt i naturkunnigheten, eller förmågan att medelst okända naturkrafter åstadkomma ovanliga verkningar; *Brimrunor* eller *Srallrunor*, kännedom om sjöfarten, samt *Bokrunor*, sannolikt konsten att använda runor i skrift.

Betraktade såsom skriftecken, har runornas första uppkomst varit mycket omtvistad; somliga hafva ansett dem först hafva begynt nyttjas med kristendomens införande; men att de äfven begagnats dessförinnan, är numera satt utom allt tvifvel. Deras betydelse var känd endast af den tidens prester, eller offerföreståndarne, och bevarades af dessa såsom en religionshemlighet; af folket betraktades dessa tecken med helig vördnad, åtminstone som en produkt af högre vetande, samt ristades ofta, utan att vara kända, på vapen, skeppstammar och dylikt, emedan de ansågos innehafva en magisk kraft att medföra lycka och seger. Deras form visar, att de varit ämnade att ristas in i hårdare föremål, såsom sten, metaller, horn, träd och dylikt. Företrädesvis valdes härtill, sedan de begynte bli allmännare kända, kaflar eller skifvor af bok; det raka strecket i hvarje runa kallas *Staf*, och hakens eller »kännestreckets« ställning till stafven bestämde runans ljudegenskap, och kallades *Mynd*. Hvarje särskild uppsats inskars för sig i en balk eller stock; häraf hafva vi ännu qvar orden *Bok* (af bokträdet), *Bokstaf*, *Budkafle* och *Balk* (en afdelning af vår lagbok). De äldsta runorna voro 16 till antalet och egde ännu såsom skriftecken, jemte ljud och namn, äfven hvar för sig vissa betydelser, enligt följande:

Form.	Namn och betydelse.	Uttal.	Form.	Namn och betydelse.	Uttal.
ᚠ	*Fe* (fä)	F.	ᛁ	*Iss* (is)	I.
ᚢ	*Ur* (urväder)	U, Å, V.	ᛆ ᛅ	*Ar* (år)	A, Á.
ᚦ	*Thorn* (törne)	Th, D.	ᛋ	*Sol* (sol)	S.
ᚬ ᚭ	*Oss* (åmynning)	O.	ᛏ	*Tyr* (krigsgudens namn)	T.
ᚱ	*Reder*, *Reid* (ridt)	R.	ᛒ	*Bjarkan* (björkfrukt)	B.
ᚴ	*Kaun*, *Kön* (böld)	K.	ᛚ	*Lögr* (lag, vatten)	L.
ᚼ	*Hagl* (hagel)	H.	ᛘ ᛰ	*Madr* (man)	M.
ᚾ ᚿ	*Naud* (nöd)	N.	ᛦ	*Yr* (pil, båge,)	Y, R.

Dessa runor, som äro de allmännaste, hafva blifvit kallade *Upsalarunor*, emedan de i rikaste mått förekomma i Upland; *Anglosachsiska* eller *Tyska runor* finnas blott på några få ställen uti södra Sverige. Upsalarunorna äro på flere sätt använde, hvaraf uppkommit *Vänderunor* (omvände) och *Stuprunor* (stupade). *Binderunor* bestodo uti, att på en lång staf tecknades flere runhakar under hvarandra, hvarigenom en enda figur kunde uttrycka ett helt ord eller namn. De begagnades äfven till hemlig skrift och kallades då *Villrunor*. Staflösa runor, som bestå af endast haken, utan staf, hafva blifvit kallade *Helsingerunor*, emedan de hufvudsakligast förekomma i Helsingland och länge af de lärde ansågos som oläsliga eller villrunor, tills slutligen Magnus Celsius år 1675 upptäckte förhållandet och tillsatte stafven, hvarefter de lästes utan svårighet. Ett slags teckenspråk, som bestod i klappning i händerna, vissa slag för hvarje figur, kallades *Klapprunor*, men utgjorde ingenting egendomligt för runorna, utan kan åstadkommas med hvilket alfabet som helst.

När med tidens lopp runornas bruk såsom skrifspråk spridt sig till folket och behofvet af flere ljudtecken uppkom, begynte man på åtskilliga sätt öka deras antal, och sålunda uppstodo de så kallade *stungna* eller punkterade runorna, som skilde sig från de gamla genom en eller flere punkter inuti figuren, hvilken förändrade deras ursprungliga ljud och såmedelst äfven ökade deras antal, sålunda kallades ᚤ Y, ᚵ G, ᛂ E och ᛔ P. Sedan genom kristendomen latinska alfabetet blef bekant, ökades runorna med ännu flere figurer, så att de slutligen voro i det närmaste lika många som de romerska bokstäfverna.

Vissa runors då varande uttalsljud är numera förloradt; så hade Thorn ett läspande ljud, liknande det engelska *th*, och Hagl uttalades hårdt, likt *gh*, och hördes framför *j*, *l*, *n*, *r*, *v*.

De så kallade runstenarne, d. v. s. med runstil gjorda inskriptioner på stenhällar, bergklintar m. m. äro de enda lemningar, som återstå af denna tidrymds språk. Riksantiqvarien J. G. Liljegren har uti sin Runlära anfört icke mindre än 1452 sådana ensamt inom Sverige, och troligen finnas ännu många flera. Genom denna sin mängd bilda dessa likasom en egen litteratur, af betydlig vigt för språkforskningarne. Många af dem äro konstrika arbeten, der inskriptionen står på en i flera sinnrika bugter sig slingrande orm, börjande vid ormens hufvud. Innehållet på en stor del vittnar väl om kristen tro; dock finnas flere, som anses hafva tillkommit under hedendomen, och tiden från år 900 till 1300 synes varit den ålder, under hvilken största delen blifvit danade. De flesta äro grafvårdar, resta öfver någon afliden; men somliga hafva uppkommit till åminnelse af något prisvärdt företag, såsom anläggandet af vägar, broar, herbergen, s. k. själahus o. s. v. Inskriptionen är äfven någon gång på vers med bokstafsrim eller alliteration. Emellertid kan af allt detta ingenting med någon säkerhet slutas om språkets beskaffenhet i sin helhet, helst ofta framskymtar stor okunnighet om ords rätta stafning hos dem. som verkstält dylika ristningar, hvadan språkets bedömande efter dessa torde bli lika felaktigt, som om vårt nuvarande språk skulle

Fig. 22. Rosander, page 61

'bedömas efter sådana grafskrifter, som t. ex. *ker viller ena tjår hustru,* jemte derfaldiga andra dylika, hvilka än i dag äro ingenting mindre än sällsynta.

II. Fornsvenskan. *Från år 1000 till 1300.*

Det föreningsband mellan nordvestliga Europas alla länder, som bestod i ett i det allra närmaste gemensamt språk och som gjorde dess alla bebyggare till ett folk, sönderföll efterhand och hvarje land antog, jemte egen regering, småningom äfven eget språk. Fornsvenskan, som på detta sätt uppstod, liknade naturligtvis i början ursvenskan, men riktades efterhand med nya ord, särdeles genom inflytande af den sig utbredande kristendomen. Runorna, som nu ej längre utgjorde hemligheter, blefvo allmännare både kända och som skrifteckeu begagnade, till dess de småningom utträngdes genom det både tydligare och vigare latinska alfabetet, som af munkarne gjordes bekant.

De nya begrepp, som åtföljde den nya gudaläran, gjorde äfven nya ord nödvändiga, och för detta ändamål användes dels sammansättningar af gamla svenska ord, såsom *radband, skärseld. vigvatten;* dels upptogos och ombildades ord på svenska från latinet och grekiskan, t. ex. *kors* (af lat. Crux), *font* (dop)*funt* (lat. Fons), och på samma sätt orden *altare, bibel, biskop, engel, fest. kloster, kyrka, oblat, prest, predika, psalm, skrifva, signa, tempel, testamente* med många flere. Troligt är, att genom religionsläraze från främmande länder ord äfven inkommo från engelskan, tyskan m. fl. språk, ehuru sådana numera svårligen kunna från riktiga svenska ord urskiljas.

Vid antagandet af de latinska bostäfverna till skrifspråk bibehölls länge runan Þ för *þ*-ljudet samt förbyttes sedan, i följd af sitt uttal, till *th,* som ända till vår tid bibehållit sig i bibel- och lagstil. Från anglosachsiskan upptogs *ð* för uttryckande af *dh.* Bland vokalljuden tecknades *å* först med *a* eller *o* och sedan med *aa; ä*-ljudet skrefs med *e* och *ö*-ljudet med *o.*

Utom runstenarne hafva vi åtskilliga andra uppsatser, som anses tillkommit under denna tidrymd, t. ex. Vestgötalagen, som tros vara författad omkring år 1220, och den äldsta handskrift deraf skrifven år 1290. För öfrigt är den svenska litteraturen från denna tid högst fattig, emedan om munkarne, tidens ende lärde, författade något, skrefs detta mest på latin. Hvad man af det som finnes kan döma rörande svenskan är, att stafsättet varit mycket obestämdt och vacklande, hvilket bäst bevisas deraf, att t. ex. det korta ordet *efter* finnes tecknadt på ej mindre än 28 olika sätt, såsom *Abtir, Ebtir, Ibtir, Ubtir, Aftar, Eftar, Ifti, Aptir, Eptir* o. s. v. Stundom fördubblas vokaler eller konsonanter utan ändamål, t. ex. *Naat* (natt), *Flerve, Monss* o. s. v.

Detta förhållande synes emellertid vara en följd af olika landskapsdialekter, samt att intet allmänt för hela riket gemensamt skrifsätt ännu hunnit utbilda sig. Att döma efter isländskan, synes umgängesspråket hafva varit både kraftfullt, rent och regelbundet samt, om än ordfattigt, likväl fullt tillräckligt för alla behof, ja till och med haft många sedermera förlorade ord för begreppsskiftningar, hvilka hos oss sakna uttryck; isynuerhet var skaldspråket rikt, och många uttryck innehålla en sinnrikhet och menniskokäunedom som visa, att den rent menskliga bildningen hos våra förfäder innehaft en vida högre ståudpunkt än man i allmänhet föreställer sig

III. Medelsvenskan. *Från år 1300 till 1523.* Under denna tid fortfor

språket att riktas med nya ord, dels från latinet och grekiskan genom de andlige, som till det mesta bade regeringsmakten i sina händer, dels från tyskan genom legotrupper under Folkungarnes regering samt dels från danskan under Kalmarunionen; äfven från franskan inkommo genom studerandes resor till Paris en mängd uttryck, i synnerhet angående litteraturen. Allt detta ökade väl ordförrådet, men verkade menligt på nationalspråket, som alltjemt vacklade från det ena uttryckssättet till det andra, utan bestämda grundsatser, och slutligen företedde en fullständig språkförbistring.

Att ett ökadt umgänge med främmande folkslag och deras språk skulle inverka på modersmålet var naturligt. Tyska konungar med åtföljande tyska embetsmän, många tyska drottningar samt framförallt de öfver hela norden utbredda hanseatiska köpmännen och handtverkarne, införde en mängd ord och talesätt från tyska språket, af hvilka vi ännu hafva qvar orden *gesims, jungfru, junker, mantel, skymf* m. fl Från latinet upptogos orden *artikel, datum, mandat, plakat, universitet* m. fl.; från franskan *kurtois, jenul, svit (suite), äfventyr (aventure)* m. fl., hvarjemte Väriagarnes resor till Konstantinopel äfven ej voro utan inverkan på språket. — Emellertid gåfvo dessa förhållanden en förut saknad väckelse åt det vittra lifvet, hvartill bidrog att norska drottningen Eufemia omkring år 1320 lät på svenska öfversätta några af Tysklands och Frankrikes romantiska dikter. såsom *Hertig Fredrik af Normandie*, *Herr Ivan lejonriddaren*, "Konung Artus", "Karl den store" m. fl ; vid samma tid anses *Konungastyrelsen* vara skrifven, ett mästerstycke till innehåll och språk, hvarjemte de yngre landskapslagarne förmodas datera sig

Fig. 23. Rosander, page 62

från detta tidehvarf, äfvensom åtskilliga sånger, S:t Brigittas uppenbarelser, Ausgarii lefverne samt stora rimkrönikan, en del af våra folkvisor m. m.

Den förkofring modersmålet under denna tidrymd erhöll, oberäknadt det ofvannämnde ökade ordförrådet, bestod hafvudsakligast deruti att sträfvare ord utbyttes mot mjukare, så att man t. ex. i stället för *mer, ther, ser, allir*, började skrifva *mik, thik, sik, alle*; i början bibehölls likväl det hårdare konsonantsystemet, t. ex. *gudelik, skipta* (gudelig, skifta); men under Kalmarunionen öfvergingo *k, p* och *t* genom danskans inflytelse i många ord till *g, f* och *d*, t. ex. *taga, skifta*, i st. f. *taka, skipta*. De forna dunkla eller skarpa vokalljuden utbyttes äfven småningom mot andra, så att t. ex. af *sun* blef *son*, af *brut* blef *brott*, af *skip* blef *skep* (skepp), af *vin* blef *væn* (vän), af *siga* blef *sæga* (säga), af *firi* blef *fore* (före) o. s. v. Från tyskan upptogos bruket af *ek, jemte* prefixerna *an, be, bi, er, ge, för (vor) und* o. s. v., samt tilläggningsstafvelserna *dom, het, skap* m. fl., äfvensom från danskan *else, ning* och obestämda artikeln *en, ett* o. s. v., genom hvilket en stor mängd nya ord blefvo bildade af förut inhemska. Efter tyskan begynte man utmärka en lång vokal genom att antingen skrifva den dubbel, t. ex. *troo, reen*, eller tillägga ett *h*, t. ex. *dhr, fahra*, hvilket senare äfven brukades i slutet af ord, t. ex. *jagh, migh, sigh, dagh, Sverighe* o. s. v. För öfrigt är uti denna tids skrifter stafningssättet mycket vacklande och obeständt genom den inverkan så många olika språk haft på den då ej ännu stadgade svenskan, så att man i slutet af tidehvarfvet finner om hvarannat tecknadt t. ex. *rike, riike, rige, riche; jak, jog, jac, jach; oc, og, och* o. s. v. (I detta sista ord har sedan språket den förhållit segern öfver både gamla svenskans *k*, latinets *c* och danskans *g*.) — Ur det kaos af förvirring, som sålunda utmärker Medelsvenskan, framgår slutligen språket mera rent och stadgadt genom den odödlige Gustaf Vasa, från hvars anträde till regeringen man räknar början till

IV. Nysvenskan. Från 1523 till vår tid.

Genom tid efter annan uppträdande lärde och sannt svenske män har språket sedan nämnde tid småningom utbildats till hvad det för närvarande är. Början gjordes af konung Gustaf 1 och hans biträdare vid reformationen, Olaus och Laurentius Petri, samt den lärde Laurentius Andreæ, hvilka antogo ett stadgadt och mera svenskt stafsätt, sannolikt för att skilja sig från danskarne. Svenska Handboken, utgifven 1529, Svenska Messan, 1531, och bibelöfversättningen, 1541, gjorde deras antagna utföringssätt allmännare kändt. Sedermera hafva många flera uppträdt och dels hindrat nya irringar, dels ytterligare bildat språket enligt tidens fordringar.

Reformatorernas hufvudsakliga åtgärder vid språket voro, att borttaga öfverflödiga främmande ord och uttryckssätt; vokalerna *å, ä* och *ö*, som redan förut voro bekanta, antogos till bruk i stället för *aa, æ* och *ø*; det svenska *a* återtogs i stället för det danska *e*, t. ex. *bida* för *bide*, och det svenska *k*, t. ex. *rike, mycken*, i stället för *rige, mygen*, utom i några ord, såsom *jag, dig, Sverige, taga*, der *g* bibehölls. I stället för Þ antogs bruket af *th; ch* behölls qvar, äfvensom bruket att utmärka lång vokal med antingen fördubbling, t. ex. *röd*, eller tillagdt *h*, t. ex. *röhd*.

Emellertid kunde språkformerna ej så hastigt stadga sig, och minst ett århundrade förgick, under hvilket uttryckssätten vacklade i striden emellan det gamla och det nya samt mellan svenska, danska och tyska former, och Svenskarnes deltagande i trettioåriga kriget hotade att ånyo förvirra språket genom tyska och franska tillsatser; handlingar, bref och skrifter från denna tid visa en så brokig blandning af diverse språk, att de ovilkorligen påminna om arlekinströjan. — Slutligen uppträdde Stjernhjelm som ny reformator af språket. Genom hans lyra föddes svenska skaldekonsten till lif och gaf språket mera böjlighet och harmoni än det förut egde. Han, tillika med Verelius och Rudbeck forskade uti fädernelandets urspråk och sökte åter frammana dess minnen ur glömskan. Många flera arbetade i samma anda; dock saknades ännu renhet och ädelhet i uttrycken, och stafsättet vacklade mellan det gamla och det nya. Vokalernas onödiga fördubbling och bruket af det öfverflödiga *h* motarbetades, och bruket af *k* i stället för *ch* påyrkades, äfvensom aflöggandet af de långsläpande slutändelserna, t. ex. *goder, verldhenne, menniskomen* o. s. v., i stället för *god, verlden, menniskan* o. s. v. Språket började behandlas grammatikaliskt, och år 1693 utgafs den första läroboken i svenska språket, af Ericus O. Aurivillius. Denna bok, med titel: «Exercitatio Academica, Continens Cogitationes de Linguæ Svionicæ, qvalis hodie maxime in usu est recta scriptura & pronunciatione», är förut så afhandla svenskan, äfven till innehållet väl mycket öfverlastad med latin, hvilket deremot icke är fallet med den af Nils Tjällman år 1696 utgifna Svenska Grammatikan, hvars svenska innehåll är rikare. Bland lärare i svenska nämnes äfven en Bureus, och Jesper Svedberg inlade mycken förtjenst om språket uti en bok, kallad «Schibboleth, eller Svenska Språkets rycht och richtighet», samt en Svensk grammatik; uti ortografien sökte han väl försvara medelsvenskan; men denna åsigt vann ej mera bifall. Den af Karl XI beslutade och under Karl XII:s tid fullbordade nya bibelöfversättningen, Svenska Psalmboken med flera allmänna böcker samt framförallt den af Karl XI utfärdade förordningen, att hvar och en, som ville begagna nådemedlen, borde kunna läsa rent i bok, gjorde språket och dess skrifsätt mera allmänt både kända och begagnade. Emellertid qvarstod ännu många af de gamla, stela

Fig. 24. Rosander, page 63

'64 Språklära.'

rmerna; många skriftställare lånade utan urskilning främmande ord och uttryckssätt, och språket d af en viss råhet och klumpighet, till dess Dalin, som ären tillkommer att stå i spetsen för as senaste utbildnings-period, med sitt exempel visade möjligheten af att göra det till ett smidigt verktyg för all slags skrifart. Af den forna, stela ordfogningen finnas hos honom få, nästan märkliga spår, och öfverflödiga främmande ord blefvo af honom och genom hans efterdöme från språket utträngde. Flere utmärkta snillen, både på vers och prosa, följde i Dalins fotspår och nderhöllo den hos allmänheten väckta kärleken för litteraturen, hvarjemte läroböcker i Svenska språket utgåfvos, bland andra «Svenska Språkets Redighet«, af 6. F. Ljungberg, 1756; «Förberedelse till en Svensk Grammatika«, af C. Brunkman, hvaraf början utkom 1767, slutet 1774; «Glossarium Sviogoticum«, af Joh. Ihre, 1769; «Svensk Grammatika«, af A. M. Sahlstedt, 1769, samt Svenska Språket i tal och skrift«, af A. af Botin, 1777. Detta oaktadt bibehöllo åtskilligt af et gamla språkets stafsätt i bibeln och lagboken, så att ett dubbelt språk begagnades, nemligen bel- och lagspråket å ena sidan och allmänna skrifspråket å den andra, utan att någotdera var llkomligt stadgadt. Ojemnheter och brister förefunnos ännu, väl obetydliga i jemförelse med rna, men tillräckliga att vanställa skrifarten; bland dessa voro obestämdheten i bruket af dubbla onsonanter samt brist på reglor för vokalerna e och ä samt o och å. År 1801 utgaf Svenska kademien en «Rättstafningslära«, ämnad att tjena till grund föf alla ords stafning, hvilkens reglor dermera blifvit till det mesta antagna; dessutom ha efter denna tid utkommit: «Försök till en årobok för nybegynnare i Svenska och Allmänna Grammatiken«, af P. Moberg, 1815; «Inledning ll Svenska Språkläran« af J. Svedbom, 1824; «Svensk Språklära« af A. Fryxell, 1824; «Svensk riklära« af C. J. L. Almqvist, 1842; «Försök till en Svensk Språklära«, af P. G. Boivie, 1834; Lärobok i Allmänna och Svenska Grammatiken«, af S. J. Filén, 1834; «Svensk Språklära«, utgifven Svenska Akademien, 1836; «Svensk Språklära«, af H. K. Tullberg, 1826; «Svensk Grammatika sammandrag«, af U. T—n. 1837; «Svenska Språkets Lagar«, af J. E. Rydqvist, 5 delar, fullständigt utkomna 1874, utan jemförelse vår språklitteraturs hufvudverk. «Ordlista« utgifven af Svenska kademien, 1874, hvilkens reglor för rättskrifning vi i allmänhet sökt följa i detta arbete, jemte ånga flera dels läroböcker, dels andra uppsatser rörande språket, genom hvilket allt detta område antagit en form, som sannolikt aldrig kan förändras. En fullständig öfverensstämmelse i alla rds stafning hör emellertid ännu till de ouppfylda önskningarnes område, emedan man om språkrarne sjelfva kan i viss fall tillämpa ordspråket: Så många hufvuden, så många sinnen. Den rincipen tycks likväl på senaste tider hafva fått allt fler och fler anhängare så väl bland vetenkapsmännen som bland allmänheten, att hvarje ord bör stafvas icke efter sin härledning utan om det uttalas, och vi skulle mycket misstaga oss om icke denna grund för stafning och framällningsätt slutligen skall bli den segrande.

I förmodan, att det kunde intressera en eller annan att se prof på språkets utveende under lika tider, anföres här slutligen följande uppställning af bönen «Fader vår«, aftecknad efter de egagnade kyrko-handböckerna under fyra af de förut omtalade tidsåldrarne:

År 1300.	År 1500.	År 1527.	År 1646.
Fadher war i himiriki	Fadher waar som är	Fader vår som är j,	Fader vår som äst i
celecht huais Þitt namn,	j himblom hälgat wari	himblomen.	himmelen, helgadt varde
illkomi os Þit rike. war-	thit nampn. Tilkome	wardhe titt nampn. Till-	titt nampn. Tillkomme
lhe Þin wili hær i jordh-	thit rijke. Warde thin	komme titt rike. Wardhe	titt rijke. Skee tin vilie
iki swa sum han war-	wili swa i jerderijke som	thin willie så på jordhen-	så på jordenne, som i
ler i himiriki. wart dag-	j bijmmerijke. Gif oss	ne som j himmelen, Giff	himmelen. Giff oss i
iet bred gif os i dagh.	i dagh waart daghlighit	oss j dagh vårt daghe-	dagh vart daghelige
o årilaat os warø mis-	brödh. Ok forlaat oss	lighit brödh, Och förlåt	brödh. Och förlåt oss
erningæ swa sum wi fi-	waara synder som wij	oss våra skuld såsom och	vara skulder, såsom och
ilatum Þem sum brut-	oc forlaatom thöm mothe	wij förlåtom, them oss	wij förlåtom them oss
ike seru wider os. oc	oss bryta. Ok leedh	skyldhoge äro, Och in-	skyldige äro. Och in-
ant os ei ledhæs i fre-	oss eij j frästilse, Wtan	leedh oss icke i frestel-	ledh oss icke i frestelse.
telse. vtan frelsæ os af	frälsa oss aaff ondho.	se, Utan frels oss från	Utan fräls oss ifrån
Þu. Amen.	Amen.	onda, Amen.	ondo. Amen. /

Var redo till att höra, och svara hvad rätt är: ty talet lägger äro in, och talet lägger också kam in, och menniskona fäller hennes egen tunga. Syr. 5: 13, 15.

Fig. 25. Rosander, page 64

Buddha-läran. Denna är en utgrening af Brahmaismen och bekännes uti Kina med alla derunder hörande länder samt Japan. Man har beräknat, att de mennniskor, som bekänna Buddhaismen, uppgå till minst 380 millioner, och då härtill läggas de till 200 millioner beräknade Brahmadyrkande Indierna finner man, att bekännarne af dessa båda grenar af samma grundreligion utgöras af omkring halfva menniskoslägtet, då detta beräknas till 1200 millioner individer.

Ordet *Buddha* betyder "gudomlig menniska" eller "helig man". Tid efter annan hafva uppträdt reformatorer af den gamla Brahmaläran, hvilka deruti åstadkommit förändringar, ungefär såsom Luther, Calvin m. fl. verkade förändringar i sin tids kristendom. De indiska reformatorerna räknas till 22, hvilka alla fått namnet Buddha och tillsammans utbildat denna religion till hvad den sedan blifvit. Om alla berättas något underverk. Den förste Buddha lefde omkring 600 f. Kr.

Han var son af en jungfru, som i en ödemark uti Siam blifvit hafvande af en solstråle; strax efter hans födelse fördes modren af englar till himmelen, och barnet fick sin första föda af en lotus-blomma, ur hvars sköte det sedan af en helig eremit blef taget och uppfostradt under namnet *Gaudama.* Redan vid 12 års ålder började han göra underverk och predika en ny lära, hvilken snart vann anhängare, af hvilka han ansågs för Buddha, hvars namn han äfven fick. Af de öfriga Buddhas äro de namnkunnigaste: *Sakia,* född öster om Ganges vid gränsen af Nepal samt *Fo,* den sista, född i vestra Indien år 20 f. Kr.

Att en religionslära, stiftad af så många personer på olika tider, skall innehålla flere skiljaktiga lärosatser, är naturligt. De sekter, som tillsammans bilda Buddhismen, öfverensstämma dock i följande satser: Brahmanska läran utgör grundvalen för den rätta tron; gudomen utgör en med enheten förenad treenighet, men befattar sig icke med de menskliga tingen och hvarken belönar eller straffar menniskans handlingar; han tillbedes bäst med tys tbetraktelse; lygden är salighetens väg; själen är utgången från gudomen och skall dit återunda; den, som fullkomligt uppfyller sina pligter, kommer genast etter döden till sällhet; men de orena straffas med att då förvandlas till djur. De hufvudsakliga punkter, hvari Buddhismen skiljer sig från Brahmaismen, äro: att Vedas icke anses såsom uppenbarelser, utan såsom en af menniskhand tillkommen förtjenstfull skrift; att kastfördelning-n mellan menniskor icke eger rum, samt att undergudar och halfgudar- endast varit heliga män, sända till menniaklighetens förbättring. De heliga allmänna religionsbuden äro här fem, nemligen: 1) Du skall icke dräpa. 2) Du skall icke stjäla. 3) Du skall icke bedrifva hor. 4) Du skall icke ljuga. 5) Du skall icke dricka starka drycker. Gudstjensten består förnämligast uti att till Buddhas bild, hvarmed hvarje pagod är försedd, frambära blommor och vällukter, under föredrag af fromma sånger och böner samt under instrumenters ljud. Till de fanatiska kroppsplågor och sjelfmord, hvarmed Brahmanerna tro sig förtjena sällheten, finnés hos Buddhisterna intet spår, ty här anses saligheten vinnas genom stilla dygder och försakelser. Religionslärarne befatta sig aldrig med verldsliga bestyr, utan lefva i sina kloster och få icke gifta sig. Uti Tibet och Mongoliet kallas presterna *Lamas,* i Siam *Talapoiner,* i Japan *Bonzer.*

Buddhisternas förnämsta land är Tibet, och den der liggande staden **Lhasa** är för dem detsamma som Rom för katolikerna. Hela denna trakt är uppfyld af kloster och i ett af dem, Putala, nära Lhassa, residerar religionens öfverhufvud, kallad *Dalai-Lama* (Stora Lama), hvilken dyrkas såsom gud och anses odödlig på det sätt, att, då han dör, tros hans ande öfvergå till hans efterträdare, den han sjelf genom testamente utväljer. Han visar sig aldrig ute, utan håller sig jemt innesluten i ett tempel, omgifven af Lamas (prester), hvilka ej allenast tjena honom, utan äfven visa honom gudomlig vördnad. Hit vallfärda menniskor, hoptals, äfven från långt aflägsna länder, för att visa Dalai-Lama vördnad. Uti en annan klosterstad, Lumbo, finnes ännu ett andligt öfverhufvud, kalladt *Bogde-Lama,* hvars alla förhållanden äro desamma som Dalai-Lamas.

Fig. 26. Rosander, page on Buddhism

Buddha samlade omkring sig många lär-
jungar, af hvilka de första voro fattigt
folk: herdar och tiggare. Ananda, Buddhas kusin, var hans käraste lärjunge, hans
Johannes, till hvilken han öfverlemnade
sina esoteriska sanningar. Buddha ansågs
kunna förrätta underverk genom handpå-
läggning, magnetisering o. s. v. Sin första
uppenbarelse fick han, säges det, under ett
bo-träd, hvilket, då det afbildas, brukar
framställas som korsformigt och kallas
"lifsens träd". Under ett dylikt träd af-
led han också vid 73 års ålder, och strax
dessförinnan yttrade han dessa ord: "Alla
sammansatta ting äro förgängliga. *An-*
den är den enda, elementära och ur-
sprungliga enheten, och en hvar af dess
strålar är odödlig, obegränsad och oför-
störbar. Akten eder för materiens illu-
sioner!" AUM!!!

Figs. 27 & 28

Clipping from scrapbook showing word AUM and envelope with
numerical calculation.

såsom skildrande grafskick, hvilka enligt fyndens och sagornas intyg under nu i fråga varande tid voro vanliga. I flere grafvar har man nämligen, vid sidan af brända eller obrända lik, träffat lemningar af hästar, betsel, stigbyglar, selar och dylikt.

410. Skeppsformig stensättning vid Blomsholm i Bohuslän, nära Strömstad.

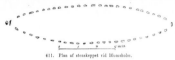

411. Plan af stenskeppet vid Blomsholm.

Liksom under föregående tid restes ofta bautastenar (fig. 407, 409, 413) till den dödes minne, men endast i de fall, då man på stenen ristat den aflidnes namn, har detta bevarats till efterverlden.

De enda skrifttecken, som under denna tid användes i Sverige, voro runor. Väl skilja de sig betydligt från dem, som under jernålderns äldre del voro i bruk, men en sorgfällig granskning har visat, att skilnaden endast beror derpå, att runornas form, och i vissa fall äfven deras betydelse, småningom ändrats. Dessutom hafva några runor fallit ur bruk, hvarigenom de under hednatidens sista århundraden begagnade, numera vanligen så kallade yngre runorna endast äro följande sexton:

ᚠ ᚾ ᚦ ᚬ ᚱ ᚴ : ᚼ ᚾ ᛁ ᛆ ᛋ ᛏ ᛒ ᛘ ᛦ
f u t h o r k h n i a s t b l m -r

Sveriges historia. I.   23

Fig. 29
Montelius, runic
alphabet

Fig. 30
Montelius on runes

Liksom i äldre tid (s. 218) hade hvarje runa äfven nu sitt namn börjande med den bokstaf som runan motsvarar[1]. Endast den sista runan ᛦ gör härifrån på visst sätt ett undantag. Denna runa står nämligen oftast, liksom den äldre runradens ᛦ, i slutet af orden och motsvarar då värt r; men stundom förekommer den äfven inuti ett ord och betecknar då ett vokalljud (vanligen y, sällan e eller æ). Namnet ýr angifver båda dessa betydelser.

Ur den äldre runradens ᛒ (a) uppkom småningom, såsom de ofta förekommande mellanformerna ᚼ (nasalt a) och ᛆ visa, runan ᚬ; i öfverensstämmelse med språkets förändring erhöll detta tecken slutligen betydelsen *å* eller *o* i stället för *a*.

Runorna ᛏ, ᚠ, ᚼ, ᛏ och ᚤ hafva också formerna ᚢ = u, ᛚ = a, ᛁ = s, ᛁ = t och ᛘ = m. Under hednatidens sista del började man att använda de så kallade »stungna runorna» ᛁ = e, ᚵ = g, ᛁ = d, ᚤ = y och ᛒ = p. Ett slags runor, i allmänhet utmärkta deraf att de sakna stafven eller det lodräta strecket, äro kända under namnet helsingerunor, emedan de nästan endast förekomma i Helsingland.

I äldre tid voro runorna ristade i räta rader (s. 218); mot hednatidens slut finner man sådant mera sällan, hvaremot inskriften i de flesta fall följde antingen utmed stenens kant eller de konstmässiga ornslingor, med hvilka i synnerhet Svealands runstenar då så ofta pryddes.

Många runstenar lära oss känna icke endast namnet på dem som läto resa minnesstoden och honom till hvars ära den restes, utan äfven hans namn, som ristade runorna och högg de ofta om ovanlig konstfärdighet och smak vitnande slingorna. Mest bekanta bland dessa äldsta nu kända svenska konstnärer, om vi få begagna detta ord, äro Ypper (riktigare än Ubbe), hvars namn finnes på nära 40 runstenar (fig. 425), Bale, Åsmund Kåresson, Torbjörn Skald, Amunde med flere, hvilka alla hafva verkat i Upland och angränsande trakter.

Ordet »runa» synes egentligen betyda hemlighet, och det betraktades väl äfven länge som en underbar hemlighet, huru man kunde genom dessa enkla streck meddela en annan sina tankar. Detta syntes så underbart, att våra förfäder trodde sig hafva Odin sjelf att tacka för runorna, liksom han äfven lärt menniskorna skaldekonsten. Men då man betraktade runorna på detta sätt, låg det ock nära till hands att tillägga dem en hemlighetsfull trollkraft, hvarför de äfven ofta användes till sådant bruk. Så läsa vi i Eddan, huru in valkyrja lär Sigurd Fafnesbane att, om han vill seger hafva, rista segerrunor å svärdets fäste och dervid två gånger nämna Ty[2]; att rista

[1] Då man ej känner någon svensk uppteckning af dessa namn, anföras de här i den form de hade på Island, hvilken form nära motsvarar den samtidiga svenska; inom parentes meddelas ordets betydelse. ᚠ kallades fé (fä), ᚾ úr (urväder), ᚦ þurs (jätte) eller ᚦ þorn (en torn), ᚬ óss (åsynjung), ᚱ reið (ridt), ᚴ kaun (bäld), ᚼ hagall eller hagl (hagel), ᚾ nauð (nöd), ᛁ íss (is), ᛆ ár (år), ᛋ sól (sol), ᛏ Týr (Ty), ᛒ bjarkan (björkfrukt), ᛚ lögr (lag, vatten), ᛘ maðr (man), ᛦ ýr (pilbåge). — De tre sätters, i hvilka den yngre runraden liksom den äldre indelades, uppkallades efter namnet på den första runan i hvarje ätt; den tredje hette således Tys ätt.

[2] Vid Gilton i sydöstra England har man funnit ett anglosachsiskt svärd, å hvars fäste runor

F. These facts, together with the division of the text into two parts, add up to the probability that the Kensington stone had been tentatively measured and outlined for an inscription of this length at the time the Hedberg sketch was drawn. At the very least, a suitable stone had been selected for the operation.

The release of the Hedberg sketch, under circumstances which have never been clarified, reveals in the present writer's opinion a compound motive on the part of someone. It was a bid for the publicity that the stone had to have if it was to accomplish its hoaxing mission before a wider audience; and simultaneously, it was a calculated attempt to obstruct too easy a solution of the runic mystery. That it did in fact contribute to that end may be seen in the contaminations found in certain other printed versions of the inscription, to be referred to below.

It would be valuable to have Breda's correspondence (to which he refers) with Siverts, cashier of the Kensington State Bank.[16] Of similar value would be Breda's original MS of the transliteration of the runes, or even the original Swedish-Norwegian adaptation—translation would scarcely be the right word—of the inscription which he not unlikely made for his own purposes.[17] The English translation in the file is probably several steps removed from whatever document was originally put before him, and one additional stage removed from the Kensington stone. Nevertheless, the gaps in the translation at the point where the stone makes mention of the skerries is significant, for it corresponds with a similar omission by Holand in a translation made by him for Winchell on August 3, 1908.[18] Both are evidently referrable to a MS that omitted *ved* 'by,' before "*2 skjar.*" Helge Gjessing, too, must have received a variant version of the inscription *along with* the photograph from which his reading was allegedly taken, for there is contamination, *viz., dhene;* cf. Iverslie to Upham some time in the year 1910: "Both Holand and Gjessing are mistaken with regard to this word, for it is not *dhene,* as they have rendered it, but *dheno.*"[19]

On April 25, 1910, A. L. Elmquist wrote to Winchell: "Have we any reason to believe that Mr. Holand's reading (and accordingly his photograph) is the one and only possible one in all cases? . . . I shall go over the photograph with Prof. von

Friesen in case the likeness is true enough to lead to a safe and correct conclusion."[20] No further record of this proposal has been found, except for Flom's letter of January 22, 1911, to Upham, which asserts that von Friesen had expressed condemnation of the stone "to your society."[21]

The sketch printed in *Svenska Amerikanska Posten* on February 28, will here be referred to as the Siverts sketch (Fig. 14).[22] Fourteen lines in length, it is relatively close to the stone, and although it shows minor deviations from the stone, it is, as previously stated, quite believable as a copy of the latter. It has the reading "*ved 2 skjar.*" This suffices to disprove any assumption of its identity with the sketch from which Breda must have worked. Holand's mistaken assertion that the Siverts sketch is on file at the MHS is owing to a mistake made by the MHS in photographing the wrong document.[23]

In *Skandinaven* for February 22, 1899, we find the following statement (translated): "It is assumed that the runes in the copy have been imperfectly copied, so that Professor Curme says that he has several times been compelled to guess at the connection."[24]

The author has not seen the copy and/or photograph supposed to have been made by Professor Curme (?) and sent to Adolf Noreen at Uppsala, nor the text sent to Christiania, where Professor Rygh had some difficulty with it.

Breda later copied Rygh's transliteration and modern Norwegian interpretation from the latter's article in *Morgenbladet* of Oslo; the following is reproduced from Breda as printed in *Symra* in 1910 (line numbers have been supplied by the present writer):[25]

[1.] göter . ok 22 . norrmen . pa . opdagelsefärd fra
     gøter . og 22 nordmaend paa opdagelsefaerd fra
[2.] vinland . of . vest . vi . hade . läger . 2 . sklear . en . dags
     vestre Vinland Vi havde leir 2 slaeder en dags
[3.] rese . norr . from . dene . sten . vi . var . ok . fiske . en
     reise nord fra denne sten Vi var og fiskede en
[4.] dagh . äptir . vi . kom . hem . fan . 5 . man . rohde . af
     dag Efter vi kom hjem fandt vi 5 maend røde av
[5.] blod . ok . ded . AVM . fräelse . af . illge (?) . har . 5
     blod og døde frelse fra Har 5
[6.] mans . ve . havet . at . se . äptir . vore . skip . 14 . dagh
     mand ved havet at se efter vore skib 14 dags-
[7.] rese . from . dene . öh . ahr . 1462 .
     reiser fra denne ø Aar 1462 .

Intimations by Holand that Rygh had made faulty readings
lose their pertinence completely.[26] One notes at once the omission
of *ved* in line 2, above, exactly as in the Hedberg sketch. Note
likewise the spelling *rese* in both line 3 and line 7 (the stone has
rise, the sketch has both *rise* and *rese*); the spelling *dene* in lines
3 and 7 (as in the sketch; the stone has *deno*); *from* in the same
lines (as in the sketch; the stone has *fro, from*). The obvious
omission in the version before Rygh of the critical word *ved* deprived him of any hint of what ᛆᛁᚠᚷᚱ might mean. A rune
for *j* is impossible in anything claiming to come from the fourteenth century; on the other hand, a compound rune (*samstav-
sruna, binderune*) seemed not unlikely in the symbol ᚠ , which is
a combination of the symbols for *l* and *e*. "Incorrectly," but very
accurately indeed, Rygh rendered the word as *sklear*, for which
he proposed a meaning apparently derived from English 'sleighs.'
His belief that the final rune of *illy* stood for *ge* was likewise
reasonable, for in the Hedberg sketch and other sketches mentioned below (including one by Holand) the rune in question
shows but a single dot (as against two dots on the stone) and
hence is distinguished from the rune for *g* only by the tiny cross
bar at the bottom; and the cross bar on an upright stave is in
runic writings—as well as in the quasi-runic Kensington document—the symbol for *e*. Rygh therefore logically treated this as
one more compound rune. Not unnaturally, he failed to translate
the meaningless word.

The fact that Rygh omitted the numeral 8, although he
guessed correctly the figure 6, makes it obvious that the 8 was
unclear, or even missing, in his text. His interpretation of ᛦ as
5 was much more in keeping with genuine runological expectations than the interpretation 10 that we now accept; in runic,
ᚹ stands for 5, whereas 10 appears not as a cipher with a superimposed 1, but as ✝. Rygh's reason for giving the date as 1462
will be clear to anyone who examines, for example, the sketches
printed in the *Chicago Tribune* for February 21, 1899 (Fig. 16),
or that in *Skandinaven* of Chicago for March 10, 1899 (Fig. 17).
The second cipher clearly shows four crossbars.

Rygh's interpretation was thus unquestionably accurate in
terms of the document sent him. In the same two sketches one
observes that an identical rune ⊕, with cross but no umlaut, is

used in the words *rohde* and *blod*, as Rygh chose to normalize them. The only alternative left to Rygh would have been *röhde* and *blöd*. Only his spelling of *norr* parallels that of the stone rather than the spelling *nor* of the Hedberg sketch. The copy sent him undoubtedly contained this telltale deviation.

As usual, Holand has understood the circumstances perfectly, as appears from pages 339–40 of *Explorations* (see page 340), "... one might just as well claim that Rygh's transcription was a draft as much as Ohman's supposed runepaper." Indeed, every bit as much a draft, and every bit as much a hoax, a hoax that not only misled Rygh but which has been utilized by Holand for half a century to confuse opponents of the inscription.

Actually, two variant sketches were printed in *Skandinaven*. The first of these appeared on February 22, 1899 (Fig. 15). Basically identical with a cut published in the *Chicago Tribune* (Fig. 16) the day before, it comprises 15 lines of text. Just as in Rygh's transliteration, the text has no clear symbol for 8 in line 1, merely a plump dot; the symbol for 3 in the last line is defective. The version in the same paper for March 10 (Fig. 17) shows a clear 8. This latter version omits the numerals and a number of the dots found in the first version, but this quasi-independence of the sketch of the previous month was doubtless owing to the newspaper draughtsman or engraver rather than to anyone around Kensington.

Certain key features constitute indisputable proof that the *Tribune* sketch and both the *Skandinaven* sketches are in the Hedberg tradition: *ved* omitted before *2 skjar; nor from; dene* twice for *deno; rese* for *rise; röhde/rohde* with the *h; ve.*

S. N. Hagen points out in *Speculum* that some of the incorrect forms "may be due to careless proofreading in the editorial office of *Symra*. It is also quite probable that Rygh was relying on a poor photograph of the inscription."[27]

Holand claims that Professor Rygh worked from a "print form," very possibly meaning a newspaper reproduction.[28] If so, this was clearly a copy in the Hedberg tradition—with *Skandinaven* influence. There is no further mystery here. The workings of these same alien genes, so to speak, are perceived in yet another sketch, one that cannot be ignored, since it was drawn and published by Hjalmar Holand (Fig. 19).

Mr. Holand acquired the stone in August, 1907. In his immigrant history of the following year he printed a runic text that he could not possibly have copied from the stone.[29] This text exhibits a number of resemblances to the Hedberg sketch and differs at the same time from Holand's own later versions. It has 12 lines of text, of which the first three, the ninth, and the tenth show the same disposition as those of the stone. Its bar sinister is comprised of a number of idiosyncrasies in spelling, some of them shared with other sketches, some unique. It reads *lager*, as do all congeners of the Hedberg sketch but not the sketch itself; *aptir* (both times), like all the sketches; *fraelse*, like all the sketches; *nor fro*, in which *nor* parallels the Hedberg, the *Tribune*, and both *Skandinaven* sketches, and *fro* follows the stone. Following accepted Hedberg tradition, it has *dene* both times; unlike the stone and unlike all sketches, it has *ok* for *og* before *ded* (possibly a mere miswriting). Likewise departing from the stone and all the sketches, Holand mistakenly uses the runic spelling for *skep*, which he however transliterates as *skip*. The familiar *rese* occurs in the last line. Holand's *illẏ* with a single dot is not from the stone but corresponds to all the sketches except the second *Skandinaven* one, which has no dot at all. He transliterates the word as "illy." To sum up: 10 deviations from the Kensington stone, and 4 characteristic deviations from the Hedberg sketch.

In a manuscript of that same year, 1908, Holand translates for Winchell as follows: "AVM. Save from‡Illy‡(the evil-fire)," in which "Illy" shows the crossbar but not the dot.[30] The manuscript sent to Winchell is important for an essential reason: It contains a complete translation of the Kensington inscription, with the significant exception of "by two skerries." All mention of skerries is omitted and the translation reads at that point: "We had camp a day's journey north from this stone."

Holand therefore had had before him while making the translation for Winchell either a text of the inscription which said nothing of skerries, or, and more likely, a text in the Hedberg tradition in which the word *ved* was omitted and ᚠ: ᛋᛂᚨᚷᚱ

consequently made no sense to him. And this once again reminds us of the difficulty that early transliterators and translators of the inscription—Breda, Curme, Kirkeberg—had at this point. It will be recalled also that Curme changed his translation in several respects after the stone itself (presumably the present stone) was sent to him. All these men, and Holand too, were led astray by variant versions of the inscription. In his book of 1908, Holand has nevertheless printed a runic version of the phrase together with a transliteration, "vedh 2 skyar," which ought to mean 'by two clouds,' but which he nevertheless "correctly" renders as though it were *skjar* 'skerries.'[31] Like the stone and the other sketches, Holand's book prints *ve* in line 10; his transliteration of the runes is "*ve(d)*" (his rune for *v* lacks the dot and is hence identical with the *m* of the word previous—an ordinary slip in copying), which is a good Dano-Norwegian word for 'at, by.' But his translation for Winchell shows "by the sea (?)" written in above the line, as an afterthought and questioningly. The text of the (presently known) Kensington stone with *ved* in line 4 and *ve* in line 10, inspires no doubt as to the meaning of the phrase; but the lack of *ved*, followed thereafter by *ve* (line 9), of the Hedberg sketch and its congeners may well have puzzled Holand. One therefore understands the caution of his contemporary letter to Winchell. Holand was confused by conflicting texts.

Further evidence of this results from a renewed comparison of the carved phrase *norr fro* 'north from,' in line 5 (Fig. 1 and endpapers), with the corresponding phrase in the Hedberg "copy" (Fig. 10, line 4), and in Holand's own published version of 1908 (Fig. 19, line 5). The stone has *norr fro;* Hedberg has *nor from;* Holand halves the difference and prints *nor fro.* The *Tribune* sketch and both *Skandinaven* sketches follow the Hedberg spelling of *nor from.* Could it be that the runecarver had planned at one time to carve the word as *nor?* Within the body of the second runic *R* are two chiselled punctures of the stone that permit of a tentative "yes" to that question. (A similar, lone chiselled dot in the first *R* of the same word is perhaps evidence of a minor miscalculation in spacing.) Noting that the word *fro* of this line is spelled *from* in line 12 (Fig. 2), one concludes that a change of intent is registered in line 5: The rune-master added a second *R* (cf. *norrmen* in line 1), and refrained from carving in the *m*, with a firm purpose in mind—that of preserving a fixed number of total characters in the inscription. As the following chapter will show, the number of letters used is not unimportant. The telltale word *nor*, to conclude, helps invest Holand's sketch with authority as having been derived from some early, independent version of the inscription, conceivably antedating the carving of the stone itself.

In 1919, Holand declared the rune for *b*, which he writes Ⴑ , in the word *blod* to be so weathered as to be illegible, and he failed to transliterate it.[32] In later versions he has transliterated the symbol as *b* while retaining the form shown above,[33] whereas others have written ᛒ , as the stone likewise shows. How was Holand able to transliterate and depict the rune as ᛒ in 1908? By 1919 he had substituted *lågir* (with *-ir* and dotted *a*) for the *lager* of 1908. We all make mistakes, and it is no part of the present purpose to ridicule Holand for his errors in copying and transliterating, all the more since many of them may not be *errors* at all.

As the man who has written at greater length on the Kensington stone, and printed more photographs, sketches, and translations in this connection than any other person, living or dead, Hjalmar Holand could perform at least one invaluable service for scholarship. That would be to give a straight, convincing explanation of the sources of his curious runic sketch from 1908.

To sum up: From the very beginning in 1898, there were demonstrably at least two local versions of the Kensington inscription—the one on the stone, and the one put out by Hedberg—and if we place credit in Holand's curious hybrid of 1908, there were at least three. Indeed, an even greater number of handwritten, preliminary versions of the inscription may have flourished in the immediate vicinity of the runesite, variants never made available to responsible investigators. In any case, no one will be found to assert that these competing runic texts date from 1362.

CHAPTER XV

"No Premeditated Ingenuities"

It is odd that our party of strangers who had wandered for many years and through thousands of miles of wilderness, could have known so definitely that they had been to *Vinland*, as stated on the Kensington stone. Vinland was surely a much attenuated geographical concept to Swedes and Norwegians of the fourteenth century. What such a party of men might have carved on a rune stone is a matter of speculation only, but puzzlement has often been expressed that the leader of the presumed expedition, Paul Knutson himself, is not mentioned even on this spurious stone. To this, two answers are here proposed: First, we have no certainty that the modern runecarver was deliberately alluding to an expedition by Paul Knutson. That is purely supposition by Holand and his echoers. Second, even if he was, so specific an identification by name would have detracted from the effect of a document that has more complexity than we have given it credit for. One must reject Holand's assertion that the Kensington inscription shows "no premeditated ingenuities."[1]

The inscription is almost certainly ambiguous in its imports and should not be taken solely as an attempt to rewrite history. Its author wanted to have some fun with the scholars while mystifying them, and in this he succeeded. In giving them disguised clues, he was encouraging them to try to *solve* the mystery posed by the text itself, although in this he largely failed, for on both sides of the Atlantic the inscription has been taken with deadly seriousness by most of its detractors, who unnecessarily impute to the original author of the playful hoax a seriousness equal to that of its adherents. In the present chapter an attempt will be made to show that the Kensington inscription evidences textual ambiguites of several kinds with regard to its vocabulary and its use of numbers. These ambiguities may possibly extend to one or more of the runes in the inscription, in particular the rune for *u* (*ü?*) or *y*. (For a parallel to the Kensington ambiguities, see D. W. Hering's discussion of the Cardiff Giant, below.)

Forty-eight years ago, C. N. Gould wrote: "A Norwegian or Swede, in my opinion more probably the latter, who had an elementary education and a large sense of humor together with considerable skill in handling tools, took it into his head to perpetrate a hoax."[2]

Respecting hoaxes, Daniel W. Hering, author of *Foibles and Fallacies of Science*, writes as follows:

'Hoax—humorous or mischievous deception' (Oxford Dictionary). Hoaxes, often silly and puerile, have sometimes risen to a dignity to command the attention of large classes of educated people, and have been audacious and clever enough to impose upon them. The imposture frequently takes the character of a posthumous work of some recognized genius in art, science, or letters, which has been unearthed in some simple but unexpected manner, and presented by its real author who poses usually as the discoverer. Sometimes it is nothing worse than a practical joke perpetrated with no special reference to pecuniary profit or to injury to the public; in other cases these results are the direct aim of the perpetrator.[3]

Another American writer on the subject is Bram Stoker, author of *Famous Imposters:* "There is a class of imposture which must be kept apart from others of its kind, or at least earmarked in such wise that there can be no confusion of ideas regarding it. This includes all sorts of acts which, though often attended with something of the same result as other efforts to mislead, are yet distinguished from them by intention. They have—whatever may be their results—a jocular and humorous intention. Such performances are called hoaxes."[4]

The classical example of an American hoax is the so-called Cardiff Giant. Quoting from Hering:

On the ninth of October 1869, several workmen employed by a Mr. Newell to dig a well on his farm near the village of Cardiff in Onandaga County, New York State, came upon a large stone or boulder which, on further excavating, proved to be a huge figure of a man, lying on his side and distorted in his limbs as if in pain. . . . Crowds flocked to the place to see it, and tales about it grew marvelously. . . . The stone figure, which had already become widely known as 'The Cardiff Giant,' was taken to New York, Boston, and other places for public exhibition, and discussions and arguments concerning its origin and character rapidly increased in number and acerbity . . . [The exhibition circular] says 'Distinguished men in all departments of science have journeyed from far and near to examine, wonder, and theorize over it . . .' [and] it cunningly implies their approval. It cites the endorsement of the State Geologist, James Hall . . .[5]

But Hall's endorsement, says Hering, was faint; in June, 1878, the hoax was analyzed in *Popular Science Monthly* by Dr. G. A. Stockwell, and again in the *Century Magazine* in October, 1902, by President White of Cornell University. It seems that the figure had been made at Fort Dodge, Iowa, of a great block of gypsum found there, and given its final shape at Chicago by a German stone-carver; that it was " 'then dotted or pitted over with minute pores by means of a leaden mallet faced with steel needles,' " after which it was stained with some preparation to give it the appearance of age, and finally, it was brought to New York and buried in 1868. The Cardiff man exhibits a number of "premeditated ingenuities" (to use Holand's phrase). Again quoting from Hering: "Like the huntsman who aims to hit his quarry if it is a deer and miss if it is a man, the sculptor so wrought this figure as to leave it open to interpretation as a petrified man or as an ancient monumental statue. And precisely this double interpretation was made, dividing the critics into two camps and increasing the interest of the public which, naturally, took sides in this controversy, and thus tacitly accepted the figure itself as unquestionably antique."[6] There is a parallel to this "double interpretation" in Hedberg's pretended identification of the Kensington inscription with "old Greek" (see previous chapter), but there the parallel ends for no one took Hedberg up on this.

James Russell Lowell, had he lived, would have enjoyed the Kensington controversy thoroughly. It was in 1862 that the author of the famous *Biglow Papers* contributed a runological essay which was printed in *The Biglow Papers: Second Series.* The full title of this little masterpiece is: "Speech of Honorable Preserved Doe in Secret Caucus. To the Editors of Atlantic Monthly."[7] Lowell's article was, among other things, a satire on C. C. Rafn and his *Antiqvitates Americanæ.* The ostensible immediate object of his essay on "lithick literature" is a rune stone which he affects to have acquired:

Touching Runick inscriptions, I find that they may be classed under three general heads: 1°. Those which are understood by the Danish Royal Society of Northern Antiquaries, and Professor Rafn, their Secretary; 2°. Those which are comprehensible only by Mr. Rafn; and 3°. Those which neither the Society, Mr. Rafn, nor anybody else can be said in any definite sense to understand, and which accordingly offer peculiar temptations to enucleating sagacity. These last are naturally deemed the most valuable by intelligent antiquaries, and to this class the stone now in my possession fortunately belongs.[8]

After thus anticipating developments of the years 1907 *et seq.*, Lowell, or rather his creature, the Rev. Mr. Wilbur, A. M., proceeds to examine his rune stone, finding to his great joy that it reads the same straight up, on the diagonal, or upside down. The interpretation follows:

HERE
BJARNA[9] GRIMOLFSSON
FIRST DRANK CLOUD-BROTHER
THROUGH CHILD-OF-LAND-AND-WATER:

that is, drew smoke through a reed stem. In other words, we have here a record of the first smoking of the herb *Nicotiana Tabacum* by an European on this continent. The probable results of this discovery are so vast as to baffle conjecture. If it be objected, that the smoking of a pipe would hardly justify the setting up of a memorial stone, I answer, that even now the Moquis Indian, ere he takes his first whiff, bows reverently toward the four quarters of the sky in succession, and that the loftiest monuments have been reared to perpetuate fame, which is the dream of the shadow of smoke. The *Saga*, it will be remembered, leaves this Bjarna to a fate something like that of Sir Humphrey Gilbert, on board a sinking ship in the 'wormy sea,' having generously given up his place in the boat to a certain Icelander. It is doubly pleasant, therefore, to meet with this proof that the brave old man arrived safely in Vinland, and that his declining years were cheered by the respectful attentions of the dusky denizens of our then uninvaded forests.

This bit of native American humor may or may not have been known to the supposed lithographer of Kensington—but it should have been. One is reminded—as was doubtless Lowell himself—of the famous "inscription" on the Runamo rock in the province of Bleking, Sweden, which puzzled scholars for 600 years until the Icelander Finnur Magnussen, speaking for the Danish Academy of Sciences in 1833, and echoing the great Saxo Grammaticus (*ca.* 1150–1220), pronounced it a genuine Old Scandinavian poem in runes on the subject of the Battle of Bråvalla.[10] But three years later the famed Swedish chemist, Jakob Berzelius, discovered that the "runes" were merely natural crevices in the rock; and modern science agrees with him.[11]

Five years after the publication of Lowell's runic humoresque, in 1867, a runic hoax was reported from the vicinity of Washington, D. C. This purported to be a Latin manuscript of the year 1117, assertedly discovered at Skálholt, an ancient seat of learning in Iceland. The manuscript dealt with explorations in Vinland and purported to record the death, at the age of twenty-five, of "Syasy" or "Suasu," daughter of Snorri and granddaughter of Karlsefni, the contemporary of Leif Erikson. And as part of the hoax, a learned Danish antiquary was reported actually to have visited this country and discovered the young lady's burial inscription in "Nevak runes," dated 1051. According to Quaife, the London *Anthropological Review* was induced to term the discovery "a very important contribution to the archaic anthropology of the American continent."[12] Quaife discusses a number of other distinguished American hoaxes as well as romantic assumptions which have often linked the round tower of Newport, Rhode Island—likely enough (in spite of Holand)[13] built about 1675 by Governor Benedict Arnold—with viking exploits of an early age. To a certain extent it was this tower which led Henry Wadsworth Longfellow to write his ballad, "The Skeleton in Armor."

One of the most famous hoaxes of all time involves, not an inscription, but skeletal remains. We refer, of course, to the alleged missing link, the jawbone of Piltdown which fooled or puzzled anthropologists for decades before it was conclusively shown to be a fraud, as described in Professor J. S. Weiner's recent book, *The Piltdown Forgery*.[14] An amateur geologist and archaeologist, Charles Dawson, found in a gravel pit at Barkham Manor, Sussex, England, portions of a skull and jawbone "of a remote ancestral form of man—The Dawn Man of Piltdown ... here was evidence, in a form long predicted, of a creature which could be regarded as a veritable confirmation of evolutionary theory."[15]

Three years later, a second skull of the same type was discovered by Dawson, who meanwhile had discovered at Barkham Manor "the earliest known bone implement,[16] a fossil slab of elephant bone shaped into a club. The Dawn Man was given the name *Eoanthropus dawsoni* and pronounced, along with his implement, to be 500,000 years old, more or less. The scientific world had split into two camps after the first discovery, the more skeptical group considering that while the cranium was that of a human, the jaw was clearly that of an ape. However, officials of the British Museum, and eventually even the great anatomist, Sir Arthur Keith, despite certain reservations, were convinced that the fossil remains were genuine. The foremost French anthropologist, Marcellin Boule, abated from his own skeptical attitude upon learning of the second discovery. The leading American anthropologist, Fairfield Osborn, who had initially stood out against British opinion, as represented by Arthur Smith Woodward, changed his mind completely: "He tells in *Man Rises to Parnassus* how he visited the British Museum after World War I in a mood of the greatest thankfulness that the bombs of the Zeppelins had spared the treasure-house of the Natural History Museum and in particular the priceless Piltdown remains."[17]

But doubt remained. Many anatomists and anthropologists privately wondered about several aspects of the case. The great Keith himself was puzzled by some features of the fossil remains to the end of his days. A dentist pointed out the ape-like arrangement of the teeth, but was ignored. Various contradictions in Dawson's story became apparent. Certain persons in a position to know details of the case not brought to public notice exhibited an unwillingness to talk. In many respects, Dawson's accounts were vague and unsatisfactory. Meanwhile, Dawson had been seen in his laboratory, experimentally staining some bones. As early as 1914, a skeptic discussed "The possibility of the bone having been found and whittled in recent times. . . ."[18] And another writes: "Mr. Dawson was a Coroner, and, therefore, understood the laws of evidence, but no Sussex jury would have been satisfied that the cleverly reconstructed skull consisted of bones belonging to the same being."[19]

Concerning Dawson, who died in 1918, Weiner says: "With all his gifts of drive and imagination . . . Dawson yet showed himself ill fitted for the exacting work of accurate historical research or of well-documented field investigation. There emerges also from our survey the certainty that Dawson was always eager for new and arresting discoveries."[20]

Weiner speaks likewise of Dawson's "anxiety for recognition," and quotes a sentence from a letter by Dawson to Woodward: " 'I gather from Keith's assistant that Keith is rather prickled as to what to make of it all, and I want to secure the priority to which I am entitled.' "[21] However, there is no evidence that Dawson attempted to sell the Piltdown remains or otherwise coin money from his discovery.

Eventually the chickens came home to roost, and in 1953 scholars of Oxford University carried out a complete investigation of the Piltdown remains. This involved chemical and microscopical analysis, in the course of which it was determined that not only had the bones been whittled and artifically stained with iron-suphate, but that a third skull in Dawson's possession at the

time of his death, had adhering to it a matrix of gravel which
"contains, in addition to iron oxide, traces of ammonium sulphate, never known to occur in nature and indicating without
doubt that the staining was produced by the use of iron alum,
which is ferric ammonium sulphate . . . an efficient and recognized method of depositing an iron salt. The artificiality of
the gypsum in the bone is confirmed completely by the virtual
lack of sulphate in the gravels and loam in the river terraces at
Barcombe Mills."[22] Weiner concludes his account with the
following sentence: "The end of Piltdown man is the end of the
most troubled chapter in human palaeontology."[23]

Professor Jansson reminds us that analogously to the situation
at Kensington, tree roots were involved in the famous hoax of
Glozel, which deceived an investigating committee appointed
by the French government.[24] Glozel is a community situated
about twenty kilometers south-east of Vichy, France. Here a
discovery of ancient artifacts was reportedly made by the
farmer, Émile Frodin in 1924. Excavations were undertaken on
the spot in 1925–27 by the amateur archaeologist Dr. A. Morlet,
who discovered alphabetical signs engraved on objects of clay,
which presently were defended by several scholars as genuine
palaeolithic or neolithic objects. It was ultimately determined,
through chemical examination among other things, that an ingenious falsification had been committed. An informative exposition of the controversy has been put forth by Count H.
Beguën, *Quelques reflexions sur Glozel*,[25] to which readers are
referred for want of a treatise on the subject in English.

We noticed that 1862 was the date of Lowell's little Scandinavian hoax. But there may have been more specific reasons
why, in the carving of the Kensington stone, 1362 was chosen
rather than 1361 or 1363. The year 1862 had been more than an
ordinary year in Minnesota history. There was, for example, the
Sioux Indian outbreak and massacre of *1862*.[26] Throughout the
90's, elderly residents of the state were reminiscing on these
events in print. The volume of the *Minnesota Historical Collections* for 1894, for example, contained no fewer than five vivid
accounts of the 1862 uprising, at least two of which had previously appeared in the *St. Paul Pioneer Press*, and four of which

prominently employed the date 1862 in their titles.[27] In the covert language of hoaxsters, 1362 might thus be a sly allusion to the Norway Lake massacre and similar bloodshed of the year 1862. The uprising of 1862 is a topic that Holand discussed at length in his book of 1908, *De Norske Settlementers Historie;* but if the date 1862 has ever had inconvenient associations for him, he has refrained from alluding to them in his otherwise exhaustive investigations of the Kensington problem.[28]

It may or may not be of importance in this connection that precisely the date 1862 occurs in interesting passages in the two books we have previously discussed, Montelius and Rosander, in the former in connection with the rune stone of Rök (see Chapter XII), in the latter at the point where the Sunday Letters of (runic and other) calendars are being discussed.[29] At all events, no longer need a refined and exact knowledge of medieval dating be assumed as a necessary condition of the Kensington fabrication. If this rune stone had to have a date, the year 1362 was as well chosen as any, and if 1362 among other things actually is "cover language" for 1862, it enhances the playful humor, apparently evidenced by apparent mystical linkage of final syllables, discussed below. Both these features would then exemplify the runecarver's predilection—one appropriate to a hoax—for incorporating more than one level of meaning into his materials.

There is, as it happens, an additional feature that points in the same direction. This feature concerns the three letters AVM, which are generally taken to signify, on the Kensington stone as well as elsewhere, *"Ave Maria"* or *"Ave Virgo Maria."*

It seems reasonable to accept the correctness of the *Ave Maria* interpretation, at least at one level of meaning. We are indebted to Holand for telling us about the Norwegian ballad from Telemark, Norway, "Hjælpe os Gud aa Maria Möy, Aa frælsæ oss alle av *illi*"[30] (Help us, Lord and Mary Maid, and deliver us all from evil), the second line of which bears an extraordinary similarity to the *"AVM fräelse af illy"* on the Kensington stone. According to Holand, the ballad was heard and recorded in Minnesota by E. Hagen as early as 1873, and was published there in 1909 and 1911. If it was known as early as 1873, many

Minnesota Telemarkings may have been familiar with it a quarter of a century later when the Kensington stone was announced. Is it merely a coincidence that Olof Ohman's immediate neighbor Nils Flaten—who had lived on his farm since 1884—was from Telemark?[31]

Our interest is in the symbol *A VM*, which one may suspect of more than one meaning. Holand unwittingly supplies a clue: "The fact that the three letters *A VM* are written without any separating marks, whereas all other words in the inscription are separated by double points, indicates strongly that the runemaster did not look upon them as separate words of a salutation, but as the initial letters of the first three syllables of one holy name. . . ."[32] Holand has here chanced upon an important aspect of the mystification, namely the double (or multiple) meaning attaching to *A VM*. There is reason to believe that *A VM* on the Kensington stone stands for the *mantra A UM* (A+U+M), representing the sacred Sanskrit syllable *OM*, a word of power.

Webster's International Dictionary[33] has this to say of *OM*, *s.v.: "interj.* [Skr.] *Hinduism, etc.* Orig., a syllable denoting assent; later, a mantra representing the triple constitution of the cosmos. The three component parts $(a+u+m)$ of the sound are the Absolute, the Relative, and the relation between them." *S.v. mantra:* "Literally, instrument of thought. Specif., Hinduism & *bahayana Buddism*, ideal, inaudible sounds constituting . . . a universal terminology. In popular use, a spell or charm. Also, a ritualistic or devotional formula." Writing on Hindu mythology in 1882, W. J. Wilkins asserts concerning *OM:* "This word occurs at the *commencement of prayers* [italics supplied] and religious ceremonies. It is so sacred that none must hear it pronounced. Originally the three letters (*a u m*) of which it is formed typified the three Vedas."[34] Spence's *Encyclopedia of Occultism* refers to *OM* as "also the name given by the Hindus to the spiritual sun, as opposed to 'Soorvj' the natural sun."[35] An extensive account of *OM* will be found in *The Upanishads* in the translation of F. Max Müller.[36]

The *A UM* theory has been mentioned by others—in the MHS Archive is a clipping on this subject from the *New York Herald* for some time in the year 1911. The clipping belongs to the Dr.

Nissen collection; its author argues that AUM was known to the early Norsemen. He supposes further that AUM is part of Masonic ritual. Freemasons state that this is not so (see below), although they recognize the syllable when it is spoken of.

In the immediate vicinity of the runesite there can be traced a certain interest in ancient Hindu lore. Holvik has called attention to the existence of a home-bound scrapbook of the Ohman homestead, an object nowhere mentioned by the otherwise so diligent Holand. Holvik borrowed the scrapbook in 1938; he sent the Montelius volume and the scrapbook to the MHS for microfilming on Oct. 14, 1949. Ohman's daughter Manda told him that the scrapbook had belonged to Sven Fogelblad. The name "Olof Ohman" is written in the margin of one of the pages. The label of the volume is worn off. The clippings in it date from 1881 to the 1930's (Ohman died in 1935). Many of the clippings seem to come from *Rothuggaren*, also called *The Radical*, published at Litchfield, Kansas, by Frans Widstrand, a Swedish-American journalist of considerable attainments. Several issues of the paper have been examined at random.[37] In June, 1881, *Rothuggaren* claimed to print 4000 copies. The scrapbook contains only one clipping on the Kensington stone, this by Andrew Anderson, pointing out that Sven Fogelblad was not a drunkard, as commonly asserted, and that if he had made the inscription it would have contained no errors. The antecedents of this volume, which certainly ought to be deposited for safekeeping with the Minnesota Historical Society, are unclear; in what way Ohman shared this volume with Sven Fogelblad is also unclear. Fogelblad, however, is the author of five of the clippings preserved in the scrapbook.

On the basis of Holvik's microfilm a digest has been made of significant items and headings covered by various newspaper clippings in the volume. The following attract one's notice: Atlantis (induced by Ignatius Donnelly's book);[38] Immortality; Mme Coué; Magnetic Healing; Prophesies (with mystical figures); Dynamiting Rock; Spiritism; Swedenborgianism; Cradle of Civilization in North America (again, a Donnelly influence); a poem called "En runa" (A Rune); Lost Art and Forgotten Secrets; Ancient Mysteries; Yogi and Ancient Religion;

Buddhism. One clipping contains a paragraph on Buddha which tells how he died under a tree. The paragraph concludes with the mystic syllable "AUM ! ! !" prominently printed in capitals (Fig. 27).

Although not necessarily itself a part of Masonic doctrine, and obviously known to others than Freemasons, the symbol "AUM" is *referred* to in manuals of Freemasonry. To quote from one of them:

It is noticeable that this notion of the sanctity of the Divine Name or Creative Word was common to all the ancient nations. The Sacred Word HOM was supposed by the ancient Persians (who were among the earliest emigrants from Northern India) to be pregnant with a mysterious power; and they taught that by its utterance the world was created. In India it was forbidden to pronounce the word AUM or OM, the Sacred Name of the One Deity, manifested as Brahma, Vishna, and Seeva.[39]

Page 580 of the Rosander volume is devoted to a discussion of Buddhism (Fig. 26); but there were doubtless many other ways by which the syllable *AUM* may have come to the attention of persons given to mystic speculation. The influence of Freemasonry in the community may have contributed something; J. P. Hedberg, who figures in the rune stone mystery, was a Mason, according to his biographical notice.[40] Theosophical influence may likewise have been at work; Ohman had such interests (see Chapter XVI).[41]

At all events, Holvik's discovery of the scrapbook is clearly of major importance to the Kensington investigation. For, recalling that *"AVM"* in the inscription is carved as a single word, without internal colons to separate the three letters, whereas colons are consistently used to separate each lexicographical unit—including *AVM*—from its neighbors on the Kensington stone, one concludes that *AUM* and *AVM* are one and the same. There is no difficulty in equating *V* with *U*. Anyone who has seen the Latin inscriptions carved on American public monuments has observed this for himself. For example, the Latin word *justitia* is carved *IVSTITIA*. The Latin capital letters *I* and *V* stand equally for *i, j* and *u, v*, respectively. The composer and/or inditer of the Kensington message would thus seem to have been

influenced here by the wide-spread notion of the essential unity
of all great religions, in this case, Christianity, Hinduism, and
doubtless also Scandinavian pre-Christian religion.[42]

Hinduism as a popular movement received its start in America
with the appearance at the Columbian Exposition in 1893 of
Swami Vivekananda and the establishment of the Vedantic
Society the following year. The Swami's appearance was attended by wide publicity, and "American ladies and American
reporters, each in their own way, made the handsome oriental
famous."[43]

The wealth of preserved materials is evidence that such themes
as runes, runology, and the early Scandinavian voyages to the
New World had a great attraction for immigrant circles during
the 80's and 90's of the last century, and that these topics were
the stuff of controversy. As judged by the columns of the contemporary Scandinavian-American press, the temper of the age
was controversial to begin with. Anyone possessed of the incli-
nation for a runic hoax would have found the time propitious.
The period was likewise a highly logical time for any potential
hoaxster—a frustrated immigrant, let us say, isolated from the
dominant elements of American culture and not well educated,
but with a speculative and antiquarian bent to have developed
an incentive in the direction of something runic.

Runological hoaxes have not been uncommon in Sweden and
the other Scandinavian countries, and still today they turn up
with great regularity. By 1915, the printed catalogue of Professor
L. F. A. Wimmer's runological collections at Copenhagen included 4 pages of entries for false runes.[44] Erik Moltke and Sven
B. F. Jansson have often referred publicly and privately to false
rune stones encountered by them. For example, of the rune
stones on exhibit at the National Museum, Copenhagen, the so-
called Herløv stone is a late production. Like the Kensington inscription, its inscription was inexpertly compounded of runic
forms of widely differing chronologies. It was found in 1876.[45]
There is an extensive list of entries for false and doubtful runes
in the book of runic bibliographies by the German runologist
Helmut Arntz.[46] Surely the world's most amusing runic hoax,
and the only rune stone carved with a message in modern Eng-

lish, was discovered in 1953 on the property of Dr. Martin Allwood at Mullsjö, Sweden, with much resultant publicity.[47] This
illustrates the continuing nature of public interest in the hoaxing
possibilities of runes.

The Kensington inscription reveals a feature never previously
remarked, which it is difficult to attribute to mere chance, and
that is a certain mystic arrangement of letters. Of the twelve
lines composing the text, the first and second out of every three
reveal a crude effect of harmony; at all events, they end with
similar or identical syllables. Here is the pattern of line endings:

1.	po	7.	röde
2.	fro	8.	AVM (Maria?)
3.	vi	9.	illu (illy?)
4.	en	10.	se
5.	sten	11.	rise
6.	äptir	12.	tvo

The only apparent exception to this "harmony" is the concluding syllable, assuming it to be such, in line 8: *A VM*. This will
be discussed presently. Dividing the text into 4 groups of 3 lines
each, we find the lines ending as follows: 1) *po, fro (vi); 2) en,
sten (äptir); 3) röde, Maria (illu); 4) se, rise (to or två).*

The four sets of "harmonizing" syllables consequently consist
of *po, fro; en, sten; röde, Maria; se, rise,* respectively. The first
two doublets call for no special comment; *se* and *[ri]se* harmonize
to the eye,[48] at least, and serve to amuse, as indeed a hoax should;
the final syllables of *röde* and *Maria* do not at first sight seem to
make a pair. And yet, in keeping with the linguistic mixtures
and variant spellings on the Kensington stone, *Maria* (a purely
hypothetical form, remember: the inscription after all reads
A VM) might just as properly be read *Mariæ (Marie),* in which
case the parallelism would be complete. The forms *Mari, Marie*
are found in modern Norwegian. On page 64 of Rosander, it will
be recalled, Biblical *frælsæ* of A.D. 1300 is equated with the
frälsa of the year 1500; the stone has *fräelse.*

Finally, those who suspect Olof Ohman of having fabricated
the runic document will not be slow to point out that the semantic multiplex *A VM/OM*, for which we have suggested two mean-

ings, may harbor yet a third interpretation: It may serve as a cryptogram for the name Ohman. By substituting for the letter *M* its runic equivalent Ψ, the name of which, *maðr*, means 'man' (in Swedish likewise written *man*), one could indeed reasonably interpret this *OM* as Ohman, to use the American spelling and pronunciation of the name (see Ohman's signature, Fig. 21). In Rosander, page 61, and in Montelius, pages 354 and 355, note, the names and values of the M-rune are clearly indicated; but no specific source need be postulated for so elementary an adaptation. Granting that this identification is logical enough, it is not offered as purported proof that Ohman himself carved the Kensington stone. He may certainly have done so. But the cryptograms as such would be equally valid if some jokester had performed the hoax in order to have fun at Ohman's expense. To be sure, the inscription contains the materials for another, and more obvious, cryptogram, one that without difficulty represents the correct Swedish form of Ohman's name. In line 7 occurs *man;* in line 12 occurs *öh.* Combined in reverse order, they give the original Swedish spelling: *Öhman.* Let us see whether this mystical aspect of the inscription is not strengthened by one further consideration, a numerological one.

We should be little interested in the search for cryptograms and secret numbers as a clue to the secret authorship of a genuine work of literature, particularly one of any bulk and reasonably established antecedents; and there is occasion to add that we have not relied on the elaborate gematric theories of Agrell and Brix.[49] Such devices are, however, singularly appropriate to an inscription already established to be a hoax.

The assignment of numerical values to runes or other letters is a very elementary device, known in the popular games of many lands as well as to secret codes (Donnelly, *The Great Cryptogram*). Furthermore, it was standard practice in Swedish runic calendars down into the nineteenth century, as even Holand has shown us while seeking to establish something different. Let us therefore proceed on the *hypothesis* that the numerals employed in the Kensington inscription were intended by their author to have some special significance. It then strikes attention that the inscription employs even numbers only: 8 Goths, 22 Norwegians,

2 skerries, 10 men slain, 10 men by the sea, 14 days' journey, the year 1362. The only apparent exceptions to this, one day and 'one day's journey,' do not contain a numeral but the word 'one' spelled out, and this 'one' is itself repeated twice to form another even number. Observe also the number of symbols that appear on the stone. For various reasons, most critics have either not considered this aspect, or have stated the figure incorrectly (221, for example).[50] The correct number is *222*, including the extra -*o* on which S. N. Hagen was the first to comment.[51]

The fact that these numbers are all divisible by 2 might be attributed to chance, to be sure. But a closer look seems worthwhile. There is reference to 22 Norwegians. The number of runes borrowed or created for the runemaster's purpose is also exactly 22. The following table shows the transliterated equivalents of the 22 runes as nearly as these can be ascertained in terms of the nineteenth-century (and present-day) Swedish alphabet, the transliterated letters being placed in proper order among the 28 letters of that alphabet:

a	b	(c)	d	e	f	g	h	i	j	k	l	m	n	o
1	2		3	4	5	6	7	8	9	10	11	12	13	14

p	(q)	r	s	t	(u)	v	(x)	y [u?]	(z)	(å)	ä	ö
15		16	17	18		19		20			21	22

If the Kensington rune Ⴘ is actually intended as *y* rather than as *u*, the result will be identical except that *y* will receive the number 19, *v* will be number 20, and *u* will disappear; *ö* will in any case remain as 22. And ö—number 22—is immediately reminiscent of the Swedish family name *Öhman*, as it is properly spelled. In the United States, however, the umlaut disappeared and the spelling ultimately became *Ohman*. Now, the 16-letter *futhork* (runic alphabet) as printed in Rosander, page 61, and Montelius, page 353, very properly has no special symbol for *ö*; it does have one for *o*. To test a chance hypothesis, let us now assign numerical values to the letters of the name Ohman in terms of that *futhork*, here transliterated:

f	u	th	o	r	k	h	n	i	a	s	t	b	l	m	R
1	2	3	4	5	6	7	8	9	10	11	12	13	14	15	16

Irrelevant to the issue is the fact that the numbering devices of *genuine* (where such can be shown to exist) runic secret writings are based on an arrangement of the *futhork* into three separately numbered *ätter* 'families,' thus:[52]

	1						2									
f	*u*	*th*	*o*	*r*	*k*	:	*h*	*n*	*i*	*a*	*s*	:	*t*	*b*	*l*	*m*	*R*
1	2	3	4	5	6		1	2	3	4	5		1	2	3	4	5

Inasmuch as there is very little about the Kensington inscription in general to remind us of *genuine* runic inscriptions, it may be assumed that in this respect as well as all others, it was based on *modern*, bookish conceptions. In the Rosander and Montelius *futhorks*, the letters *o, h, m, a, n* thus are seen to yield, respectively, 4, 7, 15, 10, 8 the sum of which is 44, or twice 22. If Ohman was indeed the runecarver, this might help explain the apparent predilection for the number 22. As a matter of fact, there is a circumstance which sheds special light on this possibility, and that involves the grouping of the runes.

In most printed sources containing runic alphabets of 16 letters, the final group is arranged in the order *t b m l R*. If the Kensington inscription had followed this prevailing system, our calculations would give us the irrelevant sum of 43. But in the two books that have already shed so much valuable light on the Kensington "mystery," namely those by Rosander and Montelius, the order in which the runes are printed is the following: *t b l m R*. This arrangement of the runes raises the position value of *m* from 14 to 15. The sum, therefore, of the position values of the runes for *o h m a n* according to the presentation in Rosander and Montelius is not 43, but 44. A reader not deeply learned in runes, but largely relying on these two books for his knowledge, would clearly consider 44 the "correct" value for these runes. The implication is obvious.

It is unclear why Holand, after stating for so many years that Olof Ohman was "fifty-four" by July 20, 1909, and hence presumably born in 1854 or 1855,[53] has now without explanation switched the date of Ohman's birth to 1859.[54] This latter date may be the correct one, in which case he was about 22 at the time of his immigration, if that took place in 1881, as still asserted by Holand.[55] But if by any chance the figure printed by Holand in 1910, 1932, and 1940 is truthful, the chances are that

Ohman was twice 22 years old when the rune stone was "unveiled" in 1898.[56]

What we have surmised as to the function of the figure 22 on the Kensington stone is in a certain sense parallel to the use of the figure 24 on some genuine rune stones, on which the older runerow of 24 characters, arranged in groups of 8, is often used for secret purposes, as on the Rök stone, which is discussed, one remembers, in Montelius.

The rune for *o* at the beginning of the second line of the Kensington text gives no meaning but is nevertheless included in the count of 222 characters in the carving. In the previous chapter we discussed a rival version of the Kensington inscription, the Hedberg sketch. The Hedberg version differs slightly from the Kensington carving in point of spelling (*i.e.*, the length of several of the words), but was nevertheless clearly intended to have 222 characters, no fewer and no more. In actuality, the Hedberg sketch has only 219 characters, because of the inadvertent omission of the very important word *ved* 'by,' in line 3 (line 4 of the stone).

On the stone, the word for English 'from' (*Sw. från*, Norw. *fra*) is spelled in line 12 as *from* but line 2 as *fro*. The Hedberg sketch has *from* in both positions. Why was the *m* omitted from line 2 of the stone? Perhaps the runecarver felt crowded at this point as he came close to the end of the line; perhaps he felt a playful urge to vary the spelling as part of the hoax. One need not think with Holand that "A forger . . . would not present different spellings for the same word."[57] This imputes too narrow and arbitrary an intention to the forger. Translate "forger" as "hoaxster," and the alleged difficulty vanishes. There is no formula for predicting what a hoaxster will or will not do. The fact remains that there is a correlation between the shortened spelling of *fro* and the otherwise functionless rune for *o* at the beginning of the line. For whether the shortening of *from* was intentional or inadvertent, the addition of the stray *o* compensates for the loss and preserves the total of 222 characters in the inscription. The letter *m* itself was not essential; on the contrary, it is one of the features that very early brought the whole inscription under suspicion. The expendable *m* is therefore replaced at another point by an *o* which is not necessary to the inscription but which keeps the total number of characters from being reduced to 221.

From another point of view, as well, the *o* may be considered a clever touch. Its presence is one more evidence of the amusing ambiguities in which a hoax may abound. The clue to this is supplied by S. N. Hagen, who, while he wholeheartedly defended the Kensington inscription, was the first to assume that -*o* can be interpreted as the remnant of a *þeno* (*deno* 'this'), the balance of the word according to this assumption having been obliterated through some accident to the stone. Taken in connection with everything else that we have learned about the Kensington inscription, however, the *o*, perched on the edge of a defect on the stone (see Fig. 1), is thoroughly in keeping with a hoax intended to mystify laymen and scholars of our day. For that selfsame defect, though it extends downward through the following line 3 of the inscription, does not appear to have removed anything else from the message on the stone (see endpapers).

Professor Flom, back in 1910, commented on the runic "author's preciseness in his numbers."[58] Although Flom did not speculate further, there can be small question that the date "1362" on the stone is humorous for "1862," the year of the Norway Lake Massacre during the great Sioux uprising which has moved Holand to repeated comment; the year of the great comet that impressed the Minnesota humorist and Baconian, Ignatius Donnelly; the year of James Russell Lowell's runic satire; the year that the cryptic rune stone of Rök, Sweden, was removed from the wall of a church. All in all, the use of numbers lends evident stature to the inscription as a product of no little care and thought.

Just as the foregoing was about to be set in type, it was learned through Professor Holvik of the existence of two documents which cast unexpected light on Olof Ohman's dabbling in numerology. Both items were "found among other loose pieces in Ohman's and Fogelblad's scrapbook."[59] The first is a Swedish newspaper article, "Sjutalet" (The Number Seven), from *Svenska Amerikanska Posten*. Dealing with the symbolism of the number seven as well as the arithmetical products of seven obtained through multiplication, it is signed by the contributor "O. T." and dated "Ala[bama], 1934." This was not long before Ohman's death. In a hand believed to be Ohman's, at the foot of the second column of the article, a sum has been performed in order to test a statement in the text that seven times 142857 is 999999, the greatest number containing six figures.

Although not dated, the second item is certainly much earlier. It has been examined in the original and is reproduced as Fig. 28. It is a "Pennysaver Envelope," yellowed with age, and bearing a one cent stamp cancelled at Chicago, Ill. The right-hand fold contains a printed indication to the effect that the envelope was patented on July 10, 1900. The document thus does not ante-date the Kensington inscription, but the numerological interest to which it bears witness may have extended back many years. The envelope is addressed to "Olof Olsman" at Route 1, Box 56, Kensington, Minnesota. The spelling "Olsman" for "Ohman" indicates the misreading of Ohman's signature affixed to a letter or coupon. Clearly, then, the envelope had been sent to Ohman in response to his request for information of some sort—possibly a descriptive brochure. The sender was an organization or publication known as "Nine Seven Seven," with an address—not ɤ77—on La Salle Street in Chicago. Almost certainly, the name possesses some numerological significance. Furthermore, a substantial portion of the face of the envelope has been utilized—in a hand apparently identical with that on the previously described item—for the testing of numbers. A mathematician to whom Holvik showed the envelope expressed the view that the calculations represent a search for "the perfect number."

CHAPTER XVI

Olof Ohman

A favorite assumption of those who favor the rune stone is that no more than a single man could have been concerned with the perpetration of such a hoax, and that if it cannot be established that this man, alone and unaided, composed, carved, and planted the stone without anybody's knowledge, then the Kensington inscription must be accepted as genuine. Presented at various times in various ways, this idea received its classic formulation from Holand in 1956: "It has become an either-or problem; either the inscription was made by Ohman, or it is authentic."[1]

Having stated this, Holand nevertheless proceeds in dead earnest, two pages later, to quote a prominent sculptor's opinion that the Kensington inscription was probably carved by *two* men.[2] By now, one is used to Holand's disregard for consistency. But whether or not the actual physical labor involved was the work of two men or of a single, ambidextrous workman, it is by no means unlikely that several men may have had a hand in preliminary stages of the hoax, at least to the extent of discussing the matter in advance. It is not likely that the hoaxing stone was brought in from distant parts. It was a local product. Surely no one will argue that the potential committer of such a hoax lived in a social and intellectual vacuum.

Just who these discussants may have been it is at present impossible to determine. Nils Flaten cannot be ruled out, and is in fact as likely a suspect as any, everything considered. The itinerant schoolmaster and former preacher, Sven Fogelblad, is generally considered to have been too indolent to have performed any physical work, at least in this connection.

Our chief authority on Fogelblad is Holand, who describes him in part as follows:

Sven Fogelblad was born December 10, 1829, in Sweden. He studied theology and the necessary classical studies that went with it in Upsala. His first public appearance is some time before 1860, when we find him as a curate under Reverend Mr. Rolander in Tomberg parish in West Gothland.

He emigrated to America about 1870. Here he was almost persuaded to re-enter the ministry as pastor of a Swedish congregation at Litchfield. But at the critical time his old enemy, drink, tripped him up.

His first appearance around Kensington was about 1885–90. He is described as a short, thickset man of about seventy years of age [when?], always cheerful and neat. He had no permanent home, but as itinerant schoolmaster used to sojourn for a few weeks at different farmhouses, getting fifty cents a month for each child taught. . . . He was extremely lazy, and was never known to have assisted in the harvest or carried in a pail of water or an armful of wood. . . . In spite of his laziness the farmers were always glad to see him because of his wealth of local news. He knew of births and deaths and other doings far and wide, and was the forerunner of the village newspaper. . . . He had been visiting for a year with a nephew in Scott county when, in 1897, he returned to Kensington to visit friends. On approaching the house of one Andrew Anderson, he suddenly felt ill, whereupon he went in there and died July 12, 1897, after a three days' attack of an unknown malady.[3]

Fogelblad's classical education and his reportorial abilities may have been more important to the genesis of the Kensington inscription than Holand cares to admit. To what extent Fogelblad's ownership—or joint ownership—of the illuminating scrapbook directly links him with the preliminaries to the hoax, can not and need not be determined. According to Holand, he died in 1897, and it is quite likely that the actual carving had not been performed by then. As to J. P. Hedberg, we have already seen that he knew a great deal more about the inscription than he was willing to acknowledge. He had apparently owned the

Montelius volume jointly with Ohman. As a Mason, too, he
would probably have come in contact with the word *A U M*. Not
only this, he was the first one to "publish" the inscription—in a
variant copy. The very circumstances of his involvement, of
course, point the finger of suspicion at Olof Ohman as the prime
mover in this affair.

Whether Ohman or not, the modern runecarver of Kensington, though naïve in respect of formal linguistics, was both
ingenious[4] and a man of humor. The idea of such a runic hoax,
despite all that has been intimated to the contrary by the
Holand school, is by no means beyond the sphere of imagination
of a relatively untutored immigrant. Indeed, such a man, particularly if a deficient knowledge of English and inadequate
opportunities for schooling in his home country had cut him off
from many of the normal cultural contacts, might well have had
a special incentive for "cultural vengeance," so to speak. The
constantly reiterated assertion that there could be no possible
motive behind such a hoax is quite without foundation.[5] The
motives presumably underlying the carving and planting of the
rune stone are no more inexplicable than those leading to any
other hoax, as Chapter XV has illustrated.

All sources are agreed that Olof Ohman was born in the
province of Hälsingland (Forsa parish), Sweden,[6] although the
year of his birth is for some reason a matter of dispute, as noted
in the previous chapter. Ohman states that he immigrated to
Douglas County from Sweden in 1879. As the U. S. Census for
1880 and subsequent periods is not open for public consultation concerning individuals, these details remain in as much
doubt as do the earliest statistics of the Kensington stone itself.
According to Professor Winchell, the farm on which Ohman was
living in 1898 was acquired by him from 1890 to 1898.[7] The
years 1884–86 Ohman spent in Sweden, according to Flom and
Jansson.[8] Somewhere along the line he married, and he had a
number of children.

Ohman was never conspicuous for prosperity. He is usually
described as an honest man incapable of fraud. According to his
daughter, Manda, he had strong Theosophical leanings and
was deeply interested in "things of the East,"[9] a statement cor-

roborated by some of the contents of his scrapbook, including material on Buddha and the syllable *A U M*. We have also noted his possession of two books of which one in particular, the Rosander volume, is closely related to features of the Kensington inscription.

In 1910, when the Minnesota Historical Society was investigating Ohman and the rune stone, it was remarked that hard feelings were evident between Ohman and Holand;[10] this was presumably in connection with Holand's sudden ownership of the stone, which—the accounts vary—cost Holand nothing or next to nothing but which he was trying to sell for a sizable sum. A full account of the negotiations between Ohman and Holand might have cleared up the entire hoax years ago. Although there is small hope of that now, it will be pertinent to quote here from Winchell's field book, now lost, from which he quotes in the MHS Report. Of considerable significance is the following sentence by Winchell: "Mr. Ohman is a rather taciturn man, and he took no pains to counteract the report that he was the imposter."[11]

Bearing in mind that Winchell was favorable to the stone, and drawing from his statement a conclusion quite different from Winchell's own, it is pertinent to note a few additional facts. First, at least down to the time of his interview with Ohman in 1909, as Winchell believed, Ohman had never felt called upon to *deny* authorship of the inscription. Second, there is nowhere any record of Ohman's having claimed that the inscription was a genuine record, or even of having tried to earn money by exhibiting the stone. Third, in announcing the discovery to the public at large, Ohman preferred to act through an intermediary— Hedberg—who in turn made no claim that the runes were genuine (far from that, Hedberg even referred to the inscription as presumably "Greek").[12] Fourth, Ohman had even called E. E. Lobeck's attention to a *whetstone* lying in the immediate vicinity of the runic field and by implication the one used by the rune-carver to sharpen his chisels. And fifth, the first to assert publicly the genuineness of the runic record was Hjalmar Holand in 1908, ten years after the find, as he has repeatedly taken pains to inform us. Olof Ohman was from that time on in an awkward predicament that lasted continuously until the time of his death in 1935. While Ohman was the object of ridicule and suspicion, another man owned—or at least exploited—the rune stone. That other man was instrumental in printing, eleven years after the fact, an affidavit respecting the stone which, if it ever existed, did not at any rate proceed directly from the hand or mouth of Ohman, yet compromised him hopelessly. That other man, though he mobilized public opinion in favor of the runic inscription, represented a school of thought that portrayed Ohman himself as an ignorant rustic. Whatever Ohman's state of knowledge up to this time, it was now too late for him to speak; and if he was in fact the author of the inscription, he could not even enjoy the satisfaction of seeing its true merits appreciated. The situation may have afforded him amusement, but also, one may feel certain, no little bitterness.

Pertinent here is a passage from the "Epilogue" of J. S. Weiner's *The Piltdown Forgery:*

So long as the weight of circumstantial evidence is insufficient to prove beyond all reasonable doubt that it was Dawson himself who set the deception going by "planting" the pieces of brain-case, our verdict as to the authorship must rest on suspicion and not proof. In the circumstances can we withhold from Dawson, the one alternative possibility, remote though it seems, but which we cannot altogether disprove: that he might, after all, have been implicated in a "joke," perhaps not even his own, which went too far? Would it not be fairer to one who cannot speak for himself to let it go at that?[13]

CHAPTER XVII

Conclusion

The chief results of the foregoing investigation will here be presented in synoptic form:

1. The Kensington stone was found in a Scandinavian immigrant community.

2. The style, spelling, grammar, numerals, and contents of the inscription on the stone forbid our thinking it medieval; but they are supremely appropriate to a writing in Minnesota dialect.

3. No reliable evidence has been adduced for believing the stone, thus inscribed, to have been extracted from the roots of a tree.

4. Very few of the assertions on which the antiquity of the inscription are based have borne analysis or scrutiny.

5. Important evidence harmful to such claims has previously been suppressed or ignored.

6. The "investigation" of 1910 was not only lacking in the necessary controls, but was in large measure dominated by private, promotional interests.

7. A superficial acquaintance with runes, sufficiently inexact to explain numerous features of the inscription, prevailed in the immediate vicinity of the runesite.

8. A subliterate familiarity with spoken Swedish of a type to

correspond closely with the colloquialisms of the inscription has been demonstrated in the immediate vicinity of the runesite.

9. Several contemporary Swedish books with contents that can account perfectly for certain unusual features of the carving are found to have been widely distributed in or by 1898 and even to have been owned by the farmer who reported finding the stone.

10. A scrapbook owned and kept by the same person sheds light on the formulation of the inscription.

11. The decades immediately preceding 1898 witnessed lively and even acrimonious public and private discussions of the Vinland voyages and much use in the newspapers of the very words *"Vinland"* and *"opdagelse"* ('discovery') which appear in the inscription. The quadricentennial Columbian Exposition at Chicago in 1892–93 brought these discussions to a focus; they were further highlighted by the actual sailing to America in the spring of 1893 of an exact replica of the famous Viking ship of Gokstad, Norway.

12. That same year witnessed the rise of Hinduism in the United States, a feature that seems connected with the word *AVM* (*AUM*=OM) in the Kensington inscription.

13. Although conclusive proof of this is impossible, the inscription contains a number of features that appear to be humorous devices. These are the cryptic use of numbers, arrangement of final syllables, and the semantic multiplex *AVM*.

14. The inscription was publicized simultaneously in several variant versions of apparently equal age with the carving—versions whose very deviations from the text on the stone are proof of their independent, and hence modern, status. The otherwise exhaustive treatises of Holand have never dealt with these versions.[1]

15. A strict interpretation of the geological opinion delivered on behalf of the Minnesota Historical Society in 1910 by Professor Winchell gives the carving a possible minimum age of fifteen years as of that date; the Ohmans and Flatens had by 1910 resided respectively 20 and 26 years on their farms at Kensington.

16. All available facts indicate that the inscription was carved in the 1890's, and probably in 1898.

The author's pains to discuss at length all the ways in which an uneducated, but intelligent Minnesota resident, a ponderer and a seeker, a man of shrewdness and humor, could have been led to conceive and, with or without accomplices, execute a rune stone hoax, have not been motivated by the urge to single out a perpetrator as such. Frankness of discussion was a condition precedent to a determination of the true genesis and purposes of the Kensington inscription. We assert as solemn opinion that the planting of such a mock runic monument—by a lay person and under such circumstances—was *not in any sense a dishonorable act*. One of the world's truly great runologists, a man of vast experience in matters involving modern runic carvings and the circumstances of their production in Sweden, that homeland of rune stones, has emphasized this:

"[It] did not become a fraud in the true sense," writes Professor Sven B. F. Jansson, "until these quantities of essays and articles were written in order to prove it genuine."[2]

The planting of the Minnesota stone was a clever and understandable hoax with both amusing and tragic consequences, and the Kensington story is an episode in the history of the development of the American frontier. It can be considered ironic that while the Kensington stone's praises are extolled in book after book, the stone itself has until recently languished in uneasy obscurity in a cellar vault. The stone has recently, to be sure, been made available for public inspection. It is high time that this classic hoax be restored to dignity as a permanent exhibit at Alexandria, where visitors from afar will witness, not an ancient runic monument, but a memorial to the pioneer settlers of Douglas County—and to the good sportsmanship of their present-day descendants.[3] We cannot better conclude this volume than by quoting once more the title of George T. Flom's article of many years ago. It reads: "The Kensington Rune Stone: A Modern Inscription from Douglas County, Minnesota."

Notes

CHAPTER I

1 A transliterated text will be found in Chapter XI.

2 For a readable account of the Vinland Voyages, see Einar Haugen, *Voyages to Vinland: The first American saga newly translated and interpreted* (New York, 1942). See Halldór Hermannsson, *The Northmen in America* (Ithaca, New York, 1909); A. M. Reeves, *The Finding of Wineland the Good* (London, 1890). The latest theories on the location of Vinland will be found in Almar Næss, *Hvor lå Vinland? En studie over solobservasjoner i de norrøne sagaer* (Oslo, n.d. [1954]), reviewed by E. Wahlgren in *Swedish Pioneer Historical Quarterly*, VII (1956), 73–75.

3 *National Geographic Magazine*, XCIV (Sept., 1948), 343. An inquiry made of the Smithsonian in 1949 by Professor J. A. Holvik was answered in part as follows on Jan. 28, 1949, by A. Wetmore, secretary of the Smithsonian: "The Smithsonian Institution has been interested in the Kensington Stone because of the definite differences of opinion that exist relative to its authenticity. . . . The archeologists of the Smithsonian have made many examinations of the Kensington Stone with great interest. We have, however, no one of our staff at the present time who is an authority on runic writing. . . . The Institution has not issued any formal statement or belief as to the authenticity of the Kensington Stone. We trust, however, that in due time a convincing conclusion relative to it acceptable to all runic scholars will be forthcoming. Until that time the Institution makes no official pronouncement though our staff members as individuals have their own personal opinions."

4 This is quoted from p. 177 of Arlington H. Mallery, *Lost America: The Story of Iron-Age Civilization Prior to Columbus* (Washington, D. C., 1951).

5 William Thalbitzer, *Two Runic Stones from Greenland and Minnesota*, "Smithsonian Miscellaneous Collections." Vol. 116. Number 3 (Publication 4021, Washington, 1951). This was translated from the Danish of Thalbitzer, "To fjærne runestene fra Grønland og Amerika," *Danske Studier, 43. Bind. Fjerde Række. 7* (København, 1946–47), pp. 1–40. See *Science News Letter*, LX (Sept. 29, 1951), 196; *Science Digest*, XXX (Dec., 1951), 79; *Time*, LVIII (Oct. 8, 1951), 56–60; *Newsweek*, XXXVIII (Oct. 8, 1951), 96 and 98.

6 Much is made of the Smithsonian sponsorship in the Book of the Month Club selection, Paul Herrmann, *Conquest by Man* (New York, 1954), "Part Seven: The Rune Stone of Kensington and the Mystery of the Greenland Vikings," pp. 217–66, especially pp. 217–27. This is a translation of Herrmann's *Sieben vorbei und acht verweht* (Hamburg, 1952), see pp. 255–65.

Herrmann's account is largely fanciful, his inexactness extending even to referring to Mr. Holand as a Swede. The German geographer Richard Hennig states that most European geographers, historians, and ethnologists incline to accept the Kensington stone, see Hennig in *Petermanns Geographische Mitteilungen*, LXXXIV (1938), 88–90, p. 90; cf. LXXXV (1939), 59; see Hennig, *Terrae Incognitae* (Leiden, 1953), Chap. 150, pp. 324–73. Hennig bases his arguments chiefly on Holand, whom he quotes extensively. James Truslow Adams, in Vol. I of his *History of the United States* (New York, 1933), was sufficiently impressed by the Kensington stone's "real claim to authenticity . . . which, however, is only a claim . . ." to reproduce a full page photograph of the stone, see Adams, p. 4 and plate opposite. In 1949, the distinguished Danish archaeologist and director of the National Museum at Copenhagen, Professor Johannes Brøndsted stated in a report to the American press in November, 1949: "After long and close study, I am personally inclined to believe that this famous runic monument is genuine." This is quoted from Holand in *Aarbøger for dansk Oldkyndighed, 1951* (København, 1952), p. 228.

7 See Chapter IV.

8 Holand accepts this attribution, which according to all available evidence was first made by himself. The repeated attacks on the Kensington stone and Holand's unfailing defense has caused a Swedish language newspaper, *Nordstjernan* of New York, to refer to the stone as being like "the boar Särimner: after it has been killed and eaten, it rises up anew in the evening." The quotation is translated from the editorial "Katolikerna anammar Kensingtonstenen" (The Catholics accept the Kensington stone), Dec. 18, 1952; see the story of *Sæhrimner* and the *einherjar* in *Grimnismál* (18), in any edition of the *Poetic Edda*.

Holand has a long list of historians and others who have commented, most of them favorably, upon the Kensington inscription, in *Westward from Vinland* (New York, 1940), pp. 318–34. Concerning his earlier book, *The Kensington Stone* (New York, 1932), Holand wrote in 1936: ". . . nearly all the fifty-odd reviews . . . expressed views favorable to the authenticity of the inscription" (*Minnesota History*, XVII [1936], 166–88, 166). Catholic support for the Kensington stone dates back to a pronouncement made in 1909 by Archbishop John Ireland that added three centuries to the asserted Catholic history of Minnesota; see *Westward*, p. 184; Francis S. Betten, *From Many Centuries: A Collection of Historical Papers* (New York, 1938), pp. 56–62; James Michael Reardon, *The Catholic Church in the Diocese of St. Paul from earliest origin to centennial achievement* (St. Paul, 1952), pp. 3–11. Reardon says (pp. 3 f.): "That inscribed stone, known as the Kensington Rune Stone, but more fittingly described as the Minnesota Rune Stone, is believed to be the oldest native historical document on the continent, if not in the Western Hemisphere, and gives our state a place in the sun peculiarly its own. . . . If it be genuine, and the consensus of competent scholarly opinion points in that direction, it proves beyond reasonable doubt that Christ was in Minnesota more than a century beyond Columbus, that representatives of the Catholic Church, one of whom may have been a priest, were in the state in Pre-Columbian days, and that the first prayer of record on the continent was borne heavenward from the shore of one of its ten thousand lakes."

See further C. S. Peterson, *America's Rune Stone of A. D. 1362 Gains*

Favor (New York, 1946); Olaf Stran[d]wold, *Norse Inscriptions on American Stones, Collected and Deciphered* (Weehauken, N. J., 1948), see pp. 48–51; this work reviewed by the author in *Scandinavian Studies*, XXII (1950), 187 f.; S. N. Hagen, "The Kensington Runic Inscription," *Speculum*, XXV (1950), 321–56; to this see E. Wahlgren, "The Runes of Kensington," *Studies in Honor of Albert Morey Sturtevant* (Lawrence, Kansas, 1952), pp. 57–70.

CHAPTER II

1 Holand, *Kensington*, pp. 1 ff., and *Westward*, pp. 97 ff. See the extended discussion in Chapters V and VI of the present study.

2 See Chapter XIV.

3 Curme's initial optimism regarding the stone and his skepticism after a personal study of it are recorded in the *Chicago Tribune* for Feb. 20, Feb. 23, Feb. 26, and March 1 and March 2, 1899; see the Norwegian language newspaper *Skandinaven*, of Chicago, for Feb. 24, 1899; the date of shipment is here stated (in translation) as "last Thursday," *i.e.*, Feb. 16, 1899. See also the article in *Skandinaven* on Mar. 1, 1899 by E. E. Aaberg, followed by an article on the stone in six paragraphs from which the following is translated: " 'I have studied the date on the stone,' says Professor Curme, 'and the meaning I attribute to it seems to be correct. But that a group of sailors from the 14th century should know the decimal system is contrary to history. Decimals were used in that age, to be sure, but only by a few scholars in southern Europe. This has contributed more than anything else to shake my faith in the original date. In that period Roman numerals were used, and those on the stone are not Roman.' "

4 *Chicago Tribune*, Mar. 2, 1899.

5 *Skandinaven*, Mar. 1, 1899.

6 This text is translated from a Swedish version of the original appearing in *Dagens Nyheter* of Stockholm for May 9, 1911: "Den s.k. runstenen är ett groft bedrägeri, utfördt av en svensk med tillhjälp af en mejsel samt en ringa kännedom om runbokstäfver och engelska."

7 As Holand has repeatedly asserted, "fortunately with the inscribed side down," *Kensington*, p. 3, *Westward*, p. 99, see his *Explorations in America Before Columbus* (New York, 1956), p. 165. Nothing can be found that corroborates this statement. An assumption sometimes made that the rune stone was used as a stepping stone to Ohman's granary was vigorously denied by Mr. John Ohman and Mr. Arthur Ohman during a personal interview on August 11, 1953, see Chapter VI, note 14.

8 *De Norske Settlementers Historie: En oversigt over den norske Indvandring til og Bebyggelse af Amerikas Nordvesten fra Amerikas Opdagelse til Indianerkrigen i Nordvesten* (Ephraim, Wisconsin, 1908). This has been consulted in the third edition of the following year; see pp. 14–21, transliteration on p. 17, photograph on p. 16.

9 See the beginning of Chapter IX.

10 See the following chapter.

11 See Chapter X for a full account. Reardon, *Catholic Church in St. Paul* (p. 9) says: "It is quite generally admitted that the well documented account of the pertinent facts as assembled by the Norwegian Society of Minneapolis, by the Minnesota Historical Society, and by Holand, cannot

be shaken. This has been very troublesome to those who believe the inscription to be a forgery."

CHAPTER III

1 Holand's earliest mention of the stone is in *Skandinaven*, Jan. 17, 1908. We shall here mention: *Harper's Weekly*, Oct. 9, 1909, p. 15, and March 26, 1910, p. 25; *Records of the Past*, IX (1910), 240–45, and X (1911), 260–71; *Journal of American History*, IV (1910), 165–84; *Wisconsin Magazine of History*, III (1919), 153–83; *New England Quarterly*, VIII (1935), 42–62; *Minn. Hist.*, XVII (1936), 166–88; *Michigan History*, XXXI (1947), 417–30; *Aarbøger, 1951*, 227–50; *Wis. Mag. Hist.*, XXXVI (1953), 235–39, 273–76.

2 New York, 1946.

3 New York, 1956. On the Kensington stone see in particular pp. 161–94, 313–50, also "Notes" and "Bibliography." The Kiwanis Club of Alexandria has made a national appeal for funds to place this book in the libraries and schools of the nation.

4 Richard Hennig, *Terrae Incognitae*, III, 372: ". . . und da die Skandinavisten in Nordamerika, nach einer mündlichen Angabe Holands vom August 1950, ihren Widerspruch gegen die Echtheit des Runensteins, im Hinblick auf die überzeugenden Beweise für die gegenteilige Auffassung neuerdings zu 95% schon aufgegeben haben . . ."

5 See Chapter X for a full discussion of the MHS investigation. The volume in question is *Minnesota Historical Society Collections*, XV (St. Paul, 1909–14), 221–86. The volume was issued in 1915, but a separate printing with the date 1910, appeared in 1912, with the pagination, 1–66.

6 *Symra* (Decorah, Iowa), V (1909), 178–89.

7 Holand, *Westward*, 131–32.

8 *Speculum*, XXV (1950), 321–56.

9 *Ibid.*, p. 324. Noreen considered the inscription to be a jumble of Swedish, Danish, and English, composed by an emigrant from Dalarna in Sweden. Hagen quotes this from Noreen's article, "Runinskrifter från nyare tid," *Föreningen Heimdals populär-vetenskapliga tidningsartiklar*, 1906, No. 7, see Noreen, *Spridda studier. Tredje samlingen* (Stockholm, 1913), pp. 48 ff. (not seen by us). Axel Kock also considered the stone a forgery (according to Professor G.T. Flom, on page 125 of his article, see Chapter IV, note 31).

10 See Chapter VIII.

CHAPTER IV

1 See under the index entry "Rune" in *Who Knows—and What among Authorities—Experts—and the Specially Informed* (rev. ed.; Chicago, 1954).

2 See Chapter III, note 6.

3 *Nordisk Familjebok. Konversationslexikon och realencyklopedi. Ny . . . upplaga.* 13 (Stockholm, 1910), *s.v.* Kensington-stenen: "Inskriftens språk är modern dansk-norska, hvarför inskriften måste vara förfalskad."

4 "Norröne runeinnskrifter er ikke påvist i Nord-Amerika." Quoted from p. 113 of M. Olsen, "De norröne Runeinnskrifter," pp. 83–113 of O. von Friesen (ed.), *Nordisk kultur. VI. Runorna* (Stockholm, 1933).

5 *Aschehougs Konversasjons Leksikon. Ny utgave*, IX (Oslo, 1948), *s.v.* Kensington-steinen: "Forskningen har tatt fullstendig avstand fra denne innskriften som må være laget i ny tid."

186

Notes to Pages 20–23

6 See Sven B. F. Jansson, " 'Runstenen' från Kensington i Minnesota," *Nordisk tidskrift för vetenskap, konst och industri utgiven av Letterstedtska föreningen* (1949), pp. 377–405, p. 398, n. 29.

7 *Collectio Runologica Wimmeriana. Fortegnelse over Ludvig Wimmers Runologiske o. a. Samlinger i Det kgl. Bibliotek*, an item in the Royal Library, Copenhagen. On Wimmer's negative views see Erik Moltke, "The Ghost of the Kensington Stone," *Scandinavian Studies*, XXV (1953), 1–14, p. 3. Writing in answer to an inquiry from the Danish librarian, Dr. Axel Anthon Bjørnbo, Wimmer declared that the Kensington stone was "an undoubted fraud" ("et utvivlsomt falsum"). Wimmer's letter of Aug. 23, 1909, is found among Bjørnbo's papers in the Royal Library, Copenhagen; the quotation is from Dr. Carl S. Petersen, "Wimmer og Kensingtonstenen," *Nordisk tidskrift för vetenskap, konst och industri utgiven av Letterstedtska föreningen*, XXVI (Stockholm, 1950), 130 f., p. 131.

8 Jansson in *Nordisk tidskrift* (1949), p. 382, has the preliminary draft of von Friesen's letter. That the latter's negative views were received by the MHS but ignored, appears in Jansson's quotation from a letter to von Friesen from Prof. G. T. Flom of Feb. 2, 1911 (see p. 382 of Jansson in *Nordisk tidskrift* [1949]).

9 *Svensk uppslagsbok: Andra, omarbetade och utvidgade upplagan*, XV (Malmö, 1950), *s.v.* Kensington-stenen: "runsten från början av 1800-talet . . . fantastisk runskrift på modern norska . . . något tvivel om att K. är en förfalskning kan icke föreligga." As late as 1940, Holand considered the inscription Swedish (*Westward*, pp. 289 ff.); but by 1956 he had evidently changed his mind (*Explorations*, p. 7): "Dialectical differences and the fact that Norse seafarers were not trained clerks will sufficiently account for every irregularity in the inscription. Even now there is no single standard of writing the Norwegian language."

10 Moltke, *Scandinavian Studies*, XXV (1953), p. 3; Holand, *Westward*, p. 326.

11 Helmut Arntz, *Handbuch der Runenkunde* (Halle/Saale, 1944).

12 Nielsen's opinions on the language of the inscription comprise pp. 73–88 (and in English summary, pp. 142–45) of J. Brøndsted, "Problemet om nordboer i Nordamerika før Columbus," *Aarbøger, 1950*, pp. 1–152, see p. 86.

13 Moltke in *Scandinavian Studies*, XXV (1953), 3; Wessén stated his opinion to the present writer in 1954.

14 "Kensington-stenen, Amerikas runesten," by Erik Moltke and Harry Andersen, constitutes pp. 37–60 of *Danske Studier* (1949–50), of which Moltke is the author of Part 1, "En alfabethistorisk undersøgelse" (pp. 37–52), and Anderson of Part 2, "En sproglig undersøgelse" (pp. 52–60). See also Moltke's article in *Scandinavian Studies*, XXV (1953), 1–14; Brøndsted in *Aarbøger, 1950*, p. 145 f.

15 See the foregoing note.

16 See note 6, above; Brøndsted in *Aarbøger, 1950*, p. 72.

17 Jansson, in *Nordisk tidskrift* (1949), pp. 393, 400.

18 See Chapter I, note 5.

19 Holand, *Westward*, p. 327. This is Holand's translation from the German of Professor Hennig, to whom Lindroth's letter containing this quotation had been sent on Jan. 11, 1938.

20 *Ibid.*, pp. 319 f.

21 *Ibid.*, pp. 320–21, p. 321.

22 *Ibid.*, p. 331.
23 *Ibid.*, pp. 157 f., p. 296, 298.
24 *Ibid.*, pp. 157 f.
25 Holand, *Kensington*, p. 96; cf. Jansson in *Nordisk tidskrift* (1949), p. 391.
26 Brøndsted in *Aarbøger, 1950*, p. 169, see p. 145.
27 In *Speculum*, XXV (1950), p. 322.
28 E. Wahlgren in *Studies*, pp. 57–70, p. 57.
29 P. 18 of a typewritten manuscript by Professor C. N. Gould, dated Mar. 19, 1910 and found with the Kensington materials in the MHS archives at St. Paul. This article had been solicited by the MHS, see MHS Report as discussed in Chapter X.
30 Curme's letter to Professor Winchell of Mar. 9, 1910 (MHS Archive).
31 G. T. Flom, "The Kensington Rune Stone: A Modern Inscription From Douglas County, Minnesota," *Transactions of the Illinois State Historical Society for the Year 1910* (Springfield, 1912), pp. 105–25; Helge Gjessing, *Symra*, V (1909), 113–26. A translation of this by E. J. Lien is in the archive. Both have been consulted.
32 See Chapter XI.
33 See note 14, above.
34 *J. Am. Hist.*, IV (1910), 177; see Holand, *Westward*, p. 252.
35 Translated from the Norwegian of Holand in *Aarbøger, 1951*, p. 227.
36 *Ibid.* See Hagen in *Speculum*, XXV (1950) pp. 321, 325. See Holand in *Explorations*, pp. 167 f.: "Many scholars, however, refused to accept these [favorable] findings. They based their objection on the fact that the inscription had been rejected by several experts when it was first found, and concluded, therefore, that it must have been forgery. They forgot, or did not know, that that early rejection was clearly based on false premises. The result has been a long controversy on questionable runes and linguistics." See *Explorations*, p. 164.
37 See Moltke in *Scandinavian Studies* (1953), p. 4.
38 Holand in *Minn. Hist.*, XVII (1936), 180.
39 *Kensington*, p. 2, and *Westward*, p. 98.
40 Text of the telegram sent to Editors of *Time* and *Life* on Feb. 4, 1954, was as follows:
    TIME MUST RETRACT UNTRUE ASSERTION THAT I CLAIM TO HAVE POSITIVE PROOF THAT OHMAN CARVED KENSINGTON STONE. STATEMENT GIVEN REPORTER BY ME CONTAINED EXPRESS DISCLAIMER OF MY ABILITY OR INTENT TO SPECIFY PERPETRATORS OF THIS MODERN HOAX. THE REQUIREMENTS OF SCIENCE AND THE DECLARED PURPOSE AND SPIRIT OF MY INVESTIGATION WERE SATISFIED BY A DEMONSTRATION THAT KENSINGTON INSCRIPTION CAN BE COMPLETELY EXPLAINED AS A MODERN FABRICATION. SHALL ADD THAT NOTWITHSTANDING THEIR SUSPICION OHMAN'S SONS WERE COURTEOUS TO ME.
                                                          ERIK WAHLGREN
    The telegram has reference to the article "A Farmer's Fun," printed in *Time* for Feb. 8, 1954. A carefully edited version of the telegram, printed in the Canadian Edition of *Time* for Feb. 22, 1954, begins: "I [DO NOT] CLAIM TO HAVE POSITIVE PROOF THAT [OLOF] OHMAN CARVED KENSINGTON STONE [TIME, FEB. 8], THIS MODERN

HOAX . . ." A slightly fuller version of the telegram is contained in the domestic edition of *Time* for Mar. 29, 1954.

CHAPTER V

1 Holand, *Kensington*, p. 1; *Westward*, p. 97, and *Explorations*, p. 162.
2 Holand, *Kensington*, pp. 34 ff., and *Westward*, pp. 110 ff.
3 *Settlementers Historie*, p. 18.
4 *J. Am. Hist.*, IV (1910), 178.
5 *Kensington*, p. 45, and *Westward*, pp. 119, 120. *Wis. Mag. Hist.* XXXIV (1953), 238; "69 years old," *Explorations*, p. 169.
6 *Danske Studier, 1946–47*, p. 1.
7 "Kensingtonstenen og 'De Lærde,' " *Kvartalskrift utgivet af det Norske Selskab i Amerika, 9de Aargang* (Eau Claire, Wisconsin, July, 1913), pp. 74–82; see p. 74.
8 *Minneapolis Tidende*, Oct. 13, 1911 (consulted in the translation of P. P. Iverslie, MHS Archive). Nissen describes a 14-year old aspen with a diameter of 11 inches. Box 10 of the MHS Archive contains two scrapbooks on the Kensington stone which between them contain 160 pages of clippings; these volumes were donated by Dr. Nissen.
9 Flom, *Transactions*, p. 120.
10 Holand, *Westward*, pp. 115–17.
11 "According to written and signed statement by Samuel Olson the tree tapered so as to have about 18 inches above the base, a diameter of about 6 inches." This is copied from p. 20 of an article, in handwritten form, by P. P. Iverslie, "Present Results of the Discussion about the Kensington Stone," dated Aug. 17, 1912. The MS is in Box 10 of the MHS Archive. The above is cited for convenience from a typed copy by Holvik. Iverslie was a believer in the Kensington stone.
12 "The Kensington Rune Stone. Preliminary Report to the Minnesota Historical Society by its Museum Committee," *Collections of the Minnesota Historical Society*, XV (St. Paul, 1915), 222–24; on this see M. M. Quaife, "The Myth of the Kensington Rune Stone: The Norse Discovery of Minnesota 1362," *NEQ*, VII (1934), 613–45; see pp. 627–33.
13 MHS Report, p. 224, cf. p. 222.
14 *Westward*, pp. 110, 112; *Kensington*, pp. 34, 36.
15 *NEQ*, p. 631, n. 41; cf. Flom, *Transactions*, p. 120.
16 *NEQ*, pp. 630 f.
17 Olson's diagram is reproduced from Fig. 1, p. 245, of the MHS Report.
18 See note 8, above.
19 Letter to Winchell from Cleve W. Van Dyke, dated April 19, 1910; cf. Quaife, p. 631, n. 42. According to the MHS Report, p. 222, the men who accompanied Olson in the digging of April, 1899, were all solicited for written comment in 1910, and of the replies that were received, "all of them [confirmed] the description by Mr. Olson." This seems to confirm Van Dyke's estimate of twelve years for the age of the tree.
20 *Westward*, p. 115, "stunted, sickly tree"; Flom, *Transactions*, p. 105, "stunted."
21 Flom does observe (*Transactions*, p. 120) that when he visited the Ohman farm, Ohman pointed out to him the spot where the poplar had stood, and Flom found that most of the timber standing there was "very young shoots of asp." But Holand, writing in *J. Am. Hist.*, IV (1910), 169, declared

that "the timber on this knoll stood large and luxuriant" [in 1898]. If the trees were "chiefly young trees," as stated by Flom in 1910, how could the timber have "stood large and luxuriant" on the same spot twelve years earlier? E. E. Aaberg, writing in *Skandinaven* for Mar. 1, 1899, declared the knoll in question to have been "treeless" twenty to thirty years previously; "since then a certain number of poplars have grown up there" (translated from the Norwegian). Aaberg's article is cited with approval by Holand in MHS Report, p. 281: "Further account of the discovery, written by a local resident acquainted with its details." It must be remembered that the tree was apparently seen by no one; only a stump and roots were put on display.

22 Depending on whether the original runic find was made in August or November, as variously claimed; see below. Another subject of dispute was the disposition of the roots, that is, whether or not the main root lay over the stone or parallel with its edge as it lay face down under the tree. Ohman's statement differed from the recollection by Sam Olson, as appears from the MHS Report, p. 223: "Mr. Olson . . . thinks the largest root ran over and across the stone, but Mr. Olof Ohman was positive that the largest root ran down into the ground at the edge of the stone, and that a smaller root ran across the upper face of the stone. This smaller root he thought was about three inches in diameter."

23 MHS Report, p. 222, Flom, *Transactions*, pp. 105 f., 120.
24 P. 169.
25 *Kensington*, pp. 34, 36.
26 *Ibid.*, p. 1.
27 *Ibid.*, pp. 292, 294.
28 *Westward*, pp. 97, 110, 112.
29 *Aarbøger, 1951*, p. 229: ". . . bare fem månter etter at steinen ble funnet . . ."
30 *Wis. Mag. Hist.*, XXXIV (1953), 235 ff.
31 Lien's translation of Gjessing's article, Archive.
32 *Records of the Past*, IX (1910), 3–7, p. 3.
33 P. 221.
34 *Transactions*, p. 105.
35 *Symra* (May, 1910), pp. 65–80, p. 70.
36 *NEQ*, VII, 613, n. 1.
37 *NEQ*, VIII (1935), 42–62, p. 62.
38 *Explorations*, p. 167: "After much study in every possible direction, the committee in April, 1910 rendered a unanimous favorable opinion on the authenticity of the inscription." See *Explorations*, p. 326: "The Minnesota Historical Society's Committee, which in 1909–10 thoroughly investigated the circumstances of the discovery of the stone . . ." See MHS Report, p. 221.
39 See note 29, above; MHS Report, p. 222.
40 *Explorations*, p. 162.
41 *Ibid.*, p. 167: "Affidavits from a number of persons were thus obtained," ostensibly by Dr. Hoegh during his "several trips to Kensington and other places." Holand does not mention his own share in the securing of affidavits nor even that he accompanied Hoegh, nor, further, does he explain why Hoegh, afterwards, mentioned only one affidavit in his own written account of the matter.
42 Holand, *Kensington*, p. 34; *Westward*, p. 110.

43 P. 221, cf. Plate III opposite.
44 *J. Am. Hist.*, IV (1910), 169.
45 P. 229.
46 *Explorations*, pp. 169 f.
47 Reconnaissance by Holvik and the author.
48 Information procured from Holvik.
49 *Kensington*, p. 48, see interpretation, p. 47; *Westward*, p. 123, interpretation, p. 122, see his Plate XVII opposite p. 203; see also Fig. 9 of present book.
50 See Figs. 3–6.
51 See note 49.
52 Holand, *Kensington*, p. 35; *Westward*, p. 111.
53 Correspondence in Archive.
54 P. 146, see p. 145.
55 *Chicago Tribune*, Feb. 18, 1899. Holand implied in 1909 that "three men" dug up the stone—who were they? See *Harper's Weekly* for Oct. 9, 1900, p. 15.
56 Archive.
57 Archive. On Hedberg, see Chapter XIV.
58 MHS Report, p. 222.
59 Archive. The MHS Report, p. 222 and note, does not even identify those of the digging party from whom answering letters were received by the MHS.
60 See previous note.
61 MHS Report, p. 224.
62 Jansson in *Nordisk tidskrift* (1949), p. 402, thinks "around 1890"; L. M. Larson suggests the early 1880's (*Minn. Hist.*, XVII [1936], 20–37, p. 36).
63 *Kensington*, p. 35; *Westward*, p. 111.
64 *Kensington*, pp. 1 f.
65 See Chapter XIV, note 1.
66 By the U. S. Census of 1890, all of Douglas County had a population of 14,606, and in 1900, 17,964.
67 MHS Report, p. 222.
68 *Explorations*, p. 162.

CHAPTER VI

1   Pp. 110 f. Cf. Holand, *Kensington*, pp. 34 f.
2   *Westward*, pp. 112 f. Cf. Holand, *Kensington*, pp. 36 f.
3   Pp. 292–95. Referred to in *Westward*, p. 113.
4   Holand, *Kensington*, pp. 294 f.; *Westward*, p. 113, refers to this.
5   *Kensington*, p. 292.
6   Flom stated on the basis of a conversation with Ohman that Ohman spoke Swedish dialect, contaminated somewhat with Norwegian, *Transactions*, p. 120.
7   MHS Report, p. 225; see Van Dyke reference, Chapter V, note 19, above.
8   Reproduced in Jansson, *Nordisk tidskrift* (1949), p. 398.
9   *Kensington*, pp. 39 f.; *Westward*, p. 116.
10 Pp. 103, 110.
11 P. 113; but see Holand, *Explorations*, p. 167.
12 *NEQ*, VIII (1935), 44.
13 *Ibid.*, p. 45.

14 Pp. 178–89; cf. Holand, *Kensington*, p. 8; *Westward*, pp. 103 f.
15 *Westward*, p. 113, n. 3.
16 *NEQ*, VIII (1935), 42–62; see also *Minn. Hist.*, XVII (1936), 166–88; *Mich. Hist.*, XXXI (1947), 417–30.
17 *Aarbøger, 1951*, pp. 227–50; *Wis. Mag. Hist.*, XXXIV (1953), 235–39, 273–76.
18 *Explorations*, pp. 167, 169.
19 Archive.
20 Archive.

CHAPTER VII

1 *Westward*, p. 105. Professor Hennig asseverates that, as contrasted with the uncertainties of linguistics, the results of natural science are "simply unassailable" ("einfach unangreifbar"), *Terrae Incognitae*, III, 350.
2 MHS Report, p. 224.
3 *Ibid.*, p. 234.
4 Adapted from p. 2 of Upham's original handwritten text, preserved in the MHS Archive.
5 MHS Report, p. 225. See Holand, *Explorations*, p. 167, and p. 162, where the stone is called "almost three feet long." In *Kensington*, p. 4, Holand says "thirty-one inches" and "two hundred and two pounds," and this is repeated in *Westward*, p. 100. But Holand's statement of 1910 makes the stone 30 inches long and 230 pounds in weight, *J. Am. Hist.*, IV (1910), 170; see Holand in *Harper's Weekly*, Oct. 9, 1909, p. 15, and *Wis. Mag. Hist.*, III (1919), 153. In a newspaper clipping found in the Archive and apparently dated Dec. 17, 1909, Holand is stated to be describing the stone as being 36 inches in length. The Kensington stone is not a perfect rectangle, but the difference in length as measured on the face along the two long sides is too slight to allow for such a discrepancy. See the following note.
6 *Aarbøger, 1950*, p. 64: "Kensingtonstenen er 0,75 m høj, 0,38 m bred; tykkelsen er foroven 0,14 m, forneden 0,02–0,07 m" (75×38 cm. with a thickness of 14 cm. above and from 2 to 7 cm. at the bottom). Jansson's figure is 78 cm.×40×15, weight over 90 kg., in *Nordisk tidskrift* (1949), p. 379. Gjessing was told 74 cm.×42×16, p. 3 of Lien's translation of Gjessing. Gjessing had not at that time seen the stone, as it was not brought to Norway until 1911.
7 Printed by Holand in *J. Am. Hist.*, IV (1910), plate opposite p. 168. On the letter H carved by Holand see Brøndsted, *Aarbøger, 1950*, p. 67.
8 See note 5, above.
9 *Explorations*, p. 167.
10 MHS Report, p. 234.
11 *Ibid.*, pp. 234 f. Compare with this Holand's assertion about the "weathered appearance" in *Explorations*, pp. 172 f. See also Flom, *Transactions*, p. 107, where he points out that the runes in the calcite area are perfectly clear and distinct; see note 14, below, likewise Figs. 1 and 2.
12 MHS Report, p. 235; cf. Holand, *Westward*, p. 99: ". . . a fair doorstep and a tolerable place to straighten nails and rivet harness straps."
13 MHS Report, p. 235; Flom, *Transactions*, p. 106; Holand, *J. Am. Hist.*, IV (1910), 170 and *Westward*, p. 99; Hennig, *Terrae Incognitae*, III, 334.
14 Oral communication, Aug. 11, 1953. The Ohmans stated that the stone lay

"near the granary," which has subsequently been torn down; upon request they pointed out the approximate former locations of the stone and the granary. They did not seem certain whether the stone lay primarily face up or face down during the years 1899–1907, and this is easily understandable; cf. Holand, *Explorations*, pp. 165 ff.: "As I went from house to house [in 1907] inquiring about past experiences, almost the only thing I heard was the story of this runic stone." One remembers that the stone weighs upwards of 200 pounds and is therefore not easily handled. It therefore seems more than probable that the stone lay face upward a large part of the time. For inasmuch as Ohman, by all accounts (see MHS Report, p. 244), had small interest in the stone after the spring of 1899, it is not to be supposed that he exerted himself gratuitously to replace the stone on its face every time some neighbor or tourist in the interval had finished inspecting the runes.

15 MHS Report, pp. 235 ff.
16 *Ibid.*, p. 236.
17 *Ibid.*
18 *Ibid.*, p. 235. Contrast with Holand's statement, *Explorations*, p. 6, that geological opinion is unanimous as to "fifty to a hundred years."
19 MHS Report, p. 236.
20 *Ibid.*, p. 234.
21 *Ibid.*, p. 248.
22 *Ibid.*, p., 248; see p. 246.
23 *Ibid.*, pp. 254 ff.
24 *Ibid.*, p. 234.
25 A chemical analysis of the iron particles might have determined whether the iron was in fact derived from such a nail, or from the chisels used in carving. It seems strange that a geologist would not have tried to determine this, in view of so obvious an alternative explanation. The extent to which the steel particles from, say, 1898, would have oxidized out by 1909, is impossible to determine.
26 *Aarbøger, 1950.* p. 67.
27 Letter to the author, June 21, 1954.
28 Report to the Modern Language Association of America, Dec. 28, 1953.
29 Gould, Archive, p. 19. See also Holand, *Westward*, p. 160.
30 Quoted from Orlando Ingvoldstad's report of a debate at Oslo between Hægstad and Holand, printed in *Norwegian-American*, Aug. 4, 1911 (Archive).
31 *Kvartalskrift*, p. 77 (translated).
32 *Transactions*, p. 107.
33 *Ibid.*
34 *Chicago Tribune*, Mar. 1, 1899.
35 *Daily Inter Ocean*, Mar. 1, 1899. Curiously, this article describes the stone as "red granite" with a weight of "about 100 pounds." Compare with note 38, below.
36 *J. Am. Hist.*, IV (1910), 179.
37 No. 556 in *Collectio Runologica Wimmeriana.* Steward (1841–1915) had historical interests and became the author of *Lost Maramech and Earliest Chicago* (Chicago, 1903). Steward's letter is incidentally mentioned, but without indication of its contents, in a tiny article by the Danish librarian,

Dr. C. S. Petersen, *Nordisk tidskrift*, XXXVI (1950), p. 131. No photographs are mentioned. (See Chapter IV, note 7.) Steward's investigation of the stone in the fall of 1899 introduces a note of uncertainty into the ordinarily accepted account of the stone's whereabouts during the year 1899. Is it literally true that the stone was returned to Ohman from Evanston in "March" of that year (MHS Report, pp. 225 f.) and that it thereafter remained continuously on his farm until it was acquired by Holand in August, 1907, as stated in Ohman's affidavit (*Kensington*, p. 35; *Westward*, p. 111)?

38 The estimate of 100 pounds is echoed in Thomas R. Henry, "The Riddle of the Kensington Stone," *Saturday Evening Post* (Aug. 21, 1948), pp. 109 f., p. 109. Steward may have meant *kilograms*.

39 Brøndsted, *Aarbøger, 1950*, pp. 64 f.

40 *Explorations*, p. 165.

41 *Ibid.*, p. 176. See Holand, *Westward*, p. 162: "at least two days . . ."

42 Oral communication of December, 1954; see Chapter XV, note 47.

43 Oral communication of June, 1956.

44 *The Dalhousie Review*, XVII (1937), 174–86, p. 180. In *Explorations*, pp. 172–73, Holand redoubles his efforts to establish the age of the inscription through evidence as to its weathering, and in so doing, publishes (p. 173) a report allegedly stemming from Professor Curme that " 'the inscription may well be 600 years old.' " Concerning this report two things must be said. The first is that the dating of this information, May 3, 1899, makes it appear that Curme at that late date favored the authenticity of the stone, whereas in fact Curme had become a skeptic by March of that year (see Chapter II, note 3). The second is that there is no article on the Kensington stone in *Skandinaven* in either of the editions for May 3, 1899 (information supplied by Professor Einar Haugen and Mr. O. M. Hovde, librarian of Luther College, respectively).

CHAPTER VIII

1 MHS Report, p. 235; see Chapter VII, note 18.

2 See Chapter II, note 6.

3 *Kensington*, p. 75, see pp. 78–95; *Westward*, pp. 90 f., 133–50; *Explorations*, pp. 154–60; G. Storm, "Studier over Vinlandsreiserne, Vinlands Geografi og Ethnologi," *Aarbøger for Nordisk Oldkyndighed og Historie (1887), II Række, 2. Bind, 4. Hefte* [Kjøbenhavn, 1888 , pp. 293–72, see pp. 365 f. In *Explorations*, p. 157, Holand refers to the royal document as "a forceful letter." It would be more accurate to call it a vague letter, and Holand himself elsewhere admits its unsatisfactory nature by referring to the manuscript as "a late and distorted copy," *Kensington*, p. 90; *Westward*, p. 145. Contrary to both Storm and Holand, the purpose of "the voyage" appears only by indirection; nor did Storm envision any such expedition to Vinland and beyond, as Holand pretends. There is no evidence that Magnus was in Bergen at this time, so that the letter is actually from Orm, in the former's name; see P. A. Munch, *Det Norske Folks Historie. Anden Hovedavdeling. Unionsperioden* (Christiania, 1862), pp. 633 f., and note 4; see pp. 583 ff.

4 The final chapter of Storm's monograph is titled "Senere Tog til de amerikanske Lande og disses mulige Eftervirkninger" (Later Expeditions to the American Territories and their Possible Effects), pp. 363–72. Storm does

not refer to the fact that no expedition to the New World could have taken place during the year 1355, when all traffic between Bergen and Iceland was suspended owing to incessant Atlantic storms. And Magnus did not rule in Norway after 1355.

5 Storm in *Aarbøger, 1887*, pp. 364 f.

6 *Westward*, p. 92.

7 See note 3, above.

8 Professor Julius E. Olson, writing in *Nordisk Tidende* (Norwegian language newspaper published at Brooklyn) for Aug. 19, 1912, gives detailed information on this, mentioning among other things his own review of Storm's monograph published in *Norden*, of Chicago; Olson further specifies a long editorial published in 1890 or 1891 in *Budskapet*, as well as discussion in *The North* of Minneapolis, a periodical much read by Swedes, Norwegians, and Danes in this country. Olson assumes that the Kensington hoax was committed about 1891. The Paul Knutson voyage from Norway to Greenland is accepted by Helge Gjessing and L. M. Larson, both of them strong opponents of the Kensington stone. Gjessing thinks there could be no connection between a voyage from Scandinavia around 1360 and the assumed Kensington voyage, where "the 8 Swedes in no case would be present" (quoted from E. J. Lien's ms translation of Gjessing's article in *Symra*, V [1909], 113–26). Gjessing's surmise is in keeping with the fact that Magnus relinquished the throne of Norway to his son Haakon in 1355. Larson wrote: "Paul Knutson was sent to Greenland in 1355 . . ." (*Wis. Mag. Hist.*, IV [1921], 384).

9 The separate printing is from *Det Norske geografiske selskabs bårbog*, IV (Kristiania, 1893): "Columbus på Island og vore forfædres opdagelser i det nordvestlige Atlanterhav."

10 *Records of the Past*, X (1911), 262, n. 7.

11 Not mentioned by Holand in his discussion of the reign of Magnus in *Westward*, pp. 134–36. Holand is very cautious here in the use of dates; in other respects, he has unwittingly assembled considerable evidence militating against the likelihood of the expedition he assumes: Magnus' unpopularity in Sweden, the disaffection of the Norwegians, the rebellion of Prince Erik, to whom Magnus "had to give . . . the greater part of his kingdom," etc. Beginning in 1355 Magnus, on top of his troubles in Sweden, relinquished the active government of Norway to his son Haakon, as even Holand tells us: ". . . in 1343 the Royal Council compelled him to abdicate the throne of Norway in favor of his son Haakon, to take effect when the latter reached his majority in 1355" (*Westward*, p. 134). On King Magnus see the section "Folkungadynastiens fall," pp. 332–48 of *Sveriges historia genom tiderna. Redigerad av Harry Maiander. Första delen. Forntiden och medeltiden* (Stockholm, 1947). For an account in English, see A. A. Stomberg, *A History of Sweden* (London, 1932), pp. 155–77; cf. Karen Larsen, *A History of Norway* (Princeton, 1950), pp. 192–96. See Absalon Tarranger, *Norges Historie. Tredje Binds første del Tidsrummet 1319–1442* (Kristiania, 1915), pp. 79–183. Munch, *Historie* p. 584, note 1, points out that Magnus was rarely in Norway, so that his letters and commands were often ignored.

With regard to the Kensington voyage, a critical remark by J[oseph] S[chafer] is highly pertinent: "However, he who would add 'a chapter' to pre-Columbian history of America must expect to be held to the most rigorous methodology in substantiating his premises" (*Wis. Mag. Hist.*,

XV [1932], 382). The Royal Antiquarian of Sweden, Dr. Ingvar Andersson, has pointed out how completely alien the Kensington inscription sounds to all those who are familiar with Swedish and Norwegian history of the fourteenth century, and adds (translated): "As an episode in a real or imagined narrative from the period of colonization and Indian wars it seems more natural." This is quoted from Ingvar Andersson, "Kring Kensington- stenen," *Nordisk tidskrift för vetenskap, konst och industri utgiven av Letter- stedtska föreningen*, XXVI (Stockholm, 1950), 132 f., p. 133. Anderson closes with the comment: "But the discussion will always remain an excel- lent point of departure for a basic seminar exercise in historical or philo- logical criticism."

12 *Terrae Incognitae* III, 324–73.

13 *Ibid.*, p. 349 and n. 1; p. 356; pp. 359 f. How little Hennig grasped of the merits of the discussion appears from his discussion (p. 337) of "der Osloer Runologe Gjessing," whom he conceives as an adherent of the Kensington stone, and his quotation in translation, *via* Holand, of a newspaper article that does not exist (p. 337 and n. 2, referring to *Skandinaven* [Chicago], May 3, 1899).

14 *Terrae Incognitae*, III, 336; see Holand, *Kensington*, p. 58: "While Hagen was generally recognized as the most learned scholar in America in the fields of Old Norse and runic inscriptions . . ." But as Hennig remarks (p. 336), quoting the "Jesuitenpater Prof. Dr. Josef Fischer-Feldkirch:" "contra facta non valent argumenta" (see also *Westward*, p. 321).

15 *Westward*, p. 323.

16 "Die Mehrzahl der europäischen Geographen neigt heute nach meinen Feststellungen dazu, die Echtheit des Runensteines von Kensington anzuer- kennen und die daraus sich gebenden geschichtlichen Folgerungen zu ziehen. Auch bei den Historikern und Ethnologen besteht anscheinend meist die gleiche Bereitschaft." Quoted from p. 90 of *Petermanns Geo- graphische Mitteilungen*, LXXXIV (1938); cf. LXXXV (1939), 59.

17 "Una spedizione siffatta, della quale, oltre a tutto, non si vedrebbe lo scopo, attuata nel modo che lo Holand suppone, potrebbe concepirsi solo se fosse stata preceduta e preparata da una lunga serie di più limitate ma ripe- tute ricognizioni verso l'interno, delle quali non si ha la benchè minima notizia." Quoted from p. 276 of Almagià's article, "Cristoforo Colombo e i viaggi precolombiani in America," *Rendiconti delle Adunanze solenni*. Vol- ume V, fascicolo 6 (Roma, 1951), 263–79.

18 Some of these contradictions are reviewed by M. M. Quaife in "The Ken- sington Myth Once More," *Mich. Hist.*, XXXI (1947), 129–61, pp. 138–42; see pp. 130 ff.

19 *NEQ*, VII (1934), 613–45, pp. 636 f.

20 *Ibid.*, p. 637, n. 54.

21 Eric Sevareid, *Not so Wild a Dream* (New York, 1946), pp. 14–27.

22 *Minn. Hist.*, XVII (1936), 171; *NEQ*, VIII (1935), 55.

23 On Greenland see Kåre Rodahl, *The Ice-Capped Island: Greenland* (London and Glasgow, 1946); *Greenland* (2nd ed.; published by the Royal Danish Ministry for Foreign Affairs, Ringkjøbing [1955]); cf. Jeannette Mirsky, *To the North! The Story of Arctic Exploration from Earliest Times to the Present* (New York, 1934); Knud Rasmussen, *Across Arctic America: Nar- rative of the Fifth Thule Expedition* (New York and London, 1927).

24 *J. Am. Hist.*, IV (1910), 172, n. 8: "Personally, I do not believe that they

made such haste, as I read the inscription to mean 41 instead of 14."

25 See Quaife in *NEQ*, VII (1934), 621 and n. 19; this is ignored in Holand's rebuttal, *NEQ*, VIII (1935), 42–62.
26 *Kensington*, pp. 136 ff.; *Westward*, pp. 189 ff. See also Quaife, *NEQ*, VII (1934), pp. 624 ff.
27 The coast of Hudson Bay at the point from which they presumably started does not ordinarily thaw before July 1. The climate in 1362 was probably not materially different from that now prevailing, although it had doubtless been warmer during the Viking age.
28 *NEQ*, VIII (1935), 60.
29 *Transactions*, p. 121, see p. 120.
30 See also Quaife, *Mich. Hist.*, XXXI (1947), 151 ff.
31 *Westward*, pp. 198 ff., cf. *Explorations*, pp. 177 ff.
32 Oral communication, August, 1953.
33 *Explorations*, pp. 177–94, p. 177.
34 *Ibid.*, see Holand's map of the explorers' route, p. 139.
35 *Explorations*, p. 178.
36 Since completion of the present book we have been able to examine a brief new article by Holand, "Was There a Swedish-Norwegian Expedition in America in the 1360's?", *The Swedish Pioneer Historical Quarterly*, VIII (July, 1957), 93–96. Contributing nothing new to the discussion, Holand wrily concludes: "Perhaps, after all, the inscription will prove to be genuine [!]. If so, it will be hailed as the most remarkable record in early American history. In that case, there will be little honor left for those who opposed it."

Professor William S. Godfrey, in his article, "Vikings in America: Theories and Evidence" (*American Anthropologist*, LVII [1955], 35–43), has removed all support for theories proffered by Holand and others that either the Newport Tower or mooring holes on Cape Cod can be connected with known or unknown Norse voyages. As for Viking weapons, an examination of thirty "Norse halberds" made recently by R. W. Breckenridge of Ames, Iowa, has revealed that all are modern. One is a piece of theatrical equipment and one, probably nineteenth century European; the other twenty-eight are tobacco cutters, manufactured for the American Tobacco Company by the (now defunct) Rogers Iron Company of Springfield, Ohio; Breckenridge in *American Anthropologist*, LVII (1955), 129–31; cf. Godfrey, p. 41.

CHAPTER IX

1 In *Nordisk tidskrift* (1949), p. 393 (translated).
2 Gould, Archive, p. 17.
3 Letter in Archive.
4 Archive.
5 *J. Am. Hist.*, IV (1910), 170.
6 *Explorations*, pp. 165 f.
7 "On the other hand it might be argued—the author is not a lawyer—that his [Sam Olson's] affidavit given under oath should be accepted; while the other unsworn statements [Olson's] should be ignored. In such a case, the whole question becomes resolved, and Mr. Quaife's elaborate argument falls flat." Quoted from Holand, *NEQ*, VIII (1935), 46 f.
8 "Such a slipshod inquiry is hardly of much value in a scientific investiga-

tion," *Minn. Hist.*, XVII (1936), 170; "This is a very careless statement by one who would pose as a defender of historical exactitude," *NEQ*, VIII (1935), 61.

9 Archive. Semasiology (see also semantics) is the science of meanings as contrasted with phonetics, the science of sounds.
10 Archive; cf. MHS Report, pp. 273 f.
11 *Kensington*, p. 113. The brackets are Holand's.
12 *Minn. Hist.*, XVII (1936), 33.
13 *Ibid.*, p. 179.
14 *Westward*, pp. 169 f.
15 P. 228, n. 4. To put it briefly, the letter by Dr. Welin is reproduced in a garbled mixture of Swedish and Norwegian.
16 C. J. Brandt, *Gammeldansk Læsebok* (Kjøbenhavn, 1857), p. 76, see p. 74.
17 *Mich. Hist.*, XXXI (1947), 417.
18 *NEQ*, VIII (1935), 59.
19 *Ibid.*, p. 60.
20 *NEQ*, VII (1934), 638.
21 *Mich. Hist.*, XXXI (1947), 417.
22 Holand, *Explorations*, p. 337.
23 *Ibid.*, p. 338.
24 The Swedish title of the book by C. J. L. Almquist is: *Svensk språklära. Tredje upplagan öfversedd och tillökad med samlingar öfver tio svenska Landskapsdialekter* (Stockholm, 1840). The runic alphabet is depicted on pp. 127–28.
25 See Chapter XIII.
26 Chapters XII and XV.
27 Chapter XV
28 *Explorations*, p. 174 (see above, Chapter IV, note 40).
29 *Speculum*, VIII (1933). 400 ff., p. 403.
30 *Ibid.*, p. 404.
31 *Ibid.*
32 *Ibid.*, p. 407.
33 *Ibid.*
34 *Canadian Historical Review*, XX (1939), 14.
35 Letter from O. M. Hovde, Feb. 1, 1957; Holand, *Explorations*, p. 173 and n. 45a.
36 *Minn. Hist.*, XVII (1936), 186.
37 *J. Am. Hist.*, IV (1910), 172, n. 8.
38 *Explorations*, p. 330.
39 *Ibid.*, p. 331.
40 *Ibid.*, p. 176, apparently a quotation from the *Minneapolis Star*.
41 *Explorations*, p. 335.
42 *Ibid.*, p. 331.
43 *Ibid.*, p. 335.
44 *Ibid.*, p. 334.
45 Axel Kock, *Svensk ljudhistoria. Andra delen* (Lund, 1909–11), pp. 1–3, pp. 2 f., see pp. 23–25.
46 *Ibid.*, p. 2.
47 *Nordisk Kultur*, XXVIII (*Palaeografi. A. Danmark og Sverige*), (Stockholm, n.d. [1943]), pp. 82–134.

48 Kristian Kaalund, *Palaeografisk Atlas* (København, 1903).
49 Kaalund's book of 1907 has the additional title: *Ny Serie*. Both portions of the following statement by Holand (*Westward*, p. 168) are false: "It appears on a wax tablet from Sogn, thus Ö. The double dots on the tablet are recognized by Kristian Kaalund, the editor . . ." The wax tablet as reproduced by Kaalund (in the work of 1907) is so pockmarked that one could say that it consists chiefly of umlauts! And Kaalund transliterates the vowel of which Holand is speaking, not by ö, but by ȯ.
50 *Nordisk Familjebok*, XII, cols. 1123 f., col 1123.
51 *Explorations*, p. 332.
52 *Ibid.*
53 *Kensington*, p. 96.
54 *Explorations*, p. 168
55 *Ibid.*, p. 164.
56 *Ibid.*, p. 176.
57 *Ibid.*, p. 165.
58 Mr. Ralph S. Thornton, on Aug. 10, 1953.
59 *Records of the Past*, IX (1910), iii.
60 Archive.
61 Archive.
62 *Records of the Past*, X (1911), 264.
63 *Ibid.*, p. 262.
64 Archive.
65 Documents in the Archive.
66 *NEQ*, VII (1934), 615, n. 5. Flom, *Transactions* (p. 119), heard "$7.50" and "$10.00." Holvik was told by Ohman's daughter Manda that the family had never received anything for the stone.
67 These persons also financed the publishing of *The Kensington Stone*, according to Quaife, *NEQ*, VII (1934). The persons in question were: C. V. Anderson, C. O. Franzen, Mrs. C. J. Gunderson, Dr. A. D. Haskell, G. A. Kortsch, Constant Larson, Phil Noonan, J. O. Shulind, T. A. Syvrud, and J. A. Wedum.

CHAPTER X

1 Flom, *Transactions*, p. 105, n. 1.
2 *Ibid.*, p. 124.
3 *Ibid.;* Jansson in *Nordisk tidskrift* (1949), p. 383.
4 Jansson in *Nordisk tidskrift* (1949), p. 383.
5 *Collections of the Minnesota Historical Society*, XV (St. Paul, 1915), 221–86. The separate printing (with misprint noted) issued in 1910, is identical except for pagination and absence of "Note Added for this Volume XV," p. 286.
6 Pp. 281–86.
7 P. 256. Cf. a statement made recently by J. M. Reardon regarding the MHS investigating committee: "All were recognized scholars capable of judging the value and force of linguistic arguments and weighing judicially the evidence adduced. In their investigation they had the help of American and European experts in runology and Scandinavian literature." Quoted from *Catholic Church in St. Paul*, pp. 3–11, p. 7. Reardon is not mentioned by Holand, *Explorations*.
8 Archive.

9 MHS Report, pp. 266 f.
10 *Ibid.*, p. 268.
11 *Ibid.*
12 *Ibid.*, p. 268 f.
13 One finds no reference to this in Holand's books.
14 Archive.
15 Archive.
16 Archive.
17 Archive.
18 Archive.
19 This is indicated by a comment written on an envelope found in the archive together with copies of an English translation of a Norwegian article on the Kensington stone by J. J. Skørdalsvold in *Kvartalskrift* (see Chapter V, note 7): "A very important discussion favoring the authenticity of the Rune Stone,—this translation being received by Professor Winchell in late November, 1913,—less than half a year before he died. I have much faith in the Rune Stone. W. W., Sept. 25, 1915."
20 Archive.
21 Archive.
22 Archive.
23 Archive.
24 Archive.
25 *Kvartalskrift*, pp. 74–82, p. 78: "Det synes lidt underligt at Øhman ikke fortalte dette til Holand eller Komitteen." We are not required to believe, however, that Ohman did *not* report the whetstone to both Holand and "the Committee." They may have simply regarded the whetstone as unimportant, inasmuch as its presence did not prove the antiquity of the rune stone.
26 Exchange of letters in the fall of 1949 between Holvik and Dr. Harold Cater of the MHS, followed by an inconclusive personal interview between them in St. Paul.

CHAPTER XI

1 As late as 1956, Holand was still repeating this, see *Explorations*, p. 324: "The fact is that all these meticulous examinations of the inscription have failed to produce any evidence that it could not have been written in the 14th century." And again: "Even the most persistent critics are now becoming aware of the futility of their criticisms and admit that they have not yet proven their claim" (*ibid.*). These claims have been echoed *ad infinitum* in the public press.
2 For general reference, see Adolf Noreen, *Altschwedische Grammatik* (Halle, 1904). There is no way of predicting the exact spelling of the inscription. Readers should further bear in mind that the reconstructed message in B represents an assumed transcription; the exact form of the runes that would have to be assumed constitutes another and different problem.
3 The Danish version is adapted from Brøndsted, *Aarbøger, 1950*, p. 68. In Norwegian, that is, the standard Dano-Norwegian literary language prevailing in Norway during the 19th century, the message would have approximately the same aspect.
4 Flom, *Transactions*, p. 120. In view of the efforts made to explain the

jumbled forms of the inscription as the result of a mixed party of Swedes and Norwegians (Holand, *Explorations*, p. 326, for example), it is pertinent to quote a sentence from Francis W. Kelsey's account of certain archaeological forgeries that turned up in Michigan beginning in 1891: "The jumble of ancient Oriental writing was explained as due to the composite character of a colony, comprising Egyptians and Phoenicians, as well as Assyrians, which in a remote period found its way from the drainage area of the Euphrates and Tigris across the seas, up the St. Lawrence and the Lakes to Michigan" (*American Anthropologist: New Series* X [1908]), 48–59, p. 53.

5   See Chapter VIII.

6   Adapted from the transliteration and German translation in Noreen, *Altschwedische Grammatik*, p. 494 (No. 22). This is a stone of the eleventh century from Rösås, province of Småland, Sweden.

7   This is the so-called Kingiktorsoak inscription from about 1328–33. Kingiktorsoak (an Eskimo name) is an island north of Upernavik, Greenland, in latitude 72° 58′ north. The island was doubtless used by the Scandinavian Greenlanders as a sealing station throughout much of the period of four centuries that Scandinavian speech and culture were maintained in Greenland beginning with Erik the Red in 982. The translation is adapted from E. V. Gordon, *Introduction to Old Norse* (Oxford, 1927), p. 166; see Gordon's discussion of runic inscriptions, *ibid.*, pp. 160–72. For a brief discussion of runes in English see Haakon Shetelig and Hjalmar Falk, *Scandinavian Archaeology* (Oxford, 1937), pp. 212–29, cf. 242–46. A German discussion of Swedish runic inscriptions will be found in Noreen, *Altschwedische Grammatik*, pp. 481–502. For more extensive treatises see Helmut Arntz, *Handbuch der Runenkunde*, as well as the latter's *Bibliographie der Runenkunde* (Leipzig, 1937); Otto von Friesen (ed.), *Nordisk kultur. VI. Runorna.* A popular discussion in Swedish is Erik Brate, *Sveriges runinskrifter (Natur och Kultur. 11) Andra upplagan* (Stockholm, 1928). An alphabetical "encyclopedia" of runology is found in columns 767–1094 of Lis Jacobsen and Erik Moltke, *Danmarks Runeindskrifter. Text* (København, 1942).

8   Of all linguists dealing with the Kensington problem whose writings have come to our attention, Jansson is the only one who has made perceptive comment on this methodological consideration; Jansson in *Nordisk tidskrift* (1949), p. 392: "Gentemot detta *konsekventa* bruk kunna givetvis enstaka singularisformer i den fornnordiska litteraturen icke anföras."

9   *The Swedish Pioneer Historical Quarterly*, VIII (1957), 25–31, p. 30.

10   Dative neuter singular and plural, respectively. On these forms see Andersen, *Danske Studier* (1949–50), pp. 55 f.

11   Dative singular masculine.

12   Dative singular feminine.

13   Translated from Jansson in *Nordisk tidskrift* (1949), pp. 394 f.

14   See K. M. Nielsen, *Aarbøger, 1950*, p. 81; Jansson in *Nordisk tidskrift* (1949), p. 395; Andersen, *Danske Studier* (1949–50), p. 56.

15   Jansson in *Nordisk tidskrift* (1949), pp. 395 f.; Nielsen, *Aarbøger, 1950*, p. 81; Andersen, *Danske Studier* (1949–50), p. 56.

16   Jansson in *Nordisk tidskrift* (1949), pp. 395 f.; Wahlgren in *Studies*, p. 62.

17   See K. F. Söderwall, *Ordbok öfver svenska medeltidsspråket* (Lund, 1884–86), *s.v.;* see also *Ordbok över svenska språket utgifven af Svenska Akademien* (Lund, 1898——), *s.v.*

18 Cf. Cleasby-Vigfússon, *An Icelandic-English Dictionary* (Oxford, 1874) and other Icelandic dictionaries.

19 The best discussion of this problem in any language will be found in the article published by E. Moltke. See Chapter IV, note 7.

20 *Ibid.* See Chapter IX, notes 50 and 51.

21 *Kensington*, pp. 120 f., cf p. 121: "Kassticka 1790." This is repeated in Holand, *Westward*, pp. 174 f.

22 Is it unreasonable to suppose that they would prefer, likewise not to remain anonymous in their plight? Notice the overwhelming extent to which genuine runic inscriptions deal in personal names. But although the Kensington stone is one of the longest inscriptions known (222 characters and 65 pairs of separating dots—not 62 as stated by Holand, *Kensington*, p. 6, and *Westward*, p. 100), not one name (AVM is a special problem) appears on it, whereas the much shorter Greenlandic stone from Kingiktorsoak with which Holand and Thalbitzer so eagerly compare it has three personal names.

23 Gjessing points this out in *Symra* (1909), 113–26, cited from Lien's translation in the MHS Archive; see p. 7 of Lien's manuscript. Holand states that Gjessing "was able to show that these numerals [those on the stone] were not an invention of the runic scribe, but were in perfect accord with runic numerals used in the Middle Ages" (*Westward*, p. 177). Holand also pretends that this "discovery" was made by Gjessing in "1909—eleven years after the stone was found—." The fact is that Gjessing cites as authority for this, a work by P. A. Munch, edited in 1848, as Holand himself acknowledges a mere five pages later (p. 182): "We have an excellent record of the early use of the decimal system with Arabic numerals in the North in a manuscript entitled *Algorismus*—a treatise on numbers—preserved to us in *Hauksbok*, a Norse manuscript of about 1320." Thereafter Holand adds in part: "P. A. Munch, who has given us a complete translation of the treatise, adds: 'After Hauk Erlendsson's time, in the beginning of the fourteenth century, the Arabic numerals are frequently found in Norwegian and Icelandic codexes, partly as chapter numbers in the margin, partly also as dates and sums.'" In a note (8) to this, Holand states: "The translation is given in *Annaler for Nordisk Oldkyndighed*, 1848, pp. 353–375. See also Gjessing in *Symra* . . . , V, 117, 118." Checking on Gjessing's exact statement we find his objection: ". . . but we should then expect to find the arabic number characters as well, instead of characters which have no similarity to the arabic [Lien translation, p. 8]." And this is the crux of the entire matter. Holand's account of Gjessing's attitude could not be more thoroughly misstated.

24 Brate, in *Sveriges runinskrifter* (1928), pp. 90 ff., gives several examples of self-dated runic objects from Sweden. The first of these is interesting for a number of reasons, but we shall at this point consider merely the date. Brate's transliteration and translation (translated) are as follows: " $-|-$ þa : iaik : uar : gør : þa : uar : þushundraþ : tu hundraþ : tiuhu : uintr : ok : atta : fra : byrþ : gus : a $+$ g $+$ l $+$ a | : aue maria : gracia : plena : | : dionisius : siþ benediktus : ✠ . When I was made it was 1228 winters from God's birth . a . g . l . a ✠ Be greeted, Maria, full of grace! Dionysius be blessed!" The cryptic letters are the initial letters of the Hebrew sentence : *atta gibbor leolam adonai*, 'Thou art strong forever, Lord!' Although Brate takes the short cut of employing Arabic numerals in rendering the date, note that the inscription writes them out: 'thousand two

hundred twenty winters and eight.' This inscription is found on the Church bell of Saleby, West Gothland, Sweden (Fig. 17 in *ibid.*).

Brate goes on to state that the oldest dated rune stone on the island of Gotland is the one at Vallstena, which has the date 1326 carved in Latin on one edge. He next mentions a Gotland inscription from Lye, which deals with historical occurrences of the year 1449 and dates itself as follows (*ibid.*, p. 94): "þa . uar . liþit . af . guz . byrþ . fiurtan . huntraþ . ar . ok . ainu . ari . minna . þen . fem . tigi . ar. Then had passed since God's birth 1400 years and one year less than 50 years." But again, the inscription has written the words out. Another rune stone from Lye, dealing with private persons is dated in almost exactly the same way, with the exception that the numeral 50 is rendered not as *fem . tigi* but as *V . tihi* (*ibid.*, p. 95). This stone likewise has a mention of Golden numbers.

25 *Westward*, pp. 181–83.
26 *Westward*, pp. 179 f.
27 *Ibid.*, p. 333.
28 For further study of this subject the reader is referred to the treatments and extensive bibliographies regarding calendars to be found in Vol. XXI of the series *Nordisk Kultur* (Stockholm, 1934), especially pp. 77–94 (Nils Lithberg, "Kalendariska hjälpmedel").
29 MHS Report, p. 242.
30 Even so careful a scholar as Stefán Einarsson has been deceived on this point: "Especially striking are the similarities between the numerals on the Kensington Stone and those given by Ole Worm in his *Fasti Danici* (1643), which hardly could have been at the disposal of a modern forger in the pioneer days of the Middle West." This is quoted from *Speculum*, VIII (1933), 403.
31 A history of Sweden by Professor Oskar Montelius, discussed in the following chapter. Professor Holvik had this examined under ultra-violet light at the Minnesota Science Museum; he reports the marginal possibility that the symbol can be explained as a freak figure in the fabric.
32 Holbrook in *Minn. Hist.*, XXXIII (1952–53), 45–52, p. 47. Urging that someone write a great novel about the Kensington stone, Holbrook remarks that "it is as impossible to prove the Kensington rune stone a hoax as it is to prove it genuine. . . . This leaves the novelist wholly free to set his imagination to work." At least one novel about the Kensington stone had already been written; this is Elizabeth Coatsworth, *Door to the North: A Saga of Fourteenth Century America* (Philadelphia, 1950).
33 Holand in *Wis. Mag. Hist.*, XXXIV (1953), 237. Even Quaife has been persuaded as to this: "The stone was found in 1898 by a dull-witted, almost wholly uneducated farmer." Quoted from *NEQ*, VII (1934), 627.
34 *Harper's Weekly*, Mar. 26, 1910, p. 25.
35 In *Explorations*, p. 7, Holand prints a noteworthy statement on runology: "The larger number of published philological opinions [by whom?] supports the authenticity of the stone, but a persistent (though notably back-tracking) minority continues to denounce it as a modern forgery. The center of controversy here lies in the fact that the inscription does not agree on all counts with textbook theory of runology. This fact will be discussed in detail, but here it must be borne in mind that the textbooks are based on what scholars have been able to piece together from medieval records, and

that those records were primarily legal documents couched in antiquated formulas while the spoken language must obviously have been changing out from under them." Only in the mind of Mr. Holand does runology have anything to do with either textbooks, manuscripts, or the spoken language. As Mr. Holand should be informed, runologists base their science directly upon the observation of runic carvings in stone or other materials. In the occasional instances when runic messages are found on parchment, these are treated like any other runic inscription. And as for the spoken language upon which Holand erects a mighty edifice of supposition, Professor Assar Janzén's recent review has dealt this absurd theory the cruelest blow of all; see note 9, above.

CHAPTER XII

1 Consulted by us in the third edition of 1883. The book contains a 44-page bibliography of "Pre-Columbian Discoveries of America" by Paul Barron Watson, together with numerous references to Vinland, Greenland, etc.

2 *Aarbøger, 1887*, pp. 293–372.

3 On this see Olson in *Nordisk Tidende* (Brooklyn), Aug. 19, 1912. For a discussion of the life works of Rasmus B. Anderson and Julius E. Olson, see Einar Haugen, "Wisconsin Pioneers in Scandinavian Studies: Anderson and Olson, 1875–1931," *Wis. Mag. Hist.*, XXXIV (1950), 28–39. For bibliographies on the Vinland voyages see I. R. Swanton, *The Wineland Voyages*, "Smithsonian Miscellaneous Collections," 107. Number 12 (Publication 3906, Washington, 1947), pp. 1–81. See also Haugen, *Voyages to Vinland*, Section II, "The Evidence of History," pp. 97–181.

4 Boston, 1892.

5 Quoted from p. 20 of Lien's translation of Gjessing's article in *Symra*, Archive.

6 Quoted from pp. 24 f. of Holvik's typed copy of Iverslie's remarks.

7 *Nordmännen i Amerika eller Amerikas upptäckt: Historisk afhandling med anledning af Columbifesterna i Chicago 1892–93* (Rock Island, 1893).

8 One of the features of the Chicago World's Fair of 1892–93 was the sailing in *via* the Great Lakes of reproductions of the three caravels, the *Pinta*, the *Niña*, and the *Santa Maria*.

9 For an account of this, see A. W. Brøgger and H. Shetelig, *The Viking Ships: Their Ancestry and Evolution* (Oslo, 1953), pp. 141 f.

10 *Antiqvitates Americanæ sive Scriptores Septentrionales Rerum ante-Columbianarum in America. Samling af de i Nordens Oldskrifter indeholdte Efterretninger om de gamle Nordboers Opdagelsesreiser til America fra det 10de til det 14de Aarhundrede. Edidit Societas Regia Antiqvariorum Septentrionalium* (Hafniæ, 1837). The volume has duplicate texts in Latin and Danish.

11 London, 1889; cf. Viktor Rydberg, *Undersökningar i germansk mythologi, 2 delar* (Stockholm, 1886–89).

12 Stockholm, 1869. N. M. Petersen was the original author.

13 Hildebrand, *Nordisk Mytologi*, p. 112, footnote (translated). The work in question is *Vues des Cordillères, et Monumens des peuples indigènes de l'Amérique; par Al. de Humboldt. Tome premier* (Paris, 1816). An English translation of vols. 1–2 had already appeared at London in 1814: *Researches Concerning the Institutions and Monuments of the Ancient Inhabitants of America with Descriptions and Views of Some of the Most Striking Scenes in*

the Cordilleras, tr. *Helen Maria Williams.* In Vol. 1, reference to Votan appears on pp. 173 f.; there are also mentions of Greenland, Vinland, the "runes" of Dighton Rock, the Taunton River rocks with their "Scandinavian" drawings, and early relations between Asia and America.

14 Quoted from p. 244 of *The Younger Edda: also called Snorre's Edda, or the Prose Edda . . .* (Chicago, 1880). For a more modern edition, see *The Prose Edda by Snorri Sturluson,* tr. Arthur Gilchrist Brodeur (New York, 1916; second printing, 1923).

15 *Wis. Mag. Hist.,* III (1919–20), 413–19, p. 416. See *Cosmos: A Sketch of a Physical Description of the Universe by Alexander von Humboldt,* II, tr. E. C. Otté (London, 1878), pp. 603 ff., where there is a discussion of early Norse explorations of America. A volume of Humboldt's writings for Swedish youth had appeared in 1867; this was *Resor i länderna vid eqvatorn. För ungdomen bearbetad af C. Goehring* (Stockholm, 1867).

16 *Minn. Hist.,* XVII (1936), 262–75, p. 275. See M. Ridge, "The Humor of Ignatius Donnelly," *Minn. Hist.,* XXXIII (1952–53), 326–30.

17 *The Great Cryptogram: Francis Bacon's Cipher in the so-called Shakespeare Plays* (Chicago, 1888). Prominently displayed on the front cover of the volume is a cryptogram in gold.

18 *Atlantis: The Antediluvian World* (New York and London, 1882). This has been consulted in *Atlantis: The Antediluvian World, by Ignatius Donnelly,* ed. Egerton Sykes (rev. ed.; New York, 1949).

19 *Ibid.,* p. 142.

20 *Ibid.*

21 *Ibid.* Sir W. Jones, 1746–94, was a Sanskrit scholar. It is of interest to note that, according to newspaper reports from Sweden, a statuette of Budda was, in 1956, dug up from the soil of Sweden in which, according to archaeological opinion, it had lain for 1700 years.

22 *Sveriges historia från äldsta tid till våra dagar* (Stockholm, 1877).

23 Ignatius Donnelly, *Cæsar's Column: A Story of the Twentieth Century. By Edmund Boisgilbert, M.D.* (Chicago, 1890).

24 *Ragnarok: The Age of Fire and Gravel* (New York, 1883).

25 *Ibid.,* p. 143.

26 *Ibid.,* pp. 152 f., see p. 344.

27 *Ibid.*

28 P. 355.

29 *Ragnarok,* p. 137; see George F. Chambers, *The Story of the Comets Simply Told for General Readers* (2nd ed.; Oxford, 1910), pp. 158 f.

30 Major John Wesley Powell made the first exploratory boat trip through the Grand Canyon in the years 1869–71.

31 Communication of June 22, 1954. Many of the names given to conspicuous features of the Grand Canyon remind one that this was the age of Richard Wagner (1813–83), greatest modern exploiter of Germanic mythology for artistic purposes.

32 Wheeler served for some years as a topographer with Major Powell.

33 Jules Verne, *A Journey to the Centre of the Earth. . . .* (Boston [1874]). See the reproduced runes on pp. 16, 88, and 245; cf. p. 18, where a typographical oversight has resulted in omission of the runes. See following note.

34 Jules Verne, *A Trip to the Center of the Earth* ([New York], 1950). Runes

are reproduced on pp. 8, 9, 58, 175; the reproduction on p. 9 corresponds to the omission on p. 18 of the earlier edition; see foregoing note.

35 *Ibid.*, p. 13.

36 The letter was to Professor Julius E. Olson; it was published in *Norwegian-American*, Sept. 8, 1911; this information procured from Professor Holvik, whose text is here reproduced.

37 See Flom, *Transactions*, p. 116, and O. E. Hagen in an article written Mar. 15, 1910, and published in *America*, apparently on April 1, following; this is pasted into p. 23 of the first of Dr. Nissen's two scrapbooks, Archive. The runic work in question is C. J. Ljungström, *Runa-list eller konsten att läsa runor. 2: a uppl. Med 4 runstensafbildningar* (Lund, Stockholm, 1875).

38 MHS Report, p. 242.

39 The original printing was consulted by the author in the Royal Library at Stockholm.

40 Information on this reprint has been obtained from Professor Holvik.

41 *Sveriges historia*, pp. 356 f.

CHAPTER XIII

1 *Transactions*, p. 116, 124.

2 Translated from *Aarbøger, 1950*, p. 85. Respecting the inscription, Nielsen continues on the following page: "The riddle of the Kensington stone is not solved, however, with this negative result. Holand has made an impressive contribution towards showing that the inscription can be from 1362. It must be the task of the scholarship to show how it can have come about in modern time. In order to solve this problem it is necessary to investigate the form and use of runes in Sweden in the 19th century, and likewise the dialect in the district that Ohman came from. The philological and runological part of the problem cannot be said to be solved until the difficult forms in the inscription can be explained through reference to their current use and when the source of the peculiar runic forms has been shown." The balance of Nielsen's conclusion (pp. 86 f.) shows that he has been impressed chiefly by Holand's statements about the roots of the tree and by the affidavits; on these see Chapters V and VI, respectively.

3 P. 4 of Fossum's letter of Mar. 7, 1910, Archive.

4 Gould, Archive, p. 10.

5 *Kensington*, p. 274.

6 Stockholm, [1857–]64. A second edition appeared 1859–61, a third in 1873. In 1881–82 appeared a revised edition: *Ny genomsedd upplaga*. The Chicago edition of 1893, according to the editor, Jacob Bonggren, was based on "1882 års genomsedda och förbättrade tredje upplaga." Bonggren's calculation apparently skipped over one of the Stockholm editions. The 1902–05 Chicago edition is differently paginated.

7 Photographed for Holvik by the Minnesota Historical Society, see Fig. 25.

8 *Minn. Hist.*, XVII (1936), 187.

9 Holand's latest statement on this is found in *Explorations*, p. 320. This view is enthusiastically accepted by Reardon, *Catholic Church in St. Paul*, pp. 3–11, *passim;* see p. 11: "With the foregoing preluding prayer to the Mother of God from the stricken hearts of these Catholic Norsemen in pre-historic

Minnesota we enter the realm of ascertainable fact and verifiable history."
10 Holand in *Wis. Mag. Hist.*, XXXIV (1953), p. 237.
11 *Decorah-Posten*, apparently on April 23, 1954, according to information received by K. M. Nielsen and contained in an article in *Berlingske Aftenavis' Kronik* of July 16, 1955 (courtesy of the author, Iørn Piø, of Copenhagen).
12 *Explorations*, p. 338.
13 *Ibid.* Italics supplied.

CHAPTER XIV

1 Archive of the Minnesota Historical Society at St. Paul.
2 *NEQ*, VII (1934), 614, n. 3.
3 *Danske Studier* (1949–50), p. 50; see Moltke's comment, pp. 51 f. Moltke considers the find "nothing less than sensational."
4 Translated from p. 54 of Holand's article, "Hvad mener de lærde om Kensingtonstenen," *Danske Studier*, 1951, pp. 49–58, see pp. 53 f. In the same issue there is brief comment by Erik Moltke and Harry Andersen, "Hvad de lærde mener om Kensingtonstenen—og Hjalmar Holand," pp. 59–63.
5 *Explorations*, pp. 338 f.
6 *Ibid.*, p. 152.
7 *Westward*, p. 98.
8 *Explorations*, p. 163.
9 *Ibid.*, p. 356, n. 35a.
10 Compare Fig. 10 with Fig. 14.
11 MHS Archive.
12 Soon thereafter, Hedberg left Kensington; by 1903 he was in business at Warroad, where he established a bank.
13 *Den kunskapsrike Skolmästaren*, pp. 61–64.
14 See the discussion of numerals in the following chapter. Holand is of the opinion that the sketch was intended by its author to represent "an exact copy, line for line, of the inscription. . . . But he soon found it too difficult to duplicate the spacing on the stone, and then used his own spacing. As in the inscription, however, he did manage to get his copy into twelve lines" (*Explorations*, p. 340). This last sentence is illuminating, for if the "copyist"—for no discernible reason—found it "too difficult to duplicate the spacing on the stone," why did he have to "manage to get his copy into twelve lines"? A study of the righthand margin of the Hedberg sketch (Fig. 10) and comparison with that of the face of the stone (endpapers) suggests an answer: The "copy," though differing in certain respects from the stone, pretends in some degree to be a facsimile of the inscription (compare in particular the first eight lines of each version); the Hedberg sketch is therefore a little hoax in itself.
15 Mr. John L. Harris of Harris and Harris, Examiners of Questioned Documents, Los Angeles. After studying photographs of the Kensington stone, the Hedberg sketch, and Hedberg's handwritten letter, Mr. Harris explained that the special characteristics of handwriting are ordinarily obliterated in the course of an attempt to imitate another mode of writing, as here represented by the runes.
16 Breda was suspicious that a man who didn't know runes (Siverts) could

make a copy so clear that a non-specialist in runes (Breda himself) could read it; Breda in *Symra* for May, 1910, pp. 65–80, p. 71.

17 Breda's transliteration (or the copy of it in the MHS Archive) shows AVM written as AUM. This spelling will be discussed in the next chapter.

18 Archive.

19 Archive.

20 Archive.

21 Archive.

22 The author of it is unknown, however.

23 Information furnished by Miss Kathryn Johnson, Assistant Curator of Manuscripts of the MHS, Feb. 13, 1957.

24 Text supplied by Holvik.

25 *Symra*, May, 1910, p. 73.

26 Holand in *J. Am. Hist.*, IV (1910), 170: "More or less faulty copies of the inscriptions were made and sent to the newspapers, where they naturally created a sensation, and many learned dissertations followed." In *Settlementers Historie*, p. 15, he referred to "fejlaktige Kopier af Runerne." In *Aarbøger, 1951*, p. 227, note 1, he writes (translated): "We know that they [Bugge, Storm, and Rygh in 1899] had not read it, because the date and a considerable portion of the inscription were not translated until many years later." The assertion as to the date is erroneous, for Curme gave the date as 1362 as soon as he had had a chance to study the stone itself, in 1899. There is therefore nothing to Holand's contention, *Explorations*, p. 313: "Ten years later, when the study of the inscription was revived, it was shown that it was dated 1362, and that the early rejection was therefore based on false evidence." In another portion of the same book (p. 164), Holand gives a different version of the rejection: The Norwegian scholars rejected the inscription because Breda in Minneapolis had rejected it, and also because of resentment over the extent of emigration to America: "He sent a report on the inscription with his conclusions to the University of Oslo, and there they were accepted without question. The story was used, publicly and privately, as a sample of 'the irresponsible trickery that characterizes the American people.' This scoffing attitude was in part a result of jealous resentment because of the great emigration to America in the closing decades of the 19th century. . . . The upper classes, therefore, had reason to feel unfriendly toward America, and the newspapers missed no opportunity to print stories about the depravity 'characteristic' of America with the hope of checking the emigration. The report came back from Oslo swiftly and sternly: the Kensington inscription was a silly, meaningless forgery." This, of course, leaves unexplained why Breda, himself an immigrant from Norway, should condemn the stone; the same applies to Professor Bothne; and what about the Americans Flom, Curme, Gould? On pp. 167 f. Holand tries once again to invalidate later repudiations of the stone (which he fails to identify by author or date) on the grounds that these objections were based "on the fact that the inscription had been rejected by several experts when it was first found" and "that that early rejection was clearly based on false premises."

27 *Speculum*, XXV (1950), 352, n. 9.

28 *Explorations*, p. 338. The solution of the Kensington mystery was thus long impeded by the circulation of these inaccurate copies. There is a parallel to

this in the case of the Piltdown skull (see Chap. XV), which for years was kept under lock and key in the British Museum and could only be studied by the anthropologists of the world through the plaster reproductions; see Francis Vere, *The Piltdown Fantasy* (London, 1955), pp. 22 ff.

29 *Settlementers Historie*, p. 17.
30 Aug. 3, 1908; Archive. Professor Kirkeberg had translated "the evil fire" in *Skandinaven*, Mar. 1, 1899.
31 *Settlementers Historie*, p. 17.
32 *Wis. Mag. Hist.*, III (1919), 155.
33 *Kensington*, p. 5; *Westward*, p. 102; *Explorations*, p. 134. Moltke in *Danske Studier* (1949–50), p. 40, has ᛒ . However, the rune is clear enough in Brøndsted's photograph, *Aarbøger, 1950*, p. 66.

CHAPTER XV

1 *Harper's Weekly*, Mar. 26, 1910, p. 25.
2 Gould, Archive, p. 19.
3 *Foibles and Fallacies of Science: An Account of Celebrated Scientific Vagaries* (New York, 1924), p. 201.
4 London, 1910, p. 249.
5 *Foibles and Fallacies*, p. 206. See Alexander Klein, *Grand Deception* (New York, 1955), pp. 126–35.
6 *Foibles and Fallacies*, p. 208.
7 *The Biglow Papers: Second Series* (Boston, 1881), No. V, 129–38. See Haugen, *Voyages to Vinland*, pp. 150 f.
8 Lowell, *Papers*, p. 131.
9 *Ibid.*, p. 134 f. "Bjarna" is an error for Bjarni; Lowell evidently did not know that the form Bjarna was merely an oblique case of the nominative, Bjarni. It would appear, then, that he had seen the name in a printed saga in the original Old Icelandic.
10 See Erik Brate, *Sveriges runinskrifter* (1928), p. 135.
11 *Ibid.*
12 *NEQ*, VII (1934), 644.
13 Holand's latest views are stated in *Explorations*, pp. 207–51.
14 Oxford, 1955.
15 *The Piltdown Forgery*, p. 1.
16 *Ibid.*, p. 10.
17 *Ibid.*, p. 12.
18 *Ibid.*, p. 164.
19 *Ibid.*
20 *Ibid.*, pp. 186 f.
21 *Ibid.*, p. 187.
22 *Ibid.*, p. 152.
23 *Ibid.*, p. 204.
24 Jansson in *Nordisk tidskrift* (1949), p. 399, n. 30.
25 Toulouse, 1927. For a brief résumé and bibliography see Winkler-Prins, *Encyclopedie*, IX (Amsterdam-Brussels, 1950), *s.v.* 'Glozel.' On such matters in general see G. Van Riet Lowe, "Pitfalls in Prehistory," *Antiquity* (1954), pp. 85–90.
26 See W. W. Folwell, *A History of Minnesota*, II (St. Paul, 1924), 109–89.
27 *Minn. Hist. Coll.*, VI (1894), 354–80: "Mrs. J. E. De Camp Sweet's Narra-

tive of her Captivity in the Sioux Outbreak of 1862"; pp. 382–400: "Chief Big Eagle's Story of the Sioux Outbreak of 1862"; pp. 401–8: "Incidents of the Threatened Outbreak of Hole-In-The-Day and other Ojibways at Time of Sioux Massacre of 1862"; pp. 438–60: "The Story of Nancy McClure. Captivity Among the Sioux"; pp. 461–74: "The Story of Mary Schwandt. Her Captivity During the Sioux 'Outbreak'—1862"; see IX, 395–449. See likewise Holand, *Explorations*, p. 6: "For several years before that time southern Minnesota was the scene of the terrible Sioux War in which 1500 pioneers were massacred."

28 Pp. 543 ff.

29 Montelius, *Sverges historia*, p. 356; Rosander, *Den kunskapsrike Skolmästaren*, p. 717.

30 *Westward*, p. 308; cf. *Kensington*, p. 269; MHS Report, p. 253. Interesting in this connection is a Danish book by P. Købke, *Om Runerne i Norden. Almenfattelig Fremstilling* (Concerning Scandinavian Runes. Popular Presentation) (Kjøbenhavn, 1879). On p. 41 occur several mentions of 'Maria' with pictures of a wooden cross from Greenland on which the word is carved in runes; there are several mentions in the book of inscriptions containing both runes and Latin words. On pp. 48 ff. occur examples of runes associated with folk-songs. A second edition of this work appeared in 1890. Similar information is contained in other works of the 1890's or earlier.

31 Holand, *Kensington*, p. 36, and *Westward*, p. 112.

32 *Westward*, p. 184.

33 Cambridge, Mass., 1950.

34 W. J. Wilkins, *Hindu Mythology, Vedi and Purānic* (2nd ed.; Calcutta and Simla [n.d.], preface dated 1882), p. 95, note. See Helmuth von Glasenapp, *Madhva's Philosophie des Vishnu-Glaubens. Mit einer Einleitung über Madhva und seine Schule. Ein Beitrag zur Sektengeschichte des Hinduismus* (Bonn und Leipzig, 1923), p. 61: ". . . Visnu [wird] mit den drei Moren der heiligen Silbe Om (A + U + M) identifiziert, und der Meditation über diese Formen wird eine übersinnliche Wirkung zugeschrieben." See John Dowson, *A Classical Dictionary of Hindu Mythology and Religion, Geography, History, and Literature* (8th ed.; London, 1953), *s.v.* 'Om,' p. 224.

35 Lewis Spence, *An Encyclopædia of Occultism.* . . . (London, 1920), p. 307.

36 *The Upanishads* (*The Sacred Books of the East.* . . . , ed., F. Max Müller, Vol. I, Part I [Oxford, 1900]), pp. 1–12 and notes. See also *Illustreret Religionslexikon, Bind II* (n.d. [København, 1950]), *s.v.*: "ÔM 1. *Aùm*, en mystisk Stavelse, kaldet Pranava, hvormed enhvr Bøn og Ceremoni i Hind. begynder og ender, Bh. Gìtà 17, 24 . . . Upanishaderne kalder den 'Vedaernes hovedsum.' Ôm symboliserer bl. a. de 3 Verdener—Âtman—Brahman—Treenigheden . . ."

37 From the files of Professor Holvik.

38 See Chapter XII of the present study.

39 *Morals and Dogma of the Ancient and Accepted Scottish Rite of Freemasonry prepared for the Supreme Council of the Thirty-Third Degree for the Southern Jurisdiction of the United States and Published by its Authority.* Charleston, A ∴ M ∴ 5632 (Richmond, Va., Reprinted. June, 1946), pp. 204 f. The materials in the volume in question are not restricted to Freemasons.

40 A. N. Marquis (ed.), *The Book of Minnesotans: A Biographical Dictionary of Leading Living Men of the State of Minnesota* (Chicago, 1907), p. 222.

41 Professor Holvik was so informed by Ohman's daughter Manda. On the syllable *AUM* see mentions by the famed Theosophical leader, Mme Blavatsky: H. P. Blavatsky, *Isis Unveiled: A Master-Key to the Mysteries of Ancient and Modern Science and Theology*, II (New York, 1878), 31, p. 39, see p. 387: "The simple truth is that modern Masonry is a sadly different thing from what the once universal secret fraternity was in the days when the Brahma-worshippers of the AUM, exchanged grips and passwords with the devotees of TUM, and the adepts of every country under the sun were 'Brothers' " (Tem or Tum, also known as Atum and Atmu, was an ancient god of the Egyptians, see *Webster's International s.v.* '*Tem*'). Mme Blavatsky speaks also of the "secret ciphers" employed by Freemasons, and gives some examples (pp. 394–98). To be noted presently is the cryptic use of numerals in the Kensington inscription. For a brief, partial history of Theosophy, see Emmett A. Greenwalt, *The Point Loma Community in California 1897–1942. . . .* (Berkeley and Los Angeles, 1955), in particular pp. 1–46. Theosophists from Adyar, India, had penetrated Sweden in the 1870's. In the 1890's, Katherine Tingley, head of the Point Loma Community, turned her attention to Sweden, which she eventually visited (1899). Ultimately she was able to purchase crown property in Sweden (on the island of Visingsö) for the establishment of a second Point Loma, which idea she later abandoned; see Greenwalt, pp. 149–53.

At least one clearly Theosophical rune stone is known. It was dug up from the ground under two feet of earth near one of the buildings of the Theosophical University at Point Loma, California, in 1926 by a Mexican laborer (Point Loma was established by Tingley in 1898 and building construction started in 1900). Only six and one half by four and one half inches in size, the rune stone is composed of fine-grained, siliceous sandstone, around the rim of which is carved a serpent—as on many Swedish rune stones—between the parallel lines of which are carved sixty-seven runic symbols in modern Swedish, translatable as follows: "Hail to thee, Sweden, the Northern seat, preserver and disseminator. Brightly shine thy light." Within the serpentine appears an elaborate Theosophical device; the serpent itself is likewise a part of Theosophical symbolism. According to geological opinion, the stone was brought in from the outside. The ground round about it not having been disturbed in twenty-five years, it was believed to have been buried by a Swedish workman and member of the Theosophical group at the time of construction of the building. The above information has been furnished by Professor Harold von Hofe of the University of Southern California.

It is worth-while to note that some writers, European and American, have considered that America was subject to Buddhist influence at a very early date; a full discussion is found in Edward P. Vining, *An Inglorious Columbus; or, Evidence that Hwui Shăn and a Party of Buddhist Monks from Afghanistan Discovered America in the Fifth Century* (New York, 1885). Among other things, this book of nearly 800 pages discusses Vinland (pp. 452–54), and claims that early Scandinavian monuments—not identified— have been found as far south as Brazil (p. 63).

42 See Chapter XI, note 24, for triple cultural influences on a Swedish church bell from Saleby, West Gothland. The three are runic Swedish, Latin (*aue : maria* etc.) (cf. *AVM* in the Kensington inscription) and Hebrew, the

latter cryptically represented by the initial letters of four Hebrew words;
Brate, *Sveriges runinskrifter*, p. 90, Fig. 17. The interesting thing about the
Saleby inscription is that its inscription combining Christian with non-
Christian elements is reproduced in the history by Montelius, p. 403 and
Fig. 463.

43 Wendell Thomas, *Hinduism Invades America* (New York, 1930), pp. 64–
133, p. 74.

44 *Collectio Runologica Wimmeriana*, pp. 43–46 (see Chapter IV, note 7).

45 Stone inspected and information obtained at Nationalmuseum, Copenhagen,
1955.

46 *Bibliographie der Runenkunde*, (Leipzig, 1937), p. 293.

47 Inspected by the author in 1954. Written in runes of perhaps the year 1000,
the stone contains 60 or so symbols and reads in part: "Joe Doakes went
East 1953. He discovered Europe. Holy smoke!"

48 *Se* contains a long vowel, whereas the second syllable (*-se*) of *rise* is properly
unstressed, phonetic [sə].

49 See for example Sigurd Agrell, *Runornas talmystik och dess antika förebild*
(Lund, 1927), a work that is speculative in the extreme; Hans Brix, *Systematiske Beregninger i de danske Runeindskrifter* (København, 1932); for
critical commentary on the cryptic theories of M. Olsen, R. Pipping, H. Brix,
and S. Agrell, see Anders Bæksted, *Målruner og troldruner* (København,
1953).

50 Flom inadvertently makes the number 211, *Transactions*, p. 105. Holand
states "220 characters" (*Kensington*, p. 6; *Westward*, p. 100).

51 Hagen in *Speculum*, xxv (1950), 322: ". . . a partly-preserved *o*-rune. This
seems to have been missed by Holand. . . . I conjecture that the word
which ended in *-o* must have been *þeno*, 'this'." Cf. Wahlgren in *Studies*,
pp. 57 f.

52 What we have surmised as the function of the figure 22 on the Kensington
stone is in a certain sense parallel to the use of 24 on many genuine rune
stones; cf. Montelius, p. 356, on the Rök stone, which has not yet been
satisfactorily interpreted, cf. Otto von Friesen, *Rökstenen läst och tydd*
(Stockholm, 1920), especially pp. 13 ff. Modern research (Bæksted) is skeptical of the cryptic theory as applied to genuine inscriptions. If it is true
that Ohman changed his name from Olsson upon immigration (Minneapolis *Star*, April 16, 1955), the cryptic theory based on the number 22
gains in validity as applied to a modern hoax.

53 *Kensington*, p. 34; *Westward*, p. 110, cf. *J. Am. Hist.*, IV (1910), 178.

54 *Explorations*, p. 162.

55 *Ibid.*

56 The figure 22 pursues us in still another way. Professor Jansson in *Nordisk
tidskrift* (1949), p. 377, has somehow ascertained that Ohman was born, as
he states, in 1856. Jansson appears to accept Ohman's "egen uppgift" (via
Holand, presumably) that Ohman emigrated in 1881 (*ibid.*); but Ohman's
statement reproduced in Holand, *Kensington*, p. 284, and *Explorations*,
p. 346, in a letter to Professor Winchell of June 6, 1910, is to the effect that
he emigrated in 1879. If the dates 1856 and 1879 are correct, Ohman may
have been 22 at the time of his emigration. The date 1879 is probably cor-

rect, for Flom, *Transactions*, p. 122, says: "Ohman came to Minnesota in June, 1879." This was on the basis of a conversation with Ohman.

The numerological point of view is capable of yielding further results. Can it be attributed to chance that the sum of all the numerals used in the inscription (aside from the date 1362) is 66? Or that the inscription employs not only an even number of total symbols (222) but that these break down into three evenly numbered components: 130 runic consonants, 80 runic vowels, and 12 runic numeral symbols? How does it happen, then, that the inscription departs from the even-numbered system in using 65 syntactical units—words or sets of numerals—together with 65 separating colons? The clue may be found in the cryptic word "AVM." It has been surmised by all investigators that this symbol represents (among other things) "Ave Maria" or "Ave Virgo Maria"; which reading is to be preferred has not previously been determined. It is surmised here that, as with the Saleby inscription described above (Chapter XI, note 24), the simpler "Ave Maria" was intended by our Kensington runemaster. If written out and punctuated in the same way as the rest of the Kensington words, the two words "Ave : Maria" would then be separated by a colon. There would then be a cryptic restoration of the prevailing system based on 22: 66 words and 66 sets of separating dots.

In assuming this, one is not reduced to conjecture alone, for examination of the word *AVM* in line 8 of the inscription (Fig. 1 and endpapers) shows a circular chisel puncture in the stone adjoining the upper righthand portion of the *V*, as if the runecarver had planned to carve two dots between the *AV* and the *M*, then abandoned the notion. Without apparent graphological significance is the fact that an occasional "dot" in the inscription is composed of two punctures which have not coalesced—the lower dot after *AVM* in line 8, and the lower dot after the last rune (in the word 'evil') in line 9. Holand seems at one time to have known that there were "66 words" in the inscription (*Records of the Past*, IX [1910], 240). His subsequent books ignore this.

The numeral 8 likewise figures in more than one connection: 8 "Goths"; *AVM* in the 8th line; the stone found in either the 8th month or on the 8th day of a month. Curiously, the addition of 8 to the number of symbols (222), gives 230, which was the reported (and disputed) weight of the stone —trimmed and carved by the runemaster—in pounds.

The number of different runic symbols employed on the stone has received indifferent treatment at the hands of investigators. Holand correctly shows 22 symbols (*Kensington*, p. 123, and *Westward*, p. 173), but never states the number, to our knowledge; Flom shows 21 (*Transactions*, plate opposite p. 112); Hagen shows 23 (*Speculum*, XXV [1950], 342); the present author treats of 22 symbols, incorrectly enumerated as "twenty-three" (*Studies*, pp. 59 f.); Moltke states the number as 22 but lists 24 (*Danske Studier*, 1949–50, p. 43; cf. p. 42.)

57 *Explorations*, p. 168. The Kensington syllable *AVM/OM* may therefore be a modern adaptation of this cryptic principle. It can be pointed out that Ómi (Swedish and English form 'Ome') is a byname of the Scandinavian god Odin, as narrated in both the *Poetic Edda* and the *Prose Edda*. Odin was the god of runes and likewise of the "Goths" (Swedes); these hold the place of honor at the beginning of the Kensington inscription.

58 *Transactions*, p. 108.
59 Holvik's letter of Sept. 24, 1957, in possession of the author.

CHAPTER XVI

1 *Explorations*, p. 174. As authority for this point of view, Holand deviously attempts to use the runologist K. M. Nielsen: "If the inscription was made in the 19th century, then the author can be none other than Ohman" (*ibid.*, cf. Nielsen in *Aarbøger, 1950*, p. 86). This is something quite different; Nielsen does not say that the inscription must be genuine if we cannot prove to everybody's satisfaction that Ohman was the author of it.

2 *Explorations*, pp. 175 f.

3 *Ibid.*, p. 347 f.

4 Jansson calls the unknown runecarver "en klipsk karl" (a shrewd fellow), Jansson in *Nordisk tidskrift* (1949), p. 400. Dr. Hoegh referred to Olof Ohman as "intelligent," *Explorations*, p. 175. Holand now states that he has "always said" that Ohman was intelligent, *Explorations*, pp. 336 f.

It is not necessary to agree with the Swedish linguist, Professor Erik Noreen, that the unknown runecarver of Kensington was a psycho-pathological type like the famous Swedish forger of historical documents, the Reverend Nils Rabenius (1648–1717); see Erik Noreen, *Svensk stilparodi och andra litterära och språkliga uppsatser* (Stockholm, 1944), p. 81; this is from the essay on "Amerikanska runor," pp. 75–82.

5 Holand, *Explorations*, p. 165: "And what could have been the motive for such a laborious forgery?" Cf. Holand, *Westward*, p. 255.

6 Professor Holvik found a letter from the church rector at Forsa, addressed to Ohman, in the Fogelblad-Ohman scrapbook, and returned it to the Ohman family.

7 MHS Report, p. 246.

8 *Transactions*, p. 122, and Jansson in *Nordisk tidskrift* (1949), p. 377.

9 See previous chapter, note 41.

10 In an undated letter (probably from 1910) to Winchell from Upham the latter warns Winchell to investigate both Ohman and Holand: "accounts of a poplar tree . . . may be a part of the deception, and the apparent ill will between Mr. Ohman and Mr. Holand may be another part." Archive.

11 P. 243.

12 Obviously not the product of a humanistic *gymnasium*, Hedberg nevertheless had opinions on this matter. His opinions must therefore have been based upon a source. Of all such sources contemporary Bible aids would have been the most easily available, both for Hedberg and for the author of the Kensington inscription. For convenience there are here adapted a few alphabetical forms from Sir Monier Monier-Williams, *A Sanskrit-English Dictionary Etymologically and Philologically Arranged with special reference to Cognate Indo-European Languages* (Oxford, 1899), "Introduction," p. xxvii:

⊗ Archaic Roman	⊗ Archaic Greek
⊗ Phœnician	⊙ Brāhma
⅄ Archaic Greek	⅄ Phœnician
† Brāhma	

13 P. 204. F. Vere, in his *Piltdown Fantasy*, is convinced that Dawson was the victim, rather than the perpetrator, of the hoax.

CHAPTER XVII

1   A partial exception to this is found in Holand's pretended analysis of the
    Hedberg sketch in his *Explorations*, pp. 338–41, concerning which he con-
    cludes, p. 341: "But it seems rather ridiculous seriously to discuss the merits
    of this runepaper in view of the circumstantial evidence of the age of the in-
    scription." See Chapter XIV, above.

2   Translated from Jansson in *Nordisk tidskrift* (1949), pp. 399 f. What pleasure
    this Swedish runologist takes in tracing Swedish influence as represented by
    genuine rune stones in foreign lands appears from his recent publication,
    Svenska utlandsfärder i runinskrifternas ljus (Svenska spår i främmande land.
    III) (Göteborg, 1956). Published by the National Society for the Preserva-
    tion of Swedish Culture Abroad, Professor Jansson's attractively illustrated
    booklet is titled in English translation: *Swedish Foreign Travels in the Light*
    of Runic Inscriptions and forms the third of the Society's publications in the
    series *Swedish Traces in Foreign Lands.*

3   It is likewise hoped that the Fogelblad-Ohman scrapbook, the Swedish
    history by Montelius, and the popular encyclopedia by Rosander can be
    placed among the treasures of the Minnesota Historical Society, where the
    Swedish grammar by Almquist has reposed these many years.

Bibliography

The following bibliography is in no sense exhaustive. It includes only the more important books and articles discussed above or consulted during the course of the investigation. Letters, manuscripts, and newspaper articles have been omitted. Valuable special bibliographies of the linguistic and historical aspects of the question will be found in many of the works cited below.

Adams, James Truslow. *History of the United States*. Vol. I. *The Rise of the Union*. New York: Charles Scribner's Sons, 1933.

Agrell, Sigurd. *Runornas talmystik och dess antika förebild*. Lund: Gleerup, 1927.

Almagià, Roberto. "Cristoforo Colombo e i viaggi precolumbiani in America," *Rendiconti delle Adunanze solenni*. Volume V, fascicolo 6. Roma: Accademia Nazionale dei Lincei (1951), 263–79.

Almquist, C. J. L. *Svensk språklära. Tredje upplagan öfversedd och tillökad med samlingar öfver tio svenska Landskapsdialekter*. Stockholm: Hörbergska Boktr. På M. Wirdsell's Förlag, 1840.

Andersen, Harry. "Kensington-stenen, Amerikas runesten," *Danske Studier* (1949–50), pp. 37–60. In two parts of which Andersen is the author of the second: "2. En sproglig undersøgelse," pp. 52–60. See also under Moltke.

Anderson, Ingvar. "Kring Kensingtonstenen," *Nordisk tidskrift för vetenskap, konst och industri utgiven av Letterstedtska föreningen*. Årg. 26, Häft 3, 1950 (1951), pp. 132–33.

Andersson, Rasmus B. *Amerikas første opdagelse. Af forfatteren gjennemset og avtoriseret oversættelse ved Fredrik Winkel Horn*. Kjøbenhavn: Gyldendal, 1886.

———. *America Not Discovered by Columbus*. 3rd ed. Chicago: S. C. Griggs, 1883.

———. (ed.) *The Younger Edda; also called Snorre's Edda, or the Prose Edda, with an introduction, notes, vocabulary and index*. Chicago: S. C. Griggs, 1880.

Arntz, Helmut. *Bibliographie der Runenkunde*. Leipzig: Harrassowitz, 1937.

———. *Handbuch der Runenkunde. Zweite Auflage*. Halle/Saale: Niemeyer, 1944.

Aschehougs Konversasjons Leksikon. Ny utgave, IX. Oslo: Aschehoug, 1948.

Bæksted, Anders. *Islands Runeindskrifter (Bibliotheca Arnamagnæana consilio et auctoritate legati arnamagnæani. Jón Helgason editionem curavit*. Vol. II). København: Munksgaard, 1942.

———. *Målruner og troldruner. Runologiske studier (Nationalmuseets Skrifter. Arkæologisk-Historisk Række*, IV). København: Gyldendal, 1952.

———. "Vore yngste Runeindskrifter," *Danske Studier* (1939), pp. 111–38.

Betten, Francis S. *From Many Centuries: A Collection of Historical Papers*. New York,: P. J. Kenedy [1938].

Blavatsky, Helene Petrovna. *Isis Unveiled: A Master Key to the Mysteries of*

215

Ancient and Modern Science and Theology. 4th ed. Vol. II. New York: J. W. Bouton, 1878.

Boer, R. C. (ed.). *Grettis Saga Ásmundarsonar (Altnordische Saga-Bibliothek. 8)*. Halle, a. S.: Niemeyer, 1900.

Brandt, C. J. *Gammeldansk Læsebok*. Kjøbenhavn: Iversens Fhdl., 1857.

Brate, Erik. *Sveriges runinskrifter (Natur och Kultur.* 11). *Andra upplagan.* Stockholm: Natur och Kultur, 1928.

Brix, Hans. *Systematiske Beregninger i de danske Runeindskrifter*. København: Gyldendal, 1932.

Brodeur, Arthur Gilchrist (ed.). *The Prose Edda by Snorri Sturluson*. Translated from the Icelandic with an Introduction. New York: American-Scandinavian Foundation, 1923.

Brøgger, A. W. and H. Shetelig. *The Viking Ships: Their Ancestry and Evolution*. Oslo: Dreyer, 1953.

Brøndsted, Johannes. "Problemet om nordboer i Nordamerika før Columbus," *Aarbøger for nordisk Oldkyndighed og Historie udgivne af Det kgl. nordiske Oldskriftselskab. 1950* (København, 1951), pp. 1–152.

Chambers, George F. *The Story of the Comets Simply Told for General Readers*. 2nd ed. Oxford: Clarendon Press, 1910.

Collectio Runologica Wimmeriana. Fortegnelse over Ludvig Wimmers Runologiske o. a. Samlinger i Det kgl. Bibliotek, København, 1915. [This is a printed catalog.]

Cleasby, Richard, and Vigfusson, Gudbrand. *An Icelandic-English Dictionary, based on the ms. collections of the late Richard Cleasby, enlarged and completed by Gudbrand Vigfusson, with an introduction and life of Richard Cleasby by George Webbe Dasent*. Oxford: Clarendon Press, 1874.

Donnelly, Ignatius. *Atlantis: The Antediluvian World*. New York and London: Harper, 1882.

———. *Atlantis: The Antediluvian World*, rev. ed. Edited by Egerton Sykes. New York: Harper, 1949.

———. *Cæsar's Column: A Story of the Twentieth Century*. By Edmund Boisgilbert, M. D. Chicago: F. J. Schulte, 1890.

———. *The Great Cryptogram: Francis Bacon's Cipher in the so-called Shakespeare Plays*. Chicago: R. S. Peale, 1888.

———. *Ragnarok: The Age of Fire and Gravel*. New York: Appleton, 1883.

Dowson, John. *A Classical Dictionary of Hindu Mythology and Religion, Geography, History, and Literature*. 8th ed. London: Routledge, 1953.

Encyclopedia of Religion and Ethics. Edited by James Hastings. Vol. IX. New York: Scribner's, 1925.

Einarsson, Stefán. Review of Hjalmar R. Holand, "The Kensington Stone," in *Speculum*, VIII (July, 1933), 400–408.

Enander, J. A. *Nordmännen i Amerika eller Amerikas upptäckt. Historisk afhandling med anledning af Columbifesterna i Chicago 1892–93*. Rock Island, 1893 [Not seen].

Flom, George T. "The Kensington Rune Stone. A Modern Inscription from Douglas County, Minnesota," *Transactions of the Illinois State Historical Society for the Year 1910* (Springfield, 1912), pp. 105–25.

Folwell, W. W. *A History of Minnesota*. Vol. II. (*Publications of the Minnesota Historical Society*, edited by S. J. Buck.) St. Paul: Minnesota Historical Society, 1924.

Fraser, A. D. "The Norsemen in Canada," *Dalhousie Review*, XVII (July, 1937), 174–86.

Friesen, Otto von (ed.). *Runorna (Nordisk Kultur, VI)*. Stockholm: Bonnier, 1933.

Fritzner, Johan. *Ordbog over det gamle norske sprog. Omarbeidet, forøget og forbedret udg.* 3 vols in 4. Kristiania: Den norske forlagsforening, 1886–96.

Glasenapp, Helmuth von. *Madhva's Philosophie des Vishnu-Glaubens. Mit einer Einleitung über Madhva und seine Schule. Ein Beitrag zur Sektengeschichte des Hinduismus*. Bonn und Leipzig: K. Schroeder, 1923.

Godfrey, William S. "Vikings in America: Theories and Evidence." *American Anthropologist*, LVII (February, 1955), 35–43.

Gordon, Eric Valentine. *Introduction to Old Norse*. Oxford: Oxford University Press, 1927.

Greenland. 2nd ed. Published by the Royal Danish Ministry for Foreign Affairs: Ringkjøbing [1955].

Greenwalt, Emmett A. *The Point Loma Community in California 1897–1942: A Theosophical Experiment*. Berkeley and Los Angeles: University of California Press, 1955.

Hagen, S. N. "The Kensington Runic Inscription," *Speculum*, XXV (Summer, 1950), 321–56.

Hastings, James (ed.). *Encyclopedia of Religion and Ethics*, IX. New York: Scribner, 1925.

Haugen, Einar. *Voyages to Vinland: The first American saga newly translated and interpreted*. New York: Knopf, 1942.

Hellquist, Elof. *Svensk etymologisk ordbok*. Lund: Gleerup, 1922.

Hennig, Richard. "Normannen des 11. Jahrhunderts in der Hudson Bai und an den Grossen Seen," *Petermanns Geographische Mitteilungen*, 85. Jahrgang (Februar, 1939), p. 59.

———. *Terrae Incognitae*. Vol. III. Leiden: E. J. Brill, 1953.

———. "Zur Frage der Echtheit des Runensteins von Kensington," *Petermanns Geographische Mitteilungen*, 84. Jahrgang (März, 1938), pp. 88–90.

Hering, Daniel W. *Foibles and Fallacies of Science: An Account of Celebrated Scientific Vagaries*. New York: Van Nostrand, 1924.

Heggstad, Leiv. *Gamalnorsk ordbok med nynorsk tyding. Ny umvølt og auka utgåve av "Gamalnorsk ordbok" ved Hægstad og Torp*. Oslo: Det norske samlaget, 1930.

Herrmann, Paul. *Conquest by Man*. Translated by Michael Bullock. New York: Harper, 1954.

———. *Sieben vorbei und acht verweht*. Hamburg: Hoffmann und Campe, 1952.

Hermannsson, Halldór. *The Northmen in America*. ("Islandica," Vol. II.) Ithaca: Cornell University Press, 1909.

Holand, Hjalmar R. *America, 1355–1364*. New York: Duell, Sloan and Pearce, 1946.

———. "Are there English Words on the Kensington Runestone?" *Records of the Past*, IX (September–October, 1910), 240–45.

———. *Explorations in America Before Columbus*. New York: Twayne, 1956.

———. "An Explorer's Stone Record Which Antedates Columbus. A Tragic Inscription Unearthed in Minnesota Recording the Fate of a Band of Scandinavian Adventurers," *Harper's Weekly*, LIII (October 9, 1909), 15.

———. "Concerning the Kensington Rune Stone," *Minnesota History*, XVII (June, 1936), 166–88.

———. "First Authoritative Investigation of 'Oldest Native Document in America'," *Journal of American History*, IV (Second Quarter, 1910), 165–84.

———. "A Fourteenth Century Columbus," *Harper's Weekly*, LIV (March 26, 1910), 25.

———. "Hvad mener de lærde om Kensingtonstenen," *Danske Studier*, 1951, pp. 49–58.

———. "The Kensington Rune Stone Abroad," *Records of the Past*, X (1911), 260–71.

———. "The Kensington Rune Stone. Is it the Oldest Native Document of American History?" *Wisconsin Magazine of History*, III (December, 1919), 153–83.

Holand, Hjalmar R., and N. H. Winchell. "The Kensington Rune Stone. Preliminary Report to the Minnesota Historical Society by its Museum Committee," *Collections of the Minnesota Historical Society*. Vol. XV, (1909–14) 221–86. St. Paul: Published by the Society, May, 1915. [Also separately printed, St. Paul, 1912].

Holand, Hjalmar R. *The Kensington Stone*. Ephraim, Wis.: Privately printed, 1932.

———. "Kensington-steinens mangfoldighet," *Nordisk tidskrift för vetenskap, konst och industri utgiven av Letterstedtska föreningen*. Årg. 26 (1950), pp. 121–29.

———. "The 'Myth' of the Kensington Stone," *New England Quarterly*, VIII (March, 1935), 42–62.

———. *De Norske Settlementers Historie. En oversigt over den norske Indvandring til og Bebyggelse af Amerikas Nordvesten fra Amerikas Opdagelse til Indianerkrigen. Med. Bygde- og Navneregister*. Ephraim, Wisconsin: Forfatteren, 1908.

———. "The Origin of the Kensington Inscription," *Scandinavian Studies*, XXIII (February, 1951), 23–30.

———. "A Review of the Kensington Stone Research," *Wisconsin Magazine of History*, XXXVI (Summer, 1953), 235–39, 273–76.

———. "The Truth About the Kensington Stone," *Michigan History*, XXXI (December, 1947), 417–30.

———. "Skandinaviske minnesmerker i Amerika fra det fjortende aarhundre," *Aarbøger for nordisk Oldkyndighed og Historie udgivne af Det kgl. nordiske Oldskriftselskab. 1951* (1952), pp. 227–50.

———. *Westward from Vinland: An Account of Norse Discoveries and Explorations in America 982–1362*. New York: Duell, Sloane and Pearce, 1940.

Humboldt, Alexander von. *Cosmos: A Sketch of a Physical Description of the Universe*. Translated by E. C. Otté. Vol. II. London: Bell, 1878.

———. *Researches Concerning the Institutions and Monuments of the Ancient Inhabitants of America with Descriptions and Views of Some of the Most Striking Scenes in the Cordilleras*. Translated by Helen Maria Williams. 2 Vols. London: Longman, 1814.

———. *Vues des Cordillères, et Monumens des peuples indigènes de l'Amérique*. *Tome premier*. Paris: N. Maze. [1816].

Jacobsen, Lis, and Erik Moltke. *Danmarks Runeindskrifter Under Medvirkning af Anders Bæksted og Karl Martin Nielsen*. København: E. Munksgaard, 1942.

Jansson, Sam. "Svensk paleografi," *Nordisk Kultur*, XXVIII. *Palæografi. A. Danmark og Sverige. Udgivet af Johs. Brøndum Nielsen*, 82–134. Stockholm: Bonnier, [1944].

Jansson, Sven F. B. " 'Runstenen' från Kensington i Minnesota," *Nordisk tidskrift för vetenskap, konst och industri utgiven av Letterstedtska föreningen.* Årg. 25, Häft 7–8, 1949 (Stockholm, 1950), pp. 377–405.

Janzén, Assar. Review of Hjalmar R. Holand, "Explorations in America Before Columbus," in *Swedish Pioneer Historical Quarterly*, VIII (January, 1957), 25–31.

Jónsson, Finnur, and Erik Moltke. *Greenland Runic Inscriptions* I–IV. I: Jónsson, F. "Grønlandske runestene," *Det Grønlandske Selskabs Aarsskrift,* 1916 pp. 63–66 [Not seen]. II: Jónsson, F. "Interpretations of the Runic Inscriptions from Herjolfsnes," *Meddelelser om Grønland udgivne af Kommissionen for ledelsen af de Geologiske og Geografiske Undersøgelser i Grønland.* LXVII (København: Reitzel, 1924), 273–90. III. Jónsson, F. "Rune Inscriptions from Gardar," *Meddelelser*, LXXVI,1929 (1930), 171–79. IV: Moltke, E. "Greenland Runic Inscriptions, IV," *Meddelelser*, 88 (1936), pp. 222–32 and plates following.

Kaalund Kristian. *Palæografisk Atlas.* 3 vols. [I]. *Dansk Afdeling.* København: Gyldendal, 1903. [II]. *Oldnorsk-Islandsk Afdeling.* 1905. [III]. *Ny Serie. Oldnorsk-Islandske Skriftprøver c. 1300–1700.* 1907.

Kelsey, Francis W. "Some Archeological Forgeries from Michigan " *American Anthropologist. New Series.* X (January-March, 1908), 48–59.

Klein, Alexander. *Grand Deception.* New York: Lippincott, 1955.

Kock, Axel. *Svensk ljudhistoria. Andra delen.* Lund: Gleerup, 1909–11.

Købke, Peter. *Om Runerne i Norden. Almenfattelig Fremstilling.* Kjøbenhavn: Wroblewski, 1879. (2. meget ændrede udg., 1890.)

Larsen, Karen. *A History of Norway.* Princeton: Princeton University Press, 1950.

Lithberg, Nils. "Kalendariska hjälpmedel," *Nordisk Kultur,* XXI. *Tideräkningen. Utgiven av Martin P:n Nilsson,* 77–94. Stockholm: Bonnier, 1934.

Ljungström, C. J. *Runa-list eller konsten att läsa runor.* 2:a uppl. Med 4 runstensafbildningar. Lund, Stockholm: Klemming, 1875.

Lowe, G. Van Riet, "Pitfalls in Prehistory," *Antiquity: A Quarterly Review of Archæblogy* (Gloucester, 1954), pp. 85–90.

[Lowell, James Russell]. *Melibæus Hipponax. The Biglow Papers. Second Series.* Boston, Houghton, Mifflin, 1881.

Maiander, Harry. (ed.). *Sveriges historia genom tiderna. Första delen. Forntiden och medeltiden.* Stockholm: Saxon och Lindström, 1947.

Mallery, Arlington H. *Lost America: The Story of Iron-Age Civilization Prior to Columbus.* Washington: Overlook, 1951.

Marquis, A. N. (ed.). *The Book of Minnesotans: A Biographical Dictionary of Leading Living Men in the State of Minnesota.* Chicago: Marquis, 1907.

Mirsky, Jeannette. *To the North! The Story of Arctic Exploration from Earliest Times to the Present.* New York: Viking, 1934.

Moltke, Erik. "The Ghost of the Kensington Stone," *Scandinavian Studies,* XXV (January, 1953), 1–14.

———. *Greenland Runic Inscriptions, I–IV.* See under Jónsson.

———. "Kensington-stenen, Amerikas runesten," *Danske Studier* (1949–50), pp. 37–60. In two parts of which Moltke is the author of the first: "1. En alfabethistorisk undersøgelse," pp. 37–52. See also under Andersen.

Montelius, Oskar. *Sveriges historia från äldsta tid till våra dagar. Första delen. Sveriges hednatid, samt medeltid, förra skedet 1060–1350. Med 532 träsnitt.* Stockholm: Linnström, 1877.

Morals and Dogma of the Ancient and Accepted Scottish Rite of Freemasonry prepared for the Supreme Council of the Thirty-Third Degree for the Southern Jurisdiction of the United States and Published by its Authority. Charleston, A ∴ M.: *5632.* Richmond, Virginia. Reprinted June, 1946.

Næss, Almar. *Hvor lå Vinland? En studie over solobservasjoner i de norrøne sagaer.* Oslo: Dreyer [1954].

Neckel, Gustav. (ed.). *Edda. Die Lieder des Codex Regius nebst verwandten Denkmälern. I. Text. 3. durchgesehene Auflage.* Heidelberg: Winter, 1936.

Nielsen, Karl Martin. "Kensingtonstenens runeindskrift," pp. 73–88 of Brøndsted, Johannes, "Problemet om nordboer i Nordamerika før Columbus," *Aarbøger, 1950* (1951). See under Brøndsted.

Nordisk Familjebok. Konversationslexikon och realencyklopedi. Ny upplaga. XIII. Stockholm: Nordisk Familjebok, 1910.

Noreen, Adolf. *Altschwedische Grammatik. Mit Einschluss des Altgutnischen (Sammlung kurzer Grammatiken Germanischer Dialekte herausgegeben von Wilhelm Braune.* VIII. *Altnordische Grammatik,* II). Halle: Niemeyer, 1904.

Noreen, Erik. *Fornsvensk läsebok. Andra bearbetade upplagan utgiven av Sven Benson.* Malmö: Gleerup, 1954.

Olsen, Magnus. "De norröne runeinnskrifter," in *Runorna, Nordisk Kultur,* VI. *Utgiven av Olof von Friesen,* pp. 83–113. Stockholm: Bonnier, 1933.

Ordbok öfver Svenska Språket utgifven af Svenska Akademien. I–XXII. Lund: Gleerup, 1898.

Petersen, Carl S. "Wimmer og Kensingtonstenen," *Nordisk tidskrift för vetenskap, konst och industri utgiven av Letterstedtska föreningen.* Årg. 26 (1950), pp. 130–31.

Peterson, C. S. *America's Rune Stone of A.D. 1362 Gains Favor.* New York: Hobson, 1946.

Quaife, Milo M. "The Kensington Myth Once More," *Michigan History,* XXXI (June, 1947), 129–61.

———. "The Myth of the Kensington Rune Stone: The Norse Discovery of Minnesota 1362," *New England Quarterly,* VII (December, 1934), 613–45.

Rafn, C. C. *Antiqvitates Americanæ sive Scriptores Septentrionales Rerum ante-Columbianarum in America. Samling af de i Nordens Oldskrifter indeholdte Efterretninger om de gamle Nordboers Opdagelsesreiser til America fra det 10de til det 14de Aarhundrede.* Edidit Societas Regia Antiqvariorum Septentrionalium. Hafniæ: Schultz, 1837.

Rasmussen, Knud. *Across Arctic America: Narrative of the Fifth Thule Expedition.* New York, London: Putnam, 1927.

Reardon, James Michael. *The Catholic Church in the Diocese of St. Paul from earliest origin to centennial achievement; a factual narrative.* St. Paul: North Central, 1952.

Reeves, Arthur Middleton. *The Finding of Wineland the Good. The History of the Icelandic Discovery of America.* London: Frowde, 1890.

Ridge, Martin. "The Humor of Ignatius Donnelly," *Minnesota History,* XXXIII (Winter, 1953), 326–30.

Rodahl, Kåre. *The Ice-Capped Island: Greenland.* London and Glasgow: Blackie, [1946].

Rosander, Carl. *Den Kunskapsrike Skolmästaren eller Hufvudgrunderna uti de för ett borgerligt samfundslif nödigaste Vetenskaper. En Handbok i nyttiga Kunskaper för alla Samhällsklasser, utarbetad efter de bästa Författare och till-*

förlitligaste Källor . . . *Med några Illustrationer samt åtföljd af en större Karta.* Stockholm: Bonnier, [1857–]64. [Several later editions].

Rydberg, Victor. *Teutonic Mythology.* Translated by Rasmus B. Anderson. London: S. Sonnenschein, 1889.

———. Viktor. *Undersökningar i germansk mythologi, 2 delar.* Stockholm: Bonnier, 1886–89.

Sevareid, Eric. *Not so Wild a Dream.* New York: Knopf, 1946.

Shetelig, Haakon, and Falk, Hjalmar. *Scandinavian Archaeology.* Oxford: Clarendon Press, 1937.

Skørdalsvold, J. J. "Kensingtonstenen og De 'Lærde'," *Kvartalskrift utgivet af det Norske Selskab i Amerika.* 9de Aargang. Eau Claire, Wisconsin, July, 1913, pp. 74–82.

Söderwall, K. F. *Ordbok öfver svenska medeltidsspråket.* 2 vols. Lund: Berlingska boktr., 1884–1918.

Spence, Lewis. *An Encyclopædia of Occultism: A Compendium of Information on the Occult Sciences, Occult Personalities, Psychic Science, Magic, Demonology, Spiritism and Mysticism.* London, Routledge, 1920.

Stoker, Bram. *Famous Imposters.* New York: Sturgis and Walton: 1910.

Stomberg, Andrew Adin. *A History of Sweden.* London: Allen and Unwin, 1932.

Storm, Gustav. "Studier over Vinlandsreiserne, Vinlands Geografi og Ethnologi," *Aarbøger for Nordisk Oldkyndighed og Historie, udgivne af Det Kongelige Nordiske Oldskrift-Selskab. II Række, 2. Bind, 4. Hefte* (1887), pp. 293–372.

Stran[d]wold, Olaf. *Norse Inscriptions on American Stones, Collected and Deciphered.* Weehauken, N. J.: Magnus Björndal, 1948.

Svensk uppslagsbok. Andra, omarbetade och utvidgade upplagan. XV. Malmö: Norden, 1915.

Swanton, I. R. *The Wineland Voyages.* ("Smithsonian Miscellaneous Collections," 107. Number 12 [Publication 3906]). Washington, D. C.: Government Printing Office, 1947.

Taranger, Absalon. *Norges Historie. Tredje Binds første del. Tidsrummet 1319–1442.* Kristiania: Aschehoug, 1915.

Thalbitzer, William. "To fjærne runestene fra Grønland og Amerika," *Danske Studier. 43. Bind. Fjerde Række. 7. Bind* (1946–47), pp. 1–40.

———. *Two Runic Stones from Greenland and Minnesota* ("Smithsonian Miscellaneous Collections," Vol. 116, No. 3 [Publication 4021]). Washington, D. C.: Government Printing Office, 1951.

Thomas, Wendell. *Hinduism Invades America.* New York: Beacon, 1930.

Torp, Alf. *Nynorsk etymologisk ordbok.* Kristiania: Aschehoug, 1919.

The Upanishads. (*The Sacred Books of the East,* edited by F. Max Müller. Vol. I. Part I.) Oxford: Clarendon Press, 1900.

Upham, Warren. "The Kensington Rune Stone, its Description, its Inscriptions and Opinions Concerning Them," *Records of the Past,* IX (January–February, 1910), 3–7.

Vere, Francis. *The Piltdown Fantasy.* London: Cassell, 1955.

Verne, Jules. *A Journey to the Centre of the Earth.* With Illustrations by Riou. Boston: Shepard, [1874].

———. *A Trip to the Center of the Earth.* Introduction by Vilhjalmur Stefansson. [New York]: Didier, 1950.

Vining, Edward P. *An Inglorious Columbus.* . . . New York: Appleton, 1885.

Wahlgren, Erik. Review of Almar Næss, *Hvor lå Vinland? En studie over sol-observasjoner i de norrøne sagaer,* in *Swedish Pioneer Historical Quarterly,* VII (April, 1956), 73–75.

———. Review of Olaf Stran[d]wold, *Norse Inscriptions on American Stones,* in *Scandinavian Studies,* XXII (November, 1950), 187–88.

———. "The Runes of Kensington," *Studies in Honor of Albert Morey Sturte-vant,* pp. 57–70. Lawrence: University of Kansas Press, 1952.

Wallace, W. S. "The Literature Relating to the Norse Voyages to America," *Canadian Historical Review,* XX (March, 1939), 8–16.

Weiner, Joseph Sidney. *The Piltdown Forgery.* Oxford: Oxford University Press, 1955.

Wilkins, W. J. *Hindu Mythology, Vedic and Purānic.* 2nd ed. Calcutta: Thacker, Spink, [1900].

Zoëga, Geir T. *A Concise Dictionary of Old Icelandic.* Oxford: Clarendon Press, 1926.

Index

This index does not aim to exhaustive listing of every occurrence of a name or subject. Within heading modifications, the abbreviation "K." refers either to the Kensington inscription, to the Kensington stone, or to both, as may be appropriate.